Watches

1850–1980

M. Cutmore

Watches

1850–1980

David & Charles

A DAVID & CHARLES BOOK

First published in the UK in 1989
First published in paperback 2002
Text and illustrations copyright © M. Cutmore 1989, 2002
Layout copyright © David & Charles 1989, 2002

Distributed in North America
by F&W Publications, Inc.
4700 E. Galbraith Rd.
Cincinnati, OH 45236
1-800-289-0963

A catalogue record for this book is available from the
British Library.

ISBN 0 7153 1461 0 (paperback)

Typeset by ABM Typographics Limited, Hull
and printed in England by Butler & Tanner Ltd
for David & Charles
Brunel House   Newton Abbot   Devon

Front cover illustration: Complicated mechanical watch made by the
International Watch Company at Schaffhausen in 1984. The decorated
movement, which may be seen through a glass cuvette, is their traditional,
fully jewelled, Lepine calibre with fine regulation which has been
continuously improved and used in high quality watches since 1930.

Back cover illustration: 'Grande Complication' hand-finished watch made
by the International Watch Company at Schaffhausen in 1984. The dial
display gives hour, minute, second, day, date and month. The mechanical
movement also allows a centre seconds chronograph, a perpetual calendar
and minute repeating.

Preface

If you look in a jeweller's shop window it is clear that most of the watches displayed are electronic, and that fashion is a dominant feature. Dramatic changes have occurred in the last decade, and a few years ago, realising that the mechanical watch with a familiar tick would soon become a thing of the past, I started to think about its history. It was immediately apparent that, although a great deal has been written about antique watches made by traditional methods, very little has been published about the post-1850 period when watches were made in factories and production rose dramatically. In 1850 about two and a half million watches were made in a year; today this quantity is produced in a single working day. This book is about the period from 1850 onwards and most of my spare time in the last five years has been spent researching the subject in libraries, museums and factories in Europe. Scores of letters have been written to various parts of the world, and as the list of acknowledgements shows, help has been forthcoming.

Although there is published information about American and Swiss activities almost nothing has been written about English watch factories or about the influence of engineering on watchmaking. About one third of this book is devoted to these aspects as a positive contribution to published knowledge. Illustrations in the book serve differing purposes. It is necessary to show the different styles of watch in the period and the significant changes in design, and the American and Swiss illustrations fulfil this task. The English photographs have, however, been chosen to enable identification of manufacturer so that movements are the main display. Many of the photographs had to be taken by the author when a watch or movement became temporarily available. These will be seen to be adequate for their purpose but not of professional quality.

The outcome is a book which has given me great pleasure to produce largely because of the welcome I received in so many places. It is clearly too short to give detailed coverage of 140 years of watchmaking, but is, however, a coherent story as a base for future work and tells of the demise of the mechanical watch and the rise of the electronic watch. It covers the rise and fall of American watchmaking, the failure of the English firms, the survival of the diminished Swiss industry and the rise of Far East watchmaking.

Contents

1 Watches and watchmaking before 1850   8

2 The changing scene   18

3 Developments in America   26

4 English conservatism   44

5 Swiss reactions   51

6 The modern watch   66

7 English watchmaking   79

8 Swiss watchmaking   132

9 American watchmaking   160

10 Watchmaking in other countries   173

11 Manufacturing principles   187

12 Electrical and electronic watches   208

13 Collecting and repair   219

Appendix: Watch sizes   229

Bibliography   230

References   231

Acknowledgements   236

Index   238

1 Watches and watchmaking before 1850

The development of watches by reducing the size of spring-driven clocks probably occurred before 1500. A watch, initialled C.W., is kept in the Wuppertal museum in Germany and is dated 1548.[1] Another early example dated 1551, signed Jacques de la Garde, can be seen at the Louvre in Paris. These two watches enable the essential components to be identified as a case, a dial with a hand to indicate the time and a movement to drive the hand through motion work (Fig 1). The spring powering the movement was contained in a drum-shaped barrel and the spring torque was kept constant by a stackfreed or a fusee and applied to the escapement through the train of wheels. The escapement was controlled by an oscillating balance.

With each vibration one tooth of the escape wheel was allowed to pass and the whole train and hand moved forward a tiny increment. Provided the balance vibration rate was constant the watch would keep good time. All the parts in the movement rotate and therefore have staffs or arbors which are supported in bearing holes in two plates. The plates are placed above and below most of the movement parts and are separated by pillars. The plates not only support the arbors and loads but also protect the fragile parts of the movement. Unfortunately the most fragile part, which is the oscillating balance, was usually placed outside the plates so losing this protection, and it needed a special upper bearing known as the cock which was pinned (later screwed) to the plate.

The stackfreed was a short-lived torque-regulating device but the fusee was used in some watches until c1900. When a fusee is used the spring in the barrel has its outer end attached to the barrel circumference and the inner end to the barrel arbor. A length of gut (later chain) is attached to and wound around the outside of the barrel circumference, the other end being attached to the fusee. The spring is wound by rotating the fusee with a key so uncoiling the gut from the barrel and recoiling it into a spiral groove cut in the cone shaped profile of the fusee (Fig 1). When the spring is fully wound the force transmitted to the fusee by the gut acts at the smallest radius and as the spring unwinds, reducing the force transmitted, the fusee radius increases to maintain a constant torque output to the train.

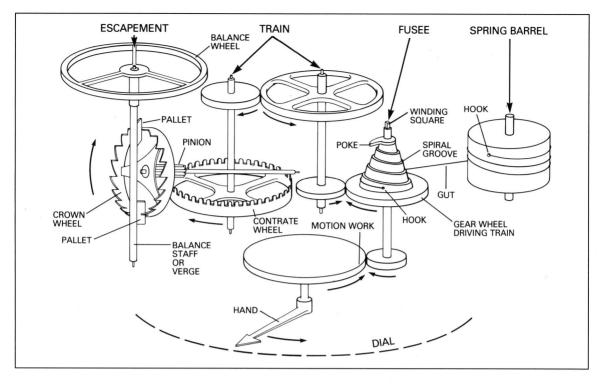

Even with this torque regulation the early watch was a poor timekeeper and the next two hundred and fifty years were spent in turning the watch into a good but relatively expensive timekeeper. Soon after this was achieved new manufacturing techniques were developed and watches became cheaper and available to everyone. Factory-made watches are the concern of this book but it is first necessary to outline the previous developments which determined the form of the watch and the methods used to make it in 1850.

In the period until 1675 improvements in the watch were limited to replacement of the fusee gut by a chain, complete elimination of the stackfreed, improvement in timekeeping by worm and wheel adjustment of the initial spring tension (set-up), and increasing complications in the information the watch could give – striking, alarm setting, day, date, moon phase, etc. The casework changed to a shape suitable for the pocket rather than hanging from the neck which was the way early watches were worn and a watchglass was fitted giving better protection to the movement from dust and damp. There were also considerable forms of case decoration, enamel work in particular became evident.

As the watchmaking craft became established in various countries so skills improved and the watches produced benefitted. In England in 1631, the Worshipful Company of Clockmakers was formed as a guild to ensure the standard and quality of the work of clockmakers and watchmakers and to ensure the proper training of apprentices.[2] This was a very significant step and no doubt contributed to the excellence of English

Fig 1 The essential components of an early watch movement; note the torque equalising fusee

watches in the eighteenth century. In due course it will be seen that some traditions become fixed in the minds of some watchmakers and in turn contributed to the demise of the industry in the late nineteenth century.

The introduction of the balance spring to the watch in 1675 by Christian Huygens and Robert Hooke was the first significant step in improving watch performance. It was equivalent to the use of the pendulum in the clock (1657). It was hoped that the use of the balance spring would cause isochronous vibrations (constant time of vibration irrespective of the arc of vibration) but it was not so and it was a further 100 years before escapement, design and balance spring fitting techniques made this possible. The timekeeping improvement caused by the balance spring was so enormous that two hands were fitted enabling time to be read to the minute and seconds hands were also occasionally fitted. Regulation of the timekeeping of the watch with a balance spring could be achieved by altering the active length of the balance spring with a pivoted pair of curb pins.

Once the balance spring watch could be regulated new faults became apparent. It was discovered that changes in temperature of the watch affected its performance. As the temperature increased, the balance spring became less stiff, causing the watch to lose. The second fault was that the position of the watch affected the timekeeping because of gravitational effects. A third was that friction in the escapement was unpredictable.

Navigation of vessels at sea depends on knowing latitude and longitude. To navigate it was necessary to keep good time so that the position of the sun could be accurately determined and the longitude calculated. In order to promote the development of a longitude quality timekeeper a prize of £20,000 was offered in 1714 by the (British) Board of Longitude for a timekeeper which would meet their specification.[3] This prize was eventually awarded to John Harrison in 1773 (the actual award-winning tests were carried out in 1761–2 and 1764). Harrison's design was ingenious but was not the eventual practical answer to the problem. He did, however, contribute two items to watch development, the first being the principle of temperature compensation for which he used a bimetallic curb acting on the balance spring and the second being the principle of maintaining power so that a fusee watch did not stop whilst being wound. A small tensioned leaf spring inside the fusee base supplied power during winding. Harrison did not provide a new escapement for his navigation instrument nor was his temperature compensation curb acting on the balance spring the final solution.

Other makers, notably in England, John Arnold and Thomas Earnshaw, invented a frictionless, detached detent escapement for use in marine chronometers and both Arnold and Earnshaw used temperature compensated bimetallic balance wheels rather than bimetallic balance spring curbs. Pierre le Roy and Ferdinand Berthoud were involved in similar work in France. In the form used in watches, the compensation balance has its rim made of two layers of metal, brass on the outside and steel inside. The rim is cut close to the balance arms (Fig 2). When temperature rises the brass expands more than the steel and the cuts allow the rim arms to bend inwards which shortens vibration time. If temperature falls the arms bend outwards increasing vibration time. Although this correction for temperature change is not perfect, this design gives a considerable improvement in timekeeping in a watch.

The timekeeping of a watch can be further improved by using special terminal curves at the ends of the balance spring. Arnold discovered the correct shape for a helical balance spring and Abraham-Louis Breguet the form of an overcoil for the spiral spring used in watches. Breguet (1747–1823) was a great watchmaker working mainly in Paris from 1762 onwards (with interruptions due to revolution and war). During his lifetime he invented several improvements including the tourbillon in which the escapement rotated to reduce errors to watch position.

In some ways it was surprising that Harrison did not approach the problem of friction in the escapement design since watchmakers were aware of the problem. The original escapement used in the first clocks and watches (Fig 1) is known as the verge escapement. There is continuous friction during its action between the teeth of the crown (or escape) wheel and the pallets on the balance staff (or verge). The first new watch escapement was introduced by George Graham in about 1726. It is known as the cylinder escapement and may well be a development of the design described in British patent 344 of 1695 to Booth, Houghton and Tompion (Graham was related to Tompion by marriage). In Graham's form, the escape wheel has a vertical arbor and teeth which project vertically from the rim of the wheel (Fig 3). These teeth give impulse to the balance by means of a special slot cut in a hollow cylinder fitted into the balance wheel staff. The working portion of the cylinder has approximately half its circumference removed so that a tooth may escape by passing through the cut-away portion at the appropriate moment during the

Fig 2 Bimetallic temperature compensation devices used in watches. The curb was never common and was not used in modern watches

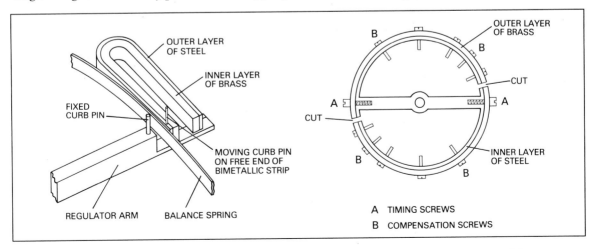

A   TIMING SCREWS

B   COMPENSATION SCREWS

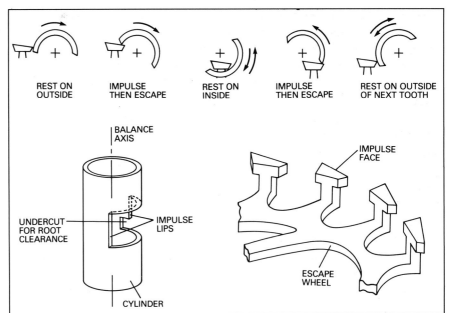

REST ON OUTSIDE   IMPULSE THEN ESCAPE   REST ON INSIDE   IMPULSE THEN ESCAPE   REST ON OUTSIDE OF NEXT TOOTH

BALANCE AXIS

IMPULSE FACE

UNDERCUT FOR ROOT CLEARANCE

IMPULSE LIPS

ESCAPE WHEEL

CYLINDER

Fig 3 The cylinder escapement

balance vibration but may rest on the outside or the inside surface of the cylinder during the remainder of the vibration. Thus this new escapement was still subject to friction problems but it is important because it was the first to be specially developed for watches and because it was still used in 1850 and indeed continued in use in factory-made watches well into the twentieth century.

Many other escapements were designed but most still had friction problems.[4] It was vital for good timekeeping that the swing of the balance should be free of friction which could be achieved by arranging the balance staff to be 'detached' from the rest of the escapement (except at the actual moment it was receiving impulse from the escape wheel). This was achieved in the detent escapement used in the marine chronometer. This escapement is relatively fragile for ordinary watch use although it was used in precision pocket chronometers.

The development of watch escapements culminated in the detached lever design introduced in 1769 by Thomas Mudge in England and at about the same time by Julien le Roy in France. The lever escapement was made in various forms in the period from 1769 to 1825 but by 1825 two successful types had emerged.[5] The only visible difference between these two forms was the shape of the escape wheel teeth (and the consequent less obvious slight differences in lever shape and action). They are known as the Swiss lever (Fig 4a) and the English lever (Fig 4b), the former having club-shaped teeth and the latter pointed shaped teeth.

There are three components in the lever escapement: the escape wheel, the lever and the balance staff. In the English lever version the pivots of these three components are usually arranged to form a right angle whereas in the Swiss lever version the pivots are arranged in a straight line or a right angle. As the balance swings in the Swiss lever, the impulse pin engages the lever fork and the safety dart enters the passing crescent on the smaller diameter part of the double roller. The pivoted lever is unlocked by the leading side of the impulse pin which protrudes below the large diameter part of the double roller on the balance staff. Unlocking causes a slight angular movement of the lever and allows the sloping face of the lever pallet to contact the leading edge of the escape wheel tooth. This edge slides over the lever pallet to the position shown in Fig 4a, giving impulse from the lever fork to the trailing side of the jewel pin (and hence to the balance wheel) which unlocked the lever. As the leading edge of the tooth reaches the end of the lever pallet, further impulse is given by the sloping face of the escape wheel tooth which then escapes (and the watch moves forward). During the impulse actions the lever has rotated so that the escape wheel (and watch) is only free to turn a small amount before it is relocked by the other lever pallet engaging a tooth further round on the escape wheel. The double impulse action is known as

Fig 4 The lever escapement; (a) shows a straight-line layout with the Swiss form of escape wheel and (b) shows a right-angle layout with the English form of escape wheel. Various roller arrangements are shown

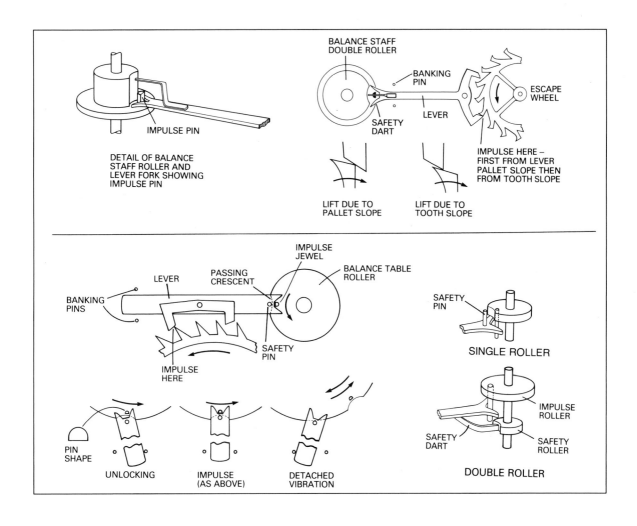

'divided lift'. The lever is pulled into deeper engagement with the escape wheel by the shaping of pallet and tooth sides and comes to rest on the banking pin. This is known as 'draw' and causes some recoil during the unlocking action. Draw is a safety measure to keep the lever out of the way of the balance which swings freely (detached) until it comes to rest under the action of the balance spring and then swings back again to unlock the train and repeat the sequence. If an accident should jerk the lever from the banking pin during the detached swing the safety dart will contact the smaller diameter safety roller and prevent any action until the passing crescent allows the correct sequence of events to occur.

The English lever (Fig 4b) works in similar fashion but all the lift is on the lever pallets operated by the tip of the pointed tooth. In most English levers a single roller is used which holds the impulse pin and also has the passing crescent cut in its edge to allow the safety pin on the lever to pass at the appropriate moment. In the English lever the 'horns' essential to the Swiss lever safety action are not required although they sometimes appear.

The lever escapement (particularly the Swiss version) has been described fully because it was successful and the watches using it were robust, reliable and moderately priced. By 1850 the lever escapement had virtually replaced all other designs except the cylinder which continued in use for cheaper watches. A few higher priced watches used other escapements and later a much cheaper form of lever was to emerge for a different market. The English form lasted in diminishing numbers until about 1914, but the Swiss form survives today.

Another development which had a considerable effect on watch design was the introduction of jewelled bearings into the escapement and train. The original British patent number 371 of 1704 was granted to Peter and Jacob Debaufre but in practice jewelling was rarely used until later and even in 1850 was limited to the escapement in all but the more expensive watches. There was a period at the beginning of the lever watch era when train jewelling became more common but the extra cost of train jewelling did not justify the results for the ordinary watch.

It is appropriate here to describe typical English and Swiss watches of about 1850. The English watch has a jewelled English lever escapement and is fitted with a fusee. The watch is wound and the hands are set with a key. It is a full plate design with all the components except the balance between the plates. Under the white enamel dial there is motion work providing differential rates of rotation for the hour and minute hands. The case is made of silver and is hallmarked with date and assay office. The Swiss watch has a jewelled Swiss lever escapement and no fusee. Instead it has a going barrel with stopwork so arranged that only the centre position of the mainspring is used so that the torque variation is not great enough to cause significant errors. The watch is wound and the hands are set with a key. The watch has a dial plate but no top plate; instead it uses a series of bridges to support the other pivots of the components. This 'Lepine' calibre is typical of Swiss watches and was introduced by Jean-Antoine Lepine in about 1790. The dial may be metal or white enamel with motion work below it. The watch may have been cased in silver in England or Switzerland. A 'Swiss' watch with a cylinder escapement would look similar except for the absence of the lever and it would be a cheaper product.

Having outlined the development of the watch to 1850, we can turn to the watchmaking methods used in this period. Disregarding for the moment the case, dial and hands and considering the watch movement as the vital part, it can be seen that if it is separated into its components we will have plates and bridges, wheels and pinions, arbors, screws, a barrel, springs, pins, a balance, jewels and various small steel and brass parts. Additionally, in English watches, we will still have a fusee and chain and there will also be an escapement in all watches. Most of these parts had been required for about 300 years and it is therefore to be expected that there would be well-established watchmaking practices. Given time and patience one man could make a complete watch and he would then be able to sign it as the maker. This would be a slow and inefficient method of manufacture and it is obvious that if a number of similar objects are to be made then some method of batch work is desirable. It is also better to let a different specialist make each part for which he will devise his own tools and techniques to ease the task.

Eventually however all these parts have to fit together to make a complete working watch movement which keeps good time. There is also a need to fit a dial and hands and to have a case made. It is therefore essential that there is a coordinator who will arrange for each part to be made in the correct sequence and for the partly finished movement to be passed on to the man who is to make the next piece. The coordinator will also need, when the complete rough movement comes back to him, to finish it by ensuring that it all works properly, as well as fitting the escapement, having the gilding done, getting case, dial and hands made and at some stage having his name engraved on the product as the 'watchmaker'. It should be noted that the specialist workers are not in a factory but at their own premises or homes and the partly finished movement has to travel from man to man. This basic system of watchmaking was used in England and on the continent from the seventeenth century and was still in operation in 1850 (Plates 1 and 2).

In England at some stage in the mid-eighteenth century the trade divided into two parts. Rough watch movements were made at Prescot in Lancashire (by the same method as that outlined above) and these were supplied in batches to finishers (or 'makers') in watchmaking centres in Liverpool, Coventry, Birmingham and London.[6,7] Information about the workers employed in Prescot, London and Coventry can be found in Hoult,[8] Rees[9] and Kemp.[6] Rees also suggests that the continental subdivi-

Plate 1 An English verge watch movement made by traditional methods. It is only part finished, the fusee is not cut and the crown wheel is unfinished. The date is c1820

15

Plate 2 *(left)* A continental movement made by traditional methods in c1820. It is thinner than the movement in **Plate 1**, has a going barrel rather than a fusee and a cylinder escapement. It is fitted with a temperature compensation curb. The construction is different with individual bridges for each wheel known as 'Lepine' calibre; *(right)* a later bridged style continental movement with a lever escapement similar to those produced by Leschot's early machines from c1840 (see **Plate 4**)

sion of labour was greater and Nussbaum[10] and Jaquet and Chapuis[11] give details of Swiss processes. The French and Swiss equivalents of Prescot were at Beaucourt and Fontainemelon.

One important aspect of this method of manufacture is that it would produce parts which would only fit one particular watch. There was no interchangeability of components. This was a considerable handicap and it was only in the middle of the nineteenth century that some organisation of size avoided the need for each watch to be individually cased. In England, the Lancashire watch size was based on overall movement diameter and pillar height but some fitting would be required at the hinging. The transfer of movements to another case is not often possible with watches of this period.

Watches made at Prescot, Beaucourt and Fontainemelon needed finishing. Rees[9] gives a list of workers needed to finish a watch in London and Cole[12] and Bickley[13] describe the processes. Weiss[14] describes the manufacture of many parts in some detail and Hatton[15] gives contemporary information. Even when watches were machine made repair work on older watches needed the traditional skills and further information can be found in Britten,[16] Saunier[17] and Finch.[18] By dismantling a watch movement of the period and reading Saunier it is possible to appreciate how it was made with quite simple tools. Experiments in making chronometer parts using period tools were described by Griffiths in 1985.[19] Some idea of production in various countries is relevant at this stage.

Geneva 1787	4,000 workers; 59,000 watches per year
Britain c1790	about 200,000 watches per year
Clerkenwell 1797	7,000 workers; 120,000 watches per year; wages 12–30 shillings per week; estimated living costs for satisfactory life 19 shillings per week
Beaucourt 1805	100,000 rough movements per year from Japy
Neuchâtel 1818	3,500 workers; 130,000 watches per year

It is also interesting to consider how watches were marketed. The Swiss products were mainly exported but much of the English product was for the home market. In a letter to the (Parliamentary) Committee investigating the Petitions of Watchmakers of Coventry written in 1816 or 1817, Samuel Smith (watchmaker) gives an indication of the travelling he did to sell his watches by visiting North and South Wales.[20] He also visited at other times much of the Midlands, Bristol, Gloucester, Manchester, etc. He says in his evidence

> . . . sell but three or four watches a year; there are but four vendors of watches in the country through which I travel who sell more than the above statement; and I, by getting orders from these different people, have for a number of years employed from thirty to forty men . . . I have sold on this journey (which is about a thousand miles in circuit) more than five hundred watches . . . At these places (Newport, Caerphilly, Cardiff, Merthyr Tydfil) I have sold six dozen, and frequently seven dozen watches in one day . . .

This is an early travelling salesman, hawking the products of his business and supporting a number of finishing workers for his rough movements obtained from Prescot. Most watchmakers must have used similar methods.

It must be clear that for all the tasks essential to making the parts of a watch there must have been a need for tools. Common tools used by many workers were therefore made and sold but the majority of workers would additionally have had their own little secret devices. Some idea of the availability of tools can be obtained from a catalogue of tools published between 1758 and 1770 by John Wyke of Liverpool.[21] The catalogue shows hand tools, lathes and important special watchmaking 'engines' for fusees and wheels.

This chapter has outlined the development of the watch and the methods used in its manufacture until 1850. It shows an industry which still has traditional manufacturing methods used for hundreds of years but which has developed its product to a robust and reliable timekeeper. With hindsight we can see that the English and European industry was due for a radical change and the remainder of this book is devoted to that change and its effects.

2 *The changing scene*

During the two hundred years that the system of watchmaking based on subspecialisation had been developed there were quite naturally upsets in the smooth way of life. Economic or political factors meant that the demand for watches would vary and there would be temporary distress in the industry during a recession. Three examples of such disturbances were the French Revolution of 1789 which severely affected the Swiss watch trade and, affecting the English trade, Pitt's tax on clocks and watches imposed in 1797[1] (replaced by income tax in 1799) and the post-war depression of 1813 which, coupled with the abuse of imports and the apprenticeship system, led to a fall in employment for qualified watch craftsmen.[2] There were also individuals who could see that the traditional method of making watches set limits to the number of watches that could be produced and to the price at which they could be made. If the price could be reduced more people could afford to own a watch. Building on the fact that many of the workers used hand-powered tools to make their pieces they began to conceive ideas of bringing all the workers and tools together. The individuals who led in this field span a period of eighty years from 1760 during which there were faltering attempts to introduce new ideas into watchmaking.

During this period another important development took place. Individual hand-powered tools were one way of making parts but better power sources were needed. Guye[3] mentions water wheels or 'in the absence of a water wheel turned by a stream, a team of oxen were used [on a treadmill], while a few large wheels were worked by human labour.' By 1774 the steam engine had been redesigned in England by James Watt and Matthew Boulton and in 1775 John Wilkinson managed to make a suitably accurate cylinder to make the new design practical. Their subsequent work, culminating in establishing the Soho foundry in Birmingham in 1795, meant that steam power was a reality.

One way of finding out what developments were taking place is to study patents. This is not easy unless a survey of patents is available. It is also not possible in countries without patent laws. In Switzerland patents were not introduced until 1888. There will also be inventors who did not take patents. If Aked's[4] survey of English horological patents is examined the earliest interesting patent is No 763 of 1761 entitled 'Machinery for the manufacture of watches' to George Sanderson. The patent principally described a 'universal engine lath for turning and cutting divers parts or belonging to a watch' and shows a set of turns with dividing plate and a four-way cutting frame which enables any of four operations to be performed on the workpiece in the machine. There are also drawings of the fittings for the lathe. It is not known if many were used.

There is a list of French horological patents by Auguste Alleaume[5] in which the earliest interesting patent is No 63 of 17 Mars 1799 to Sieur Frédéric Japy of Beaucourt, 'pour diverses machines d'horlogerie'. This is an important patent for Japy did go into production using the ten machines described in this patent and no doubt others before and after the patent date. The firm of Japy was founded at Beaucourt, France, in 1750 by Fritz Japy.[6] The most significant step in the history of this firm was however due to the patent holder Frédéric Japy (1749–1812) who served his apprenticeship in Switzerland and returned to Beaucourt[3] in 1771 where he started to make ébauches[7] (unfinished rough movements). His success enabled the business to expand and in 1776 he purchased from, or had made by, Jean-Jaques Jeanneret-Gris of Le Locle a set of machines to enable him to mass-produce verge escapement ébauches. Nussbaum[8] states '[Jeanneret-Gris] had to take to the Japys at Beaucourt his machines for cutting out brass parts and plates and for forming fusees and barrels'. There is a difference of opinion between French and Swiss sources[7] about the designer of the machines but there is no doubt about their user nor of the patent to Japy. The ten machines described and illustrated in the patent, which will be developments of those of 1776, consist of:

 1 A circular saw for cutting brass sheet into strips.
 2 A lathe for plates, fusees, barrels, collets, slides and racks.
 3 A machine to cut wheel teeth.
 4 A machine for pillar making.
 5 A press tool to make balances.
 6 A press tool for train wheels.
 7 A vertical drilling tool.
 8 A tool to rivet pillars.
 9 A screw head slitting tool.
10 A draw bench for the potence groove.

The production figures Japy achieved are quite staggering but sources are not consistent. By 1780 he employed 50 workers and made 43,000 pieces per year or by 1795, 40,000 pieces per year and by 1805 100,000 pieces per year.[7] Jaquet and Chapuis[9] suggest that, by 1793, 40,000 ébauches were supplied to the Jura industry annually. This dependence on Japy disturbed the Swiss who founded an ébauche factory in Fontainemelon to supply their own industry. Photographs of Fontainemelon ébauches are shown in Guye.[3] Similar steps were taken for the Geneva industry by the firm of Sandoz & Trot who imported tools from Besançon, France and in 1820 another firm founded by Humbert and Daries also started making ébauches in Geneva.[9] Japy's products were 'identical' verge escapement ébauches. The parts were not interchangeable but the system was the beginning of mass production. If his 50 workers made 43,000 rough movements per year this represents about 16 per man-week compared with perhaps 1 or 2 per man-week by traditional methods. The ébauches still needed to be finished but because they were identical the finishing processes were simpler. After finishing, the parts would still not be interchangeable.

Interchangeable parts for weapons were an ideal desired by military men. It would then be possible to take damaged firearms on the field of battle and make some usable firearms. There is debate about the first successful armourer to achieve this objective but the principle was introduced in France by Blanc in about 1790. Previous to this there are records that Christopher Polhem was making interchangeable parts for clocks by precision measurement in Sweden in 1720.[10] Following Blanc were John Hall (1811 US patent), Simeon North and Eli Whitney in America, all of whom were making firearms. To make interchangeable parts by mass production for a rifle is one problem, to do it for a tiny watch is another. The manufacture of interchangeable parts requires at least three elements: precision tools and machines, precision measuring devices and some system of mechanical drawing and dimensions to specify size exactly. If all the parts are not made on the same site by the same man then the three elements above must be universal. This situation did not exist in 1800. The micrometer was improved in England in 1805 by Henry Maudslay, drawing techniques were mooted in 1795 by Gaspard Monge in France[11] in his *Géométrie descriptive* and were developed in England and France over the next thirty years. True interchangeability of watch parts would take about 100 years to perfect, but the first steps started in about 1830.

Returning to the Aked patent list[4] we find the name Pierre-Frédéric Ingold (1787–1878). Ingold was born in Bienne and became a watch worker both in his native Switzerland and in France which included some time in Breguet's Paris workshop.[3] He is reported to have contacted Japy with ideas which were probably too advanced to be practical. Ingold envisaged large-scale production of interchangeable parts for watches which was not a popular idea with Swiss finishing watchmakers. He returned to Paris in about 1835 and tried to form the 'French or Parisian Watchmaking Company' to fulfil this ideal (different sources give different names) but he was not successful. A similar unsuccessful story is told of a company at Versailles[12] (perhaps this is the 'French' as opposed to the 'Parisian' company). The company prospectus stated

The company is already in a position to satisfy all orders for watches from 200 to 600 francs; it can multiply the number of its productions by means of the perfect machines which it possesses. By the aid of those machines the principal parts of a watch are made of uniform size and great quickness; the precise exactness is an invaluable advantage, which alone renders the establishment without a rival of its kind.

Ingold came to England in about 1840 to found the British Watch and Clockmaking Company for which there were three prospectuses in 1842. Aked[4] lists three patents; No 9,511 and No 9,752 of 1842 which were six-month holding patents, and No 9,993 of 21 December 1843 which gave full details of the plate machine and a wheel press with an important four-pillar guide system for the punch and die.

The involved story of this company is told by Carrington.[13] It was not successful because the company, to be established by Act of Parliament, failed when the second reading of the Bill was rejected on 31 March 1843. The company had argued that the division of labour in the watchmaking trade was wasteful and that the application of machinery would revitalise the industry. The opposition argued correctly that there was as yet no patent detail and suggested Ingold was a speculator. This may have been a good legal argument but there is no doubt that the trade contributed much to the defeat. Two documents were written by a committee, one listing seven objections including lack of patent specifications, monopoly, market flooding and dissatisfaction of practical watchmakers which were not particularly damning arguments. The second reports a visit to the premises in Dean Street.

At an interview, 22nd March, 1843, on its premises at 75, Dean Street, Soho, they were then requested, urged, and challenged to exhibit proof of the working of their machinery before your committee. The favour was claimed on behalf of the trade at large. This request was refused upon the most frivolous and contradictory pretexts. The committee advisedly declares its firm persuasion that the company is not in a capacity to make good its assertion upon the subject of letters patent which have been taken out to secure these newly-invented machines to the company; the committee would remark that the specifications have not yet been enrolled.

In spite of these reports the machines existed and Torrens[14] comments that the plate machine was a hollow mandrel lathe with a double swing rest and an indexed chuck. With the machine it was possible to produce a complete watch plate finished on both sides with a single insertion into the chuck. The chuck had to be set by hand to the indexed position for each separate operation of drilling, tapping, turning, etc, and the drill, tap, tool, etc, had to be fed by hand. These operations had to be repeated for each individual plate so that the degree of interchangeability depended on the skill of the operator to make identical settings. The

settings were based on both polar and rectangular co-ordinates so that Ingold had anticipated the design principle of the pointing machine and the jig borer by considerable period of time. It is no wonder that with such advanced ideas his reception was cool in the trade.

Some watches were made, presumably with the machines and some survivors are described and illustrated by Carrington.[13] There is also a drawing of a watch with a different serial number in a letter dated 1890 to the *Horological Journal*.[15] (Plate 3 shows a frame and two watches.) The machinery proposed by the company was supposed to be capable of making 300 watches per day which would have been an enormous step forward but two points need making. The watches would still have required finishing as subsequent experience showed that true interchangeability was not easily achieved. Some selective fitting would have been necessary. The second point concerns the plate machinery which would have required great operator skill in each setting. Modern production machines with few exceptions are set and dedicated to a specific task and do not require continuous operations of resetting.

With his failure in England Ingold went to America for a time where it is feasible, in spite of lack of evidence, that he may have influenced the formation of the American companies. Aaron Dennison, the traditional founder of the post-1850 American watchmaking industry apparently never met Ingold.[16] Ingold's machines were sold[3] in about 1863 and according to Gannay,[16] in 1886, one was at the factory of Gillett and Bland in Croydon. Whether they were using it is not clear. After a relatively short period in America, during which time he made a watch with a special lever escapement, Ingold returned to Switzerland in 1857. At some stage in his career Ingold invented a milling fraise (cutter) for shaping the curves of gear teeth for watch wheels and it is this invention which has preserved his name.

The next venture in Europe took place in Switzerland and was a move towards an increase in the rate of production by standardising the models. The ideas were not as ambitious as those of Ingold but because it was an existing firm which initiated the work it was bound to be adopted if a successful method could be evolved. Georges-Auguste Leschot (1800–84) was born in Geneva. In his early days he introduced draw into lever escapements and continuing his interest in these escapements devised several machines for their manufacture. In 1839 the Geneva firm of Vacheron and Constantin, which was founded in 1819 from the original Vacheron watchmaking shop of 1755, decided after some years of trials to standardise their watches by using machine manufacture and asked Leschot to work for them. They required 'gilt movements with lever or cylinder escapements to be manufactured, for which the cases can be made to a standard size for each calibre'.[9] Leschot devised a pantograph machine which, from a template six times full size, would accurately make the holes in the plate.

Since the watches had the Lepine calibre with bridges rather than a top plate the same system could be used for the pressed-out bridges when finishing the profiles, milling out recesses, etc.[3] Leschot had to devise other machines to make the remaining parts of the movement, some of which had tools fitted in sliding blocks working between adjustable stops. Whether this is an original idea is not clear but it is an essential production step. The basic pantograph machine was 1,000mm long by 520mm wide and 6mm thick. Illustrations of this and other Leschot machines can be seen in Guye[3] and some of the watches in Jaquet and Chapuis.[9] Production by these methods was very successful and in a letter dated 24 December 1842,[3] M. Vacheron states 'the barrels are machined in every detail; at the moment, we are organising what is required for cutting out drums with their teeth ready made. Today, we have recessed about 1,500 of them to prepare them for this operation'. Indeed the rate of production of ébauches was in excess of the needs of Vacheron and Constantin so that they were able to supply other manufacturers (Plate 4). Leschot's achievements were a big step forward for rapid production and uniformity in all parts of the watch movement but it is absolutely certain that these movements would still require finishing processes and once finished the parts would not be interchangeable.

Interchangeability was demonstrated at the 1851 exhibition in London by the Swiss maker Antoine Le Coultre but this was achieved with special hand-finished parts.[7] With Leschot's work, Vacheron and Constantin were world leaders but they were to lose this lead because their machines would not handle hardened steels. As a result, subsequent heat treatment was needed for some parts causing distortion and their machines were in no way automated needing considerable operator attention for hand feeding, etc. They remained European leaders for some time as further general progress was discouraged by the secrecy with which they blanketed their methods.

As will be seen in Chapter 3 crucial developments took place in America after 1850. It is therefore necessary to examine the state of watchmaking in that distant country which Europeans had always regarded as an export market. Whereas in Europe there were strong traditions in all trades, America did not have this background. There is evidence of watchmaking in America but these were early colonists who continued these European occupations but would be more truly 'makers' Some parts would have been imported. By studying a list of American watchmakers and companies,[17] about forty makers can be found working between 1760 and 1850. There were bound to be more than this but it is obvious that the scale of watchmaking was very small indeed. Many would probably be watch importers or finishers of European products. From the names it is possible to find some pioneers whose watches have survived. These include Luther Goddard (1762–1842) who imported hands, dials, springs, verges, pinion wire and chains but made the remain-

Plate 3 British Watch and Clockmaking Company products (*left*) a frame without internal parts; (*right*) a complete watch; (*centre*) the movement of another watch. It may be that if the company had survived it would have sold complete watches and ébauches for finishing. The watches were thin and small by contemporary English standards of 1840

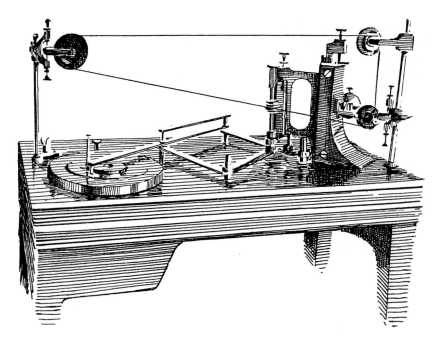

Plates 4 Leschot's pantograph machine together with a Vacheron and Constantin movement produced by his machines in c1842

ing steel and brass parts of the movements and the cases. In all Goddard made about 530 watches and his son a further 60, mainly during a period of import restriction between 1809 and 1812. Illustrations of these watches show them to be English in style.[18]

Makers like Goddard were using traditional methods and tools but with less subdivision of labour. Special tools such as wheel engines would be self-made or imported. At the same time the American clockmaking industry was already using new ideas. Harrold[18] suggests that Harland, who died in 1807, may have made a few watches but he had already been thinking about production methods for clocks with interchangeable parts. Daniel Burnap and Eli Terry (1772–1852) turned these ideas into a reality and Terry in particular made 3,000 clock movements in a year by simple mass-production methods.[7] The arms industry was also busy making interchangeable parts in the first quarter of the nineteenth century. Both Terry and the arms industry were working in Connecticut which may have influenced the Pitkin brothers of East Hartford, Connecticut to attempt to make watches using machines to produce interchangeable parts.

Henry Pitkin (1811–46) was the watchmaker and James Pitkin (1812–79) the businessman. They designed the 'American Lever Watch' and machines to make most of it. They had to import dials, hands, springs and balance jewels like other makers. Production started in 1838 and about 350 watches were sold locally which encouraged them to move to New York in 1841. However, this was not a successful move and after about 500 were made they abandoned the business in 1842.[19] Watches still exist and one is illustrated in Britten.[20] It is an important watch for it was the first to be made by machine with reputedly interchangeable parts although there is no doubt that the interchangeability would require considerable fitting skills. The watch had an English lever escapement, no fusee and conical wheel pivots running in hardened screws set into the plates.

Thus both in Switzerland and America there is evidence of imminent change but Aked[4] shows no English initiatives. Consulting patents is not a certain method of detection, for not all inventors use patents and indeed examination of the United States Horological patent extractions of Eckhardt[21] does not show any patents relevant to the watchmakers above.

It is worth summarising what had been happening and the conclusions that can be made about the changes which were beginning to occur in the watchmaking industry.

1 Traditional methods of outworker manufacture based on subspecialisation were being questioned by the concept of concentrating all the watchmaking operations at one site; a factory. This would offer considerable economies of time wasted in moving the parts from one place to another and enable closer control of the processes.
2 The availability of steam power meant that machinery could be developed to increase production rates. Machines needed to be fitted with preset stops to enable the operator to make a number of similar parts. The start of mass production.
3 A need for interchangeable parts was recognised as essential for efficient assembly of mass-produced parts.
4 It was not yet realised that the new method was capital intensive. Machines were expensive and to be profitable needed to be fully utilised to avoid bankruptcy.

3 Developments in America

With the closure of the Pitkin venture in New York in 1842 there was a pause in the progress of machine watchmaking in America. There was no doubt a small-scale traditional watch industry operated by a number of apprenticed, trained men and one such man was Aaron Dennison (1812–95).

Dennison was apprenticed to a clockmaker in Brunswick, Maine, for three years. As a forerunner of things to come he made a model of an automatic machine for cutting clock wheels during this period.[1] In 1833, aged twenty-one, he went to Boston to learn about watchmaking and repairing. Here he worked for a year with Currier and Trot before setting up independently as a watch repairer. This venture was short lived and he went to work for Jones, Low and Ball under their foreman Jubal Howe (Tubal Hone in some books) who had himself been apprenticed to Goddard. Two items that Dennison observed during this period were the poor finish and mechanical imperfections of many imported watches. Dennison left Boston for a short stay in New York where he made contact with Swiss and English tradesmen and then returned to Boston to set himself up again, this time as a tool and material dealer and watch repairer. This firm was known as Dennison, Adams & Company. During this period of material dealings the Dennison Standard Gauge for mainsprings was devised. The material and repair business became A. L. Dennison & Company in 1846 with Nathan Foster as partner. Partners were always necessary to Dennison because a business needed capital. Dennison would always provide ideas, drive and some expertise in a venture but he continually needed financial backing. Fortunately his enthusiasm, industry and trustworthiness always helped him to find a backer. By nature Dennison must have been restless and unsatisfied for although he was apparently successfully pursuing a career in watches he had concurrently been involved with his family in retail jewelling, silk farming and paper box manufacture.

Dennison met Edward Howard in 1842.[2] Howard, who had clockmaking experience, was a partner in the firm Howard & Davis who owned a plant in Roxbury at which they made clocks, scales, weights, sewing machines and other speculative products. Howard was willing to try watch manufacture and he and Dennison discussed this in about 1845. In 1849 Dennison employed Nelson Stratton in his own material and repair business. Stratton had been an apprentice in the Pitkin factory when they were building their machines in 1837. It may therefore not be entirely fortuitous that in 1849 Howard and Dennison decided to proceed with their watchmaking project.

Capital was again required and this was provided by Howard and Davis ($10,000) and by Howard's father-in-law, Samuel Curtis ($20,000). The firm of Dennison, Howard and Davis was set up in 1850. It had been decided that at first it might be necessary to import some parts (springs and dials) and they would certainly need to find out how to make these for the future. It was also vital to get information of gilding techniques. Dennison, therefore, went to England to solve these problems and whilst there wrote his report on the traditional methods of watchmaking in use, concluding[3]

> my theory of Americans not finding any difficulty in competing with the English, especially if the interchangeable system and manufacturing in large quantities was adopted, may be accepted as reasonable.

Whilst Dennison was away, a small section of the Howard and Davis plant was set aside for the manufacture of the first watch. In this space Dennison, on his return, designed and built an eight-day watch for machine production with a single going barrel rather than a fusee.[4] It was not successful in its timekeeping capabilities.

The exact order of events at this time is, not surprisingly, unknown and early texts[5, 6] do not agree with later versions.[4] A new factory was built in the grounds at Roxbury and was completed early in 1851. After the failure of the eight-day watch, Stratton, who had moved to the new company with Dennison when it was formed, designed an English style thirty-hour watch with going barrel as the first production model. This was not to Dennison's liking and he had his eight-day watch redesigned and built with two mainsprings by David and Oliver Marsh. Only a small number was made before it was abandoned. There are certainly illustrations of an eight-day watch with single mainspring in Harrold[4] and of an eight-day watch with two mainsprings in Abbott.[5] All these eight-day watches are engraved 'Howard, Davis & Dennison'. The first hundred thirty-hour watches were produced early in 1853 and marked 'Warren' and the next nine hundred 'Samuel Curtis'. Illustrations of these are shown in Harrold.[4] Like the products, the firm changed its name frequently in this period:

1850   Dennison, Howard and Davis (or Howard, Davis and Dennison)
1850   American Horologe Company
1853   Warren Manufacturing Company
1853   Boston Watch Company

but continued with the same thirty-hour watch (Plate 5).

Plate 5 A movement from the Boston Watch Company at Waltham made in c1855 which bears the names of the founders of the firm. The jewels and regulator scale give the movement an English look

There were also some problems in other areas. The thirty-hour watch at first used English lever-style escape wheels with pointed teeth but these proved vulnerable and a change was made to Swiss lever-style escape wheels. Dials and gilding still presented difficulties in spite of Dennison's visit to England and further visits were made by the dialmaker to Liverpool, England, and by Stratton to Coventry, England, for gilding skills. Many of the early machines were not satisfactory due to inaccuracy and problems of measurement and in 1852 Charles Moseley, an experienced machinist, joined the company to assist in solving these problems. The size and layout of the factory at Roxbury were not ideal and in 1853 the Waltham Improvement Company was formed to buy land and provide capital for a new steam-powered factory at Waltham about 10 miles (16km) from Boston. This was completed in 1854 and was surrounded by housing for the workers. Pictures of both factories can be found in Abbott.[5] Dennison moved into the original farmhouse on the land to complete a watchmaking community. There were 90 to 100 workers producing 30 to 40 watches per week, a rate which was in fact about half that achieved by the traditional methods in use in Switzerland at that time.

With all these problems it might be concluded that the project was a disaster but it was the first realistic attempt at mass production of watches by machinery with interchangeable parts and with hindsight it is possible to see why the problems arose.

1 Ambitious eight-day watch design.
2 Inadequate knowledge of some manufacturing processes.
3 Inadequately accurate machinery.
4 Lack of knowledge of plant layout and space requirements.
5 Dennison could not be expert in everything; watch designer, foreman, driving force, businessman, etc. He was best suited to being a factory superintendent.

There was a final financial problem. The time scale from formation in 1850 until the first watches were sold in 1853–4 was not good for investors who would want a good return on their money in the next few years to make up for the 'lost years'. Unfortunately in the period from 1854–7 it was not possible to achieve these returns because of a recession and debts began to increase. In May 1857 the company was assigned bankrupt and auctioned.

Fortunately there were observers in the trade who had realised the potential that had been demonstrated by Dennison and Howard with their English-style watches in standard sizes with standard parts. There was considerable manipulation before the inevitable collapse. Howard had a scheme to obtain the factory and contents and Dennison had a different one. Details of the manoeuvring can be found in Moore[2] and eventually the Dennison group made the successful auction bid for a combination involving the gold watchcase-making firm Tracy and Baker with two thirds of the funding to be supplied by Robbins and Appleton who were watch wholesalers. Royal E. Robbins made the bid for $56,000 and the new firm was called Tracy, Baker and Company. However, Baker soon withdrew and in the same year, 1857, the name became Appleton, Tracy & Company. There were other name changes in the next few years:

1858 Waltham Improvement Company and Appleton, Tracy merged
1859 American Watch Company
1885 American Waltham Watch Company
[1906 Waltham Watch Company]

During the period from 1857 to 1892 Robbins was in charge and due to his financial stake had a controlling interest in the firm. However, his purchase in May 1857 did not include everything at Waltham, for Charles Rice had a chattel mortgage which enabled him to take away some watch material and machinery. This was installed in the old Roxbury plant with Howard as a manager and some Waltham workers. There, watches were produced under the name Howard and Rice. Within a year Howard managed to settle his debt and purchase the new company which he renamed E. Howard & Company. There were now two machine watchmaking companies in America. Early watches from Howard are illustrated in Harrold.[4] (Plate 10.)

Plates 6 and **7** A Waltham Chronodrometer engraved 'Appleton, Tracy & Co' made c1859. **Plate 6** shows the dial. The sweep seconds hand takes four minutes to rotate and the subsidiary lower dial hand takes four seconds. The time is recorded on the upper dial. The watch is a timer but the stop button stops the whole watch and there is no reset mechanism. **Plate 7** shows the movement (see also **Plates 37** and **41**)

Although Dennison had favoured the Robbins group purchase he did not really get on with them but Robbins found he needed Dennison's expertise as factory superintendent and Dennison became a salaried employee. This was not easy for Dennison as he felt it was his business and it was obvious that in due course he would have to leave; perhaps when Stratton or Moseley became competent to run the plant.

At this stage both Appleton, Tracy & Co and Howard & Co were producing attractively priced (compared with imports) watches of standard size which suited the public and the casemaking firms. Spare parts were interchangeable (albeit on a limited scale requiring some fitting) which suited repairers. Thus, provided nothing untoward happened, the American watchmaking industry was under way. However, the costs of the exercise were large and as Harrold[4] observes the Boston Watch Company could supply a $20 watch in 1857 but it had cost $150,000 to find out how.

The trade recession of 1857 which had contributed to the final collapse of the Boston Watch Company continued and Robbins' new company had to struggle to survive. Robbins himself explains some of the early problems in a speech celebrating the millionth watch.[6] In this speech he gives credit to Dennison, Howard and Davis for laying the foundations of machine watchmaking. He then explains how the factory was kept going by persuading the workers to accept a 50 per cent pay cut in November 1857 rather than for the factory to remain closed as it had been in October. Moore[2] gives some financial data which illustrate the problem.

	SALES	CASH SPENT
June 1857	$789	$6,690
September 1857	$5,286	$5,097
November 1857	$167	– [50% pay cut]
March 1858	$7,894	–

Robbins kept the watches produced at minimal cost which he pledged in various ways to borrow money to keep going. By autumn 1858 the worst was over and he was able to sell the watches. In 1858–9 Robbins sold the now profitable watch company to the Improvement Company and the complete unit was named the American Watch Company in which he held a controlling amount of stock and of which he was the manager. Robbins[6] estimated that his 'paper' profits for two years' work salvaging the watch company were $70,000. During the difficult period Robbins had employed a number of key staff at high rates of pay and after a short period of profitable operation more difficulties arose due to the outbreak of the Civil War in 1861. This time Robbins cut production to a minimum to reduce the possibility of large debts and kept only the skilled, essential workers employed. Early in 1862 Dennison was discharged for a variety of reasons, basically an inability to allow Robbins to manage without interference, which culminated in Dennison's desire to produce a

Plate 8 A Nashua Watch Company product of c1862

Plate 9 A Waltham 'William Ellery' grade threequarter plate watch based on the Nashua company design which they acquired in 1862

new cheap 'soldier's watch'. Since the firm already marketed two cheap lines (C. T. Parker model and P. S. Bartlett model), Robbins considered this an unwarranted expense. However, the new watch was somehow produced in 1861–2 as the William Ellery model and was a great success accounting for 45 per cent of the sales (30 per cent of the cash value) by 1865.[2] (Plates 8 and 9.)

When Dennison was dismissed he brought a suit for breach of contract. With the success of the Ellery watch the company settled out of court in late 1863, paying Dennison his salary since dismissal, employing him as agent to furnish foreign material and making their records right in relation to the dishonourable discharge.[1] The agency did not in fact materialise for Dennison also wanted to act as sales agent in England which Robbins would not allow. In 1863, Dennison went to Europe and eventually achieved success (see Chapter 7).

What can be concluded about Dennison's contribution to the future of watchmaking? Although he departed to Europe he left behind a factory, albeit salvaged by Robbins' financial skills, which was the first of many American firms. There are a number of points which can be deduced from the years 1850–62.

1 Watchmaking in America was a proven new industry which could create new job opportunities and because there was no traditional watchmaking industry would destroy no *American* jobs. It could therefore be expected that there would be expansion and new firms providing fierce competition.

2 Mass production of interchangeable parts (with some fitting) was a realistic proposition with properly designed machinery.

3 New special machinery was required with new high standards of accuracy.

4 The basic machining processes needed had been established often by adapting traditional methods but more importantly by rethinking the processes in the light of new developments. They can be broadly divided into four groups:

(a) Lathe processes using fixed tools with rotating work; needed for round parts such as arbors, pillars, plates, screws, etc.

(b) Milling-type processes using moving tools with fixed work; needed for non-round parts such as contouring, sinks, gear wheel teeth, pinion teeth, etc.

(c) Pressing or stamping processes in which press tools consisting of a die and punch lined up by block and pillars made bridges, wheel blanks, etc. This was a very important process for the watchmaking industry. It was advanced considerably in Europe by the precision made possible by the four-pillar block of Ingold (1843) and the two-pillar block of Retor (1854)[7,8] and presumably Dennison used similar tools. The block kept the die and punch in their correct relative positions.

Plate 10 A Howard watch of
c1860 with Mershon's patent
regulator and Reed's patent
barrel

(d) A range of processes using special tools peculiar to watchmaking.

5 It was beginning to be recognised that machines needed to be dedicated to a single purpose. Continuous resetting by an operator was not ideal for interchangeability.

6 There was a need for measurement systems to check parts and for a recognised system of sizes.[9] Gauges needed to be designed which used a measurement system common to all makers and all repairers and which used a common system of units. There was a considerable number of individual systems in Europe but in America there was no need to use traditional methods.

7 There was a need to be able to communicate manufacturing information by means of a widely recognised system of drawing.[10] 'It is desirable to note here that an essential difference between the old and the new methods shows itself at this point . . . now a book of drawings is furnished to the foreman who has to set the machines . . .'

8 There was a need for engineers as well as watchmakers in the industry. The engineer had to translate the watchmaker's design into machines and processes to produce the parts. This did not mean that the watchmaker was redundant, his knowledge and skill was still needed in the design of a successful product. In an article considering the 'mechanical manufacture of a watch' it is pointed out that anyone wishing to set up in this business needs three vital assets: sufficient capital, a good mechanical engineer and a competent watchmaker. The writer emphasises the role of the watchmaker in what is to be an engineering

34

environment in that his design from both the manufacturing and horological viewpoint is the keystone for success. It must first be made by hand and be completely satisfactory before the engineer can proceed with planning the production in quantity.[11]

9   One factor which was not yet fully appreciated was the cost of starting a successful factory system and many firms would later discover this problem. The main cause of trouble was the time taken to set up the factory and to market the watches so that there might be three or four years of capital input before any returns could be expected. The investors needed to be patient and the overall manager needed some financial skills.

10 In this survey there is no mention of automatic machinery.[12] The industry first envisaged was still labour intensive. The use of machines in a factory was to increase production and promote interchangeability, not to reduce the workforce.

The role of the engineer in the new method of watchmaking is worthy of further consideration. Since there was no special watchmaking machinery available one of the first steps on setting up a new factory was to design and manufacture suitable machines to produce the parts for the watch.[13] This was done with the ordinary machine and hand tools available at the time. It soon became apparent that an engineer who could set up a new watch factory was in demand and might frequently change firms. An example of this type of person is Charles Moseley. His history reads[5,12]

1852   Dennison, Howard and Davis for whom amongst other achievements he designed the split chuck lathe; first with a moving collet and later with fixed collet for interchangeable accuracy. This chuck became standard for many watchmaking lathes
1859   Nashua Watch Company
1862   American Watch Company
1864   The National Watch Company of Chicago (Elgin)
1877   Own Business

As machines became standardised in form some engineers left the watch companies to form watch machine tool companies to supply new factories with suitable machines. An example of this approach is Ambrose Webster.

1857   Appleton, Tracy and Company for whom he designed and developed various machines and introduced a single standard measurement system.[5]
1876   Joined Fisher and Whitcomb to form the American Watch Tool Company who supplied machine tools to, for example, the Waterbury Watch Company in America and to the Rotherham Watch Company in Coventry, England.[14]

Plates 11 and **12 Plate 11** shows a 'P.S. Bartlett' grade Waltham watch of c1890. **Plate 12** shows the Waltham full-plate style of the period with a finely adjustable regulator. The handset mechanism is engaged by the lever at 5 o'clock which can be pulled out

Plate 13 *(left)* A Waltham
movement of c1882; *(right)* a
Swiss watch made to look
American and given a
fictional manufacturer's
name (Brooklyn Watch
Company)

Another interesting pioneering engineer was Charles Vander Woerd who worked for the Boston Watch Company and their successors till 1883 (with a short spell at Nashua, 1859–62). During this time he invented a number of machines including an *automatic* pinion cutter (1864) and an *automatic* screw-making machine (1874). Screw-making machines could also be set up or adapted to rough out pinions and staffs and machines for this purpose were patented by Woerd in 1882 (US patent 268,340) and 1885 (US patent 320,942).[15] This range of machines is particularly interesting because they were exhibited in action, together with examples of watches produced at the time, at the 1876 Philadelphia Centennial Exhibition and the 1885 Inventions Exhibition in London.[16] The impact of these exhibitions on European watchmaking is considered in Chapters 4 and 5.

At the time of the Philadelphia Exhibition, which was a great success for the American Watch Company, the prudence of this display of machines was discussed. Robbins replied, 'Only sixteen machines will be showed out of some thousands we make use of', suggesting that no real information could be gained. This view was also expressed later by D. H. Church (1849–1905), who joined the American Watch Company in 1882 and was probably the last great machine designer at Waltham. Some of his machines were in use for fifty years[2] and from about 1920 new machinery was usually purchased from specialist suppliers. In an interview,[17] Church said 'For a long time we used to patent my machines but a few years ago we gave that up . . . since the machines could not well be imitated and they wouldn't be much use outside Waltham . . .'

In this survey of engineers at Waltham one important designer has not yet been mentioned. E. A. Marsh, with the company from 1865 to 1910–11, who apart from his contribution to machine design was the author of a book about the development of automatic machinery; a very important document.[12]

The period from 1859 to 1883 was one in which the American Watch Company prospered but from 1883 the effect of competition from other firms brought about a return to more usual business conditions. Several changes occurred in this twenty-year period, one of which was a slow move towards the use of automatic machinery. Here the engineers were forcing the pace for the management was not at first keen on this expensive investment but in due course with increasing competition automatic machines became vital in reducing costs. Such machinery needs less men and many of those needed require little skill. Another change was to simplify the watch design to reduce the number of parts and to ease assembly. The results of the various changes were to alter the production rate from 40 per day with 200 workers in 1859 to 2,000 per day with 1,200 workers in 1883. This increased production and manpower and required

Plate 14 An Elgin railroad quality watch of c1869

Plates 15 and **16 Plate 15** shows an Elgin watch of c1910 in an engraved gold-plated case with screw-on front and back. **Plate 16** shows the watch movement to be of good quality with 17 jewels and micrometer adjustment of the regulator

a bigger factory. This was achieved by steady alterations and additions and was complete by 1883. Robbins' method of management was always conservative so that he built and maintained a healthy company providing good dividends for the necessary investors. The period can be illustrated with some figures.[2]

	Dividend	Production; sales (millions)	Swiss imports; value (millions)
1865	22%	44,632; –	226,000; $3*
1870	20%	55,042; –	330,000; $4*
1876	6%	84,737; $1	75,000; $1.5
1883	8%	350,000*; $3.5	150,000*; $2.5

(*estimated figures)

The impact of production at Waltham and other factories on Swiss imports is marked. In 1859 virtually 100 per cent of watches sold in America were Swiss imports but by 1883 the Swiss had only 40 per cent of the market. Not only were Waltham products satisfying a large part of the American market but because of the need to keep machinery at full production to be profitable they were seeking their own export markets. A

London office was opened in 1873 and it appears that Aaron Dennison was approached to work for the company as he was then living in England. Dennison and Robbins could not agree terms and Dennison's son Edward was hired by Stratton who was in charge of the London office. Soon after this Dennison started in the business of making watch cases in Birmingham, England, and quickly secured an order from Waltham for most of their watches sold in England. By 1882 Waltham watch sales were £100,000 per annum in England and by 1887 Dennison was making 50,000 cases per year for Waltham alone.[18] (See Chapter 7.)

A typical American watch movement of 1880 would be made in several qualities and be sold over a range of prices depending on the materials used, brass or nickel; the finish, gilding or decorated; the amount of jewelling, 7 to 17; and the adjustments made for accuracy. Not all watch movements sold to the retail jewellers would be cased so that the retailer or purchaser could, because of the standard sizes (6, 8, 10, 12, 14, 16, and 18), choose his own case, again available in a variety of styles and materials over a range of prices.[19] All the watch movements would use a going barrel and a Swiss lever escapement. Most would have a patented safety device between the barrel containing the mainspring and the centre wheel,[15] the earliest patent being to G. P. Reed in 1857 (US patent 17,055). These devices protected the gear and pinion teeth if the (still imported) mainspring broke. This was usually arranged by having the centre wheel pinion screwed with a coarse thread to the centre wheel arbor so that the normal spring torque kept the pinion tight. If the spring broke the sudden

Plates 17 and **18 Plate 17** shows an Elgin dress watch in a gold plated case c1915. **Plate 18** shows the unusual case style and the relatively low-quality 7-jewel movement

Plate 19 A Tremont Watch Company product of 1866. This ill-fated Dennison venture founded in 1864 was based on imported Swiss components assembled in American plates. The company became the Melrose Watch Company in 1866 and in 1871 the remnants were moved to England to found the Anglo-American Watch Company (see Chapter 7)

reverse shock allowed the pinion to fly up the coarse thread and disengage the train. Watches with this feature are often marked 'safety pinion'. Winding was by key in the older design but by button from 1867–8. Handset was by key or by lever under the bezel engaging the gearing and wind button with the hands. The original full plate design in the English style lasted to the turn of the century but threequarter plate models which were thinner were also available from about 1860 (Plates 8 to 22).

Catalogues of spare parts for movements were available for dealers[20] and by examination of one type of movement it is possible to calculate the number of parts of each grade of watch and the price of everything except the plates which were not priced but were available. Repairs involving plates required the watch to be returned to the factory, this was probably due to the selective fitting required. Of particular significance in 1885 was the ability of a watch dealer to hold a stock of those parts most frequently required, or be able to get a less common part quickly, and repair watches with certainty and minimum fuss. This was a completely new method of watch repair which was not feasible with the traditional method of manufacture used in Europe.

Typical American watch factories of the period are described in journal articles of 1869 and 1884.[21,22] These illustrate and describe many of the processes used and show differences in the use of machinery. Perkins[13] gives a more technical description of a factory in 1874 and describes the processes of punching, plate making, wheel and pinion making, lever making, jewelling, etc.

So far only the developments at Waltham have been considered for the period from 1850 to 1883 but the success achieved was bound to stimulate competition. The first competitor to the Robbins' organisation was Howard, the other survivor of the 1857 bankruptcy. Howard's first contribution to American development was to change from the full plate style and make watches with a variety of top plate arrangements.[4] He was prepared to introduce other new features, one of the best known being Reed's safety barrel (Plate 10). Howard also featured Reed's whiplash regulator (US patent 49,154 of 1865) which was later used by other American and Swiss firms (Plate 35).[23] The company, which Howard left in 1882, were known for their high-quality watches and they only produced about 800,000 by the end of the century.

The first completely new company was the Nashua Watch Company which proposed to produce high-quality threequarter plate watches using more machinery to produce completely interchangeable parts. For this scheme, Moseley, Vander Woerd and Stratton left Waltham in 1859 to join the new company. However, in 1862 financial problems caused the company to be sold to Waltham who took on the men, the factory and the stock successfully incorporating the Nashua Watch into their products (Plate 8).

Plate 20 A Columbus Watch Company (1882–1903) watch of c1884. The company developed from a watch-importing business and made watches of both average and railroad quality

The Civil War boom (William Ellery) encouraged more firms to start. In 1864 The National Watch Company of Chicago (Elgin), the Newark Watch Company, the United States Watch Company, the Tremont Watch Company and the New York Watch Company were created. Of these five companies only The National Watch Company (Elgin National Watch Company from 1874) was successful and gave Robbins competition. Elgin did finally produce more jewelled watches than the Waltham Company.[4] The Tremont Watch Company (Plate 19) leads directly to Europe and is discussed in Chapter 7. The New York Watch Company, despite a series of failures, did eventually become the Hampden Watch Company and survived till 1930 when it was sold to Russia as a complete factory to establish their industry (Chapter 10).

By 1883 there were four other successful companies producing jewelled watches to compete with Waltham, Elgin, Hampden and Howard.

Plates 21 and **22 Plate 21** shows a Peoria Watch Company product of c1886.

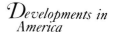

Plate 22 shows the movement with fine regulation; it is also described as 'adjusted'. The company, which existed from 1885 to 1895, had a background in the failed Newark, Cornell, US Marion and Fredonia Watch companies and was probably doomed to failure from the start

None were making watches in quantity as can be seen by the totals of movements produced by 1885.

Springfield Illinois Watch Company	280,000
Lancaster Watch Company	100,000
Rockford Watch Company	100,000
Columbus Watch Company (Plate 20)	120,000
Howard	430,000
Hampden	450,000
Elgin (Plates 14 to 18)	1,800,000
Total	3,280,000
Waltham	2,600,000

Waltham's total product is about the same as all the others put together but their share of the market (excluding imports) had fallen from 100 per cent to 30 per cent.

Robbins' reaction to this competition was to reorganise his management team. Ezra Fitch was appointed as General Manager in 1883. Fitch, with a sales background, understood marketing and would shape the products to meet changing tastes and competition. Other successful makers would pursue similar policies.

This chapter has shown how a new industry was established in America in a period of twenty-five years (1851–76). In 1876 the Philadelphia Exhibition enabled European visitors to see the threat provided by this development. (Later American watchmaking is considered in Chapter 9.)

4 English conservatism

'Ces brigands-là, pour faire le pain, se servant de
la vapeur, qui est une invention du diable'
Alphonse Daudet (1840–97)

During the eighteenth century, English watchmakers established a reputation for making the best watches. In the latter part of the century, continental makers started to produce thinner watches using the Lepine calibre with a going barrel instead of a fusee. The cylinder escapement was also being used in an increasing number of continental watches. In particular the Swiss Jura industry produced and exported large numbers of cheap watches so that by the mid-nineteenth century the production figures showed a changed situation.

	England	*Switzerland*
1800	200,000	200,000
1850	200,000	2,200,000

The losers in this change were the English ébauche workers in Prescot and Coventry and from time to time they protested. The watch 'makers' who sold watches continued to sell English watches to customers who wanted them and could afford them but also sold cheaper Swiss watches, which were often illegally imported to avoid duty, to other customers. Thus was born the English view that English watches were best and there would always be a market for them as the rival Swiss makers were for the cheaper end of the market. The Swiss also made better-quality watches but these were initially as expensive as their English counterparts.

In 1850 the American watch industry was born and by 1885 they were producing about a million good-quality lever watches a year made by machinery with 'interchangeable' parts. These were sold at prices to compete with both the English and the Swiss products. Whereas the Swiss export-based industry knew they had a lot to lose to the American makers, the English who still sold 200,000 per year could see no problem and indeed were still convinced that hand-finished fusee watches would remain superior to the machine-made product. The evidence of this attitude can be seen in the discussions that took place amongst the members of the British Horological Institute in the period from its foundation in 1858.[1] A summary of a selection of meetings illustrates the arguments.

1862 *Discussion on the best practical means of improving the watch trade*[2]
The number of watches sold was increasing but the number made in England was decreasing as Swiss imports rose (42,000 in 1853, 160,000 in 1862). There are 800 parts in an English watch and 100 in a Swiss watch. A going barrel could be satisfactory but a fusee looks English. There was forewarning of US problems, the formation of co-operatives was suggested. There was a lack of gauges, drawings and a system for uniform balance springs. Cheapness needs interchangeability. English buyers do not like cylinder escapements. Swiss watches are not good timekeepers.
(A committee for standards was set up in 1861–2.)

1867 *Discussion on the state of the watch trade*[3]
France, Switzerland and America are increasing production but Britain is not. What has the measurement committee been doing? There was a defeatist reply about difficulties. A correct comment that the Institute cannot regulate the trade. The paper admits machines can be useful and suggests that before long US watches will come to Britain in tens of thousands. A report in the *Clerkenwell News* suggesting that the Institute retards progress by opposing change in any shape or form is denied.

1869 *A lecture on American watch manufacture*[4]
Wycherley's methods (qv) are not used enough and the number of parts in an English watch is too large. Vendors do not like machine-made watches as there are too few repair jobs. A large amount of manual labour is still used in America for machine-made watches so that unemployment fears are not realistic. Interchangeability for depthing is satisfactory in ordinary watches (this was a common fear). There is a need to get rid of the fusee for machine manufacture. We have lost trade abroad to America because there is a lack of repairers overseas and an interchangeable parts system helps. London watches were more solid, more permanent and much better finished than any watches manufactured in any country with or without machinery. The public need to appreciate this; once they did, English watches would take the lead all over the world. English watch manufacturers have nothing to fear from America. (Plate 23.)

1874 *American Watch Manufacture*[5]
A description of the Elgin factory. Question — Are all parts interchangeable? Answer — All except escapements. Question — Do they use the fusee? Answer — No. Parts were shown and the comments were that they were not suited to the finer grades of watch.

(1876   English Watch Company, Ehrhardt, Philadelphia Exhibition.)

1879   *Discussion on Fusee*[6]

The adoption of keyless watches will drive the fusee out. We must accept this for the public does not want the fusee, only the trade. (Is this a crack in the armour?)

1880   *Further discussion on the Fusee*[7]

No greater misfortune could befall the English watch trade than the substitution of the going barrel for the fusee by accidental drift. A decision must be made but remember *keyless watches will not supersede others, it is a fashion.* Stick to the fusee. Some comments on repair problems in distant places.

1880   *English watch manufacture*[8]

The speaker purchased an ordinary English watch and stripped it down for critical analysis. He concluded that some design changes were needed to simplify manufacture. There was some shoddy work and the use of pins made assembly difficult when compared with the use of screws.

(1880   Rotherham buy machines.)

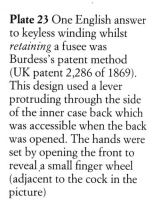

Plate 23 One English answer to keyless winding whilst *retaining* a fusee was Burdess's patent method (UK patent 2,286 of 1869). This design used a lever protruding through the side of the inner case back which was accessible when the back was opened. The hands were set by opening the front to reveal a small finger wheel (adjacent to the cock in the picture)

1880 *The present system of English watch manufacture*[9]

Cheap English watches are not required but we should improve our old lines. The author proposes more subdivision of the work but organised under one roof.

1884 *Machine Watchmaking*[10]

One London factory uses foot-powered tools and it takes three months to achieve the daily production of a large American factory. There are some signs of increasing acceptance of limited numbers of machine-made watches.

(1885 Inventions Exhibition in London.)

1886 *Report on Inventions Exhibition*[11]

A description of American machines in action making parts covering barrel making and *automatic* screw and pinion making with conclusions about the *customers'* needs. These are reasonable timekeeping at a low price and this is what machinery offers in quantity. There is a large market for lower-priced watches. Machinery needs quantity runs of identical parts, etc. Thus the big problems here are still gauging, measurement and education. The author of this paper was soon involved in the formation of the Lancashire Watch Company.

(1899 Formation of Lancashire Watch Company.)

1901 *The advancement of machine watchmaking in England*[12]

The paper discusses the Swiss trade, the Merchandise Marks Act and the current English situation. The demand is now for cheap watches to suit the mass of the people and this has virtually squeezed out the fusee. Ordinary watches are now made from drawings, master plates, gauges and tools consisting of presses, lathes, etc. The rising influence of engineering is noted and the necessity to use the full capacity of machines.

What can be concluded from these few examples of the continuous discussions from 1858 on? It would not be correct to blame the Institute for this lack of positive thinking. Any institute can only reflect the views of its members and since the leading members were traditional makers who made a comfortable living selling their share of 200,000 watches per year (plus imports) they would not be enthusiastic about changing the system. This attitude is shown in the suggested model answer to a City and Guilds examination question on the manufacture of a threequarter plate watch.[13] This answer clearly explains the traditional method of hand-to-hand passing of parts. At this time seven factories were making over 60 per cent of English watches. The answer is correct but the question is not forward thinking.

One of the problems has been discussed in Chapter 3, namely the need for capital and the need to manufacture on a large scale. The business of

Plate 24 This 1875 advertisement shows the machine-made watches available to the British purchaser. Waltham opened a London office in 1873 to penetrate the English market

changing to machine manufacture was risky and even those that tried (Chapter 7) largely ended in failure with losses to their shareholders. Much of this failure was a lack of understanding of marketing and being able to shape the product to suit the largest possible range of customers with the smallest possible number of different parts and sizes else the costs became too great. The scale of operations attempted was always too small but big production needs skilful marketing and expert salesmen. Marketing was something Englishmen did not appear to understand. The supplier made the watches and the customer had little real choice. If the English maker refused to study the market the Swiss and Americans would. The Swiss needed to be aware of the market as their business was export based and the Americans were new, forging a new industry in an environment where risk capital was available from fortune hunters.

The English maker did not realise that the Swiss and Americans would not be satisfied with only part of the market but would want a share in the higher price end which the English maker thought he could keep. With a large manufacturing base it is possible to make a superior model for the higher priced market by extra finish on the basic parts which were mass produced. Englishmen did not believe this was possible. In short, the customer now dictated whereas before the (English) maker dictated. There was now a real choice available to all buyers and less and less people chose the English product (Plate 24).

There were two further consequences of not establishing a healthy machine-based watch manufacturing system. The first was a commercial loss, for by 1890 Swiss, German and American makers realised that there was an enormous untapped market for customers who wanted a watch which was even cheaper but still reliable. This need was supplied from 1890 to 1980 in large quantities by the pin lever watch (Roskopf watch, dollar watch). For cheapness, mass production was essential and only one completely unsuccessful British attempt was made by the ailing Lancashire Watch Company. The second consequence of no watch industry was more serious for such an undertaking is vital in wartime when imports are not available. In 1938 Britain had to build a new watchmaking capability and after the war, in an attempt to preserve this skill, the Government encouraged Smith, Ingersoll and Newmark to commence pin lever watch manufacture. Their success was limited because the customer in the end preferred Swiss imports and the day of the cheap mechanical watch was soon to finish with the development of the more accurate and cheaper LCD electronic watch.

There were some temporary bright spots in this gloomy picture. Patent number 880 of 1867 to John Wycherley of Prescot (1818–91) effectively acknowledged the need for the production of ébauches with interchangeable parts and enabled him to advertise in the 1872 Kelly Directory 'sole manufacturer of interchangeable machine made movements'. The patent states:

The chief object of this Invention is to affect an economy in manufacture of the parts constituting the framework of watches, and to form them with such accuracy as to render the parts interchangeable instead of (as is now the practice) making and fitting the parts for each watch separately.

Wycherley attended a meeting about his system of manufacture in September 1867.[14] At this meeting a letter was read out clearly stating this viewpoint. He *guaranteed* all plates of a particular size to be identical and all frame fittings to fit the plate so that all cases could be identical. He marked the plates ready for drilling so that when drilled by the 'maker' all the wheels supplied would be correctly depthed. There was also a letter from Rotherham, a leading Coventry maker, who tested seven frames with one set of materials and found the parts to be interchangeable.

In spite of this success and the fact that Wycherley supplied many movements to makers from his factory his contribution to watchmaking was outdated when patented because he was still trying to fit in with the traditional method. He should have opened an American-style mass-production enterprise and he also should have abandoned the fusee. However for this he would have needed large financial backing. Rotherham, by ordering American machinery in 1880, made their break with tradition. A description of Wycherley's factory is found in his obituary.[15] The factory was built in 1866 specifically to make movements and was a large building in Warrington Road, Prescot. There were three floors and steam power was used. There were, when production got into full swing, about one hundred and twenty employees about one third of whom were girls. Judging by the number of watches found bearing the initials JW under the dial, indicating a Wycherley ébauche, his venture was very successful.

The remaining bright spots were the attempts by a number of firms between 1871 and 1930 to found or sustain an English watchmaking *industry*, all of which failed due to a variety of reasons but which could be summarised as:

(a) too small and too late, these being of their own making.

(b) failure to understand marketing, again a self-made problem.

(c) World War I (1914–18) and subsequent slumps.

However most firms had made good profits during the war years which may have prolonged their solvency. English firms are examined in Chapter 7.

5 Swiss reactions

Swiss watchmaking was established in Geneva in the second half of the sixteenth century and flourished under a restrictive Guild system. The division of labour method of manufacture described in Chapter 1 was used and is known in Switzerland as *établissage* where the maker *(établisseur)* did the final finishing *(repassage)* and marketed the product. At the beginning of the eighteenth century a new centre of watchmaking materialised in the Jura in north-west Switzerland traditionally 'founded' by Daniel Jean Richard (1665–1741) of La Sagne in 1681. This centre grew rapidly and made watches that were cheaper than those from Geneva and of several qualities to satisfy a wide market. This part of Switzerland had close ties with the French watchmakers and, for example, bought ébauches from Japy (Chapter 2). The success of the Jura industry was such that its production was nine times that of Geneva by 1855.

In order to promote better watches the Swiss started simple performance trials and formed several Société d'émulation (Geneva 1776, Neuchâtel 1791) which aimed to 'contribute to the public good'. These societies formulated competitions to encourage improvements in watches such as the cutting of teeth and the manufacture of balance springs.[1] By 1850 the Swiss had achieved a very satisfactory state based on using simple machines, such as those of Leschot, and hand finishing to utilise both lever and cylinder escapements (Plate 25). The industry was producing over two million watches per year (England 200,000) and selling to a large export market including the United States and England. The workforce in 1870 was 34,000 of which threequarters were outworkers. The impact of the American watch industry on Swiss exports to America was dramatic, a fall from 330,000 in 1870 to 75,000 in 1876. The American industry made 200,000 watches in 1875–6. This was something to cause concern and Edouard Favre-Perret was sent to the 1876 Philadelphia Centennial Exhibition to see what was happening. Here machinery and watches were exhibited and it was the latter which particularly interested Favre-Perret. He borrowed a fifth-grade Waltham watch for a personal trial and was so impressed by its performance that he had it stripped down and examined by an expert who reported,[2] 'I am completely overwhelmed; the result is incredible; one would not find one such watch among fifty thousand of

our manufacture'. The point being made was that American machine-made watches were of better quality than the Swiss were exporting and that they needed to pay attention to this facet to defeat the threat to their vital export industry.

The Swiss were aware that the interchangeability of American watches was not perfect and hand fitting was used so that they did not need to make a *dramatic* change in their manufacturing method. They did improve quality and started to adapt their industry to introduce more machinery for processes suitable for modification. Repassage continued but the emphasis on outworkers changed so that by 1905, when 51,000 workers were employed, threequarters were now in small factories. The small units suited the village-centred industry which was caused by the climate and geographical locations in difficult country. They also introduced some new ideas of their own.

Plate 25 Two Swiss watches with barred Lepine calibre, cylinder escapement movements of standard quality. They could be cased in a variety of styles: *(top)* this case has a transparent blue enamel bezel and back over engine-turned metal; *(bottom)* this one is of high domed, cast silver

Plate 26 A pin lever escapement watch with Roskopf calibre made or marketed by Roskopf's son Fritz-Edouard. The case is cast with a railway engine picture and was supplied to Belgian railway workers according to Roskopf's biographer

Plate 27 A Roskopf watch in a blued steel case with gold-plated hinges, bezel, etc. The movement maker is unknown

Plate 28 A good-quality Roskopf movement of c1910 which has been identified as a 24 ligne Oris calibre 9. It is contained in a nickel-plated case with an enamel dial inscribed 'Oris patent non magnetic lever'

A very important advance in the history of watchmaking was initiated by Georges-Frédéric Roskopf (1813–89). Roskopf was born at Niederweiler in Germany and went to Switzerland to learn French in 1829. After working for four years he became an apprentice with J. Biber at La Chaux de Fonds to learn about horology and watchmaking. In 1835 he married a widow with two sons and with her financial help set up as an établisseur to make cylinder and lever watches for export to North America and Belgium.[3]

He sold this business in 1850 and became manager of the La Chaux de Fonds factory of the Wurzburg firm B. J. Guttmann until 1855 when he set up in business with his son Fritz-Edouard and Henri Gindraux as Roskopf, Gindraux & Co. This lasted for two years when his son decided to open his own business in Geneva and Gindraux went to the horological school at Neuchâtel. It was at about this time that Roskopf began to think of a watch 'à la portée de tout les bourses' (within reach of all purses) to be sold for 20 francs, a price today we recognise as too high. Although it is not clear it seems obvious that Roskopf was still working as an établisseur and developed his ideas by trial and error until he was satisfied. Initially he thought of the cylinder escapement but after discussion with M. J. Grossman adopted the simple detached pin lever escapement (Chapter 6) for his new watches.

Roskopf designed a new calibre in which he reduced the number of parts, simplified escapement fitting, had good driving torque and had an improved winding method. The watch was to keep good time so that the materials and workmanship had to be of a high standard and was to be placed in a robust case made of base metal. In this new calibre he abandoned the traditional centre wheel and engaged the wheel on the large-sized barrel with the third wheel pinion achieving the aims of less parts and good torque. Hand drive through motion work is directly from the barrel. To enable simple fitting he designed the escapement to be assembled on its own separate adjustable platform so that it could be added to the watch as a complete unit which he called a 'porte échappement'. Although he used keyless winding, handsetting was initially by finger pressure as in a clock but soon changed to keyless hand-set methods. Finally, in his oversize barrel, he arranged to use Adrien Philippe's patent free mainspring without stopwork for which he paid a royalty of 25 centimes per watch (few other watches except eight-day designs use this system). For dials he proposed to use printed card, but fearing the action of the chemicals used in papermaking on the movement, he settled for conventional enamelled ones at a cost of 25 centimes each rather than 1 centime for the card.[3] (Paper dials were used in cheap watches within twenty years.)

The Roskopf calibre is shown in Fig 5 and one of his early products was shown at the Universal Exhibition in Paris in 1868 where it was awarded a bronze medal. It is surprising to note that the English press do not mention this new watch.[4] Roskopf patented his calibre (French patent 80,611 of 25 March 1868; there was no Swiss patent system) as 'un genre de montre avec porte échappement' in which it states 'il est facile de changer le genre d'echappement, ancre (lever), cylindre (cylinder) etc', and indeed it is possible to find Roskopf calibre watches with jewelled lever escapements rather than pin lever which is usual and is shown in the patent drawing. He called the watch 'Montre de prolétaire' (people's watch). (Plates 26 to 28.)

Plate 29 A watch made in c1870 by E. Francillon in the new factory at St Imier

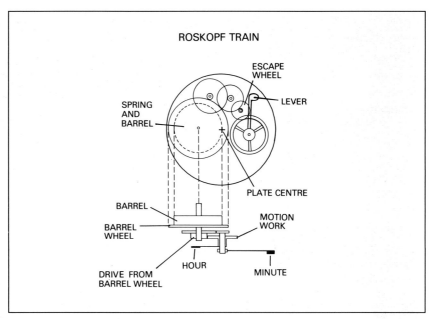

Fig 5 The Roskopf calibre showing the large-size barrel driving the third wheel pinion since the second or centre wheel is not used. The *lower* part of the diagram shows the hands driven from the barrel

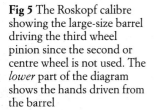

Plate 30 An interesting 16 ligne size watch with a cylinder escapement marketed in 1885 by Louis Brandt. On the back is a gambling machine which is operated by the slide lever on the side. The game shown involves playing cards but other designs were made with roulette, etc

Roskopf was an établisseur so that he did not make his own watches but finished them from bought-out ébauches and parts. For the new calibre this took time and patience to arrange, for not only were his ideas new but he was proposing to produce a watch which some people felt might affect the market by being considered an inferior product. This is a similar reaction to that seen in England when any proposal for change was made (Chapter 4). In the end Roskopf ébauches were made by the Société d'horlogerie de Malleray and were completed in Doubs by M. Chatelan. The escapement was assembled by Adolphe Jacot of Dombresson from parts acquired from various sources by Roskopf.[3]

Roskopf knew of the American market when his ideas were being developed because he had made watches for export. He should also have been aware of their new machine-based industry; indeed it is possible that it is this same G. F. Roskopf who in about 1873 assisted Jacob Schweizer with finance in the development of the Swiss automatic screwmaking machine[5] (Chapter 11). However the 'People's Watch' was a new idea predating the American Waterbury and Ingersoll types and Roskopf is clearly the creator of the concept of a cheap watch for everyone. We now know his standards were too high and such watches needed to be much cheaper and in the early years of the twentieth century his calibre was used by Swiss makers to produce a very cheap pin lever watch to compete successfully in the export markets with the American and German mass-produced 'dollar watches'. These new 'Roskopf Watches' did not have the 'porte échappement' and were not made in the quality Roskopf envisaged so that the name 'Roskopf' became associated with inferior products. Erroneously, the pin lever escapement was also blamed for poor

Plate 31 Two unidentified good-quality Swiss movements; well jewelled with lever escapements they may have been intended for America (see **Plate 32**). They were made c1890

performance whereas in truth it was the quality of finish and assembly associated with cheapness.[6] This is no reflection on Roskopf, watches made to his specification between 1880 and 1910 were of satisfactory quality and performance and are attractive repairable watches rather than throw-away designs. However Roskopf pointed the way and the Swiss industry was able to survive the impact of cheap watches by adapting his ideas to the market place. An indication of the forthcoming cheap watches can be found in the report of a visit made in 1905 to a factory making Roskopf watches.[7] Roskopf died in 1889 so that he did not see these changes. His son, F. E. Roskopf, also made good-quality Roskopf calibre watches, many of which were apparently used by Belgian railway workers[3] (Plate 26).

Jacob Schweizer (mentioned above) was another innovator in the history of Swiss watchmaking. He devised a form of automatic lathe which was particularly suited to making precise small parts for watches. Initially it was for making balance collets but it was quickly adapted to making screws and later all manner of small parts (Chapter 11). The vital feature of the design (the sliding headstock) owes nothing to the American machines and indeed the Americans copied his idea.[5] Although Schweizer was an inventor who soon turned his talents to other fields his contribution to watchmaking was enduring and indeed his ideas are still used today in precision engineering lathes. Once the Swiss automatic lathe became established other machines were devised, often by specialist Swiss firms, and slowly the whole Swiss horological industry rose to its

Plate 32 Two good-quality Swiss lever movements sold in America: *(left)* movement has a trademark and is engraved 'Benedict, 691 Broadway, New York'; *(right)* movement engraved 'Richard Oliver, New York' is marked under the dial 'Agassiz' and is a Longines product (winding wheel missing)

Plate 33 A jaquemart watch which strikes. It was made by Louis Brandt in 1891 and is operated by the slide lever on the side

59

position of dominance resulting in exports rising from 3 million watches in 1885 to 17 million in 1913.[2] These exports, however, were not to America but to Europe and the British Empire.[8] (Plates 29 to 38.)

The total number of Swiss watchmakers listed in the 1901 Kelly Directory is 713. Of this total 75 are located in Geneva, 258 in La Chaux de Fonds, 88 in Bienne, 47 in Tramelan and 37 in Le Locle, showing the large size of the Jura industry compared to the Geneva industry. Many of these 713 would be associated with a small community and would not be large. The production of watches in 1899 was 6.7 million employing a total of 50,000 workers. An 'average' factory can be postulated by division as having about 70 associated workers including its percentage of home workers and the production would be about 190 watches per week. Thus this small 'average' factory produced as many watches as contemporary English factories but with less workers due to the efficiency of the Swiss system (Chapter 7). It is possible to find out something about larger, well-known factories from contemporary visit reports.

At Messrs Stauffer, Son and Co, 'Atlas' watch factory[9] in the Jura in 1885 there was a 30-horsepower steam engine, gas lighting, a winter heating boiler and 300 machines producing 60,000 watches per year. (This factory was six times the size of the 'average'.) A new building had electric lighting. There were fourteen workshops, some for forges and presses, each press making 1,800 items in a ten-hour day. In other workshops, pieces were drilled, turned, etc by a multitude of machines. Automatic machines were used for gears and wheels. Pivoting was done separately (possibly after automatic roughing out). Cases were made at the factory and all the machines were specially made on site (it is however likely that automatic lathes would have been bought rather than made, for these were available in Switzerland). The parts were assembled and went to the finishing and adjusting departments from which the watch emerged ready to be worn.

Another report[10] of a visit to J. J. Badollet and Co in 1888 shows that there were hand-controlled lathes with American chucks (automatic closing by lever) and with hand-operated cutter turrets which were used to finish plates from the press or to make barrels and barrel covers. It is not clear if these were their own machines or purchased machines. The report gives an estimate of the number of operations (pressing and drilling etc) needed to make a plate with associated cocks and bridges for a barred Lepine calibre watch as 216. Dies and punches were used for steel work in ordinary watches but for good watches pantograph-based contouring machines were used. Leschot's machines at Vacheron and Constantin also used pantographs. Screws and taps came from specialist firms. These could be made by Muller and Schweizer at their factory in Solothurn using Schweizer's lathes. Finally there is a description of a machine to make barrel arbors having cutters with complex motion regulated by stops and moveable discs. This could be a description of a cam-

Plate 34 A watch with a 19 ligne Lepine calibre movement and a lever escapement made by Louis Brandt in 1895

Plate 35 An Omega chronograph watch of 1898 with a 19 ligne Lepine calibre movement which has a lever escapement and a form of Reed's whiplash regulator patented in America in 1865. The case is silver with a decorated back

Plate 36 An Omega watch of 1899 with a 19 ligne Lepine calibre movement. The silver case has floral engraving and the dial is white with translucent blue enamel numerals. The dial dots are blue and gold and the hands are Omega's own style

operated automatic lathe. Although there is no mention of steam power it would seem likely that this was used nor is size mentioned but the description suggests a fairly large factory.

There is a letter[11] regarding the Longines exhibit at the International Inventions Exhibition in London in 1885 which includes some useful information. The Longines works were built in 1866–7 for the production of watches on the gauged and interchangeable principle. By 1885 it was enlarged and had steam and water power. At the exhibition interchangeability was demonstrated by holding twenty-four plates on straight wires so that it was possible to see through all the tiny jewel holes. This would not guarantee interchangeability unless the parts to go into the holes were also accurate. Barrel manufacture is described in the letter in an unspecified automatic machine. Cases were made at the factory. Towards the end of

Plate 37 A gold-plated brass case containing a poor-quality cylinder escapement movement. In spite of this it makes an attractive picture. The slide on the side stops the whole watch as on many watches described as chronographs (see **Plates 6, 7** and **41**)

the letter the large amount of final fitting and adjustment required is honestly admitted 'these boasted appliances will take you so far . . . [require] a high degree of manipulation'. The factory output was 1,000 watches per week. The purpose of this letter is to point out that the reports on the Waltham exhibit in London in 1885 (Chapter 4) suggest that America is ahead of Switzerland in machine production which the writer suggests is not true. Irrespective of the truth of the claim it is clear that by 1885–8 the Swiss makers were well on the way to wiping out the problems that Favre-Perret had highlighted in 1876.

The Swiss made one more significant step in the nineteenth century. They realised the complexity and size of their industry (713 makers in 1901) and they set up a Chambre Suisse d'horlogerie in 1890 as a consultative body for the industry.[1] This was a first step in a series of activities to form a cartel to protect their vital export industry. This policy has continued to the present day (Chapter 8).

Plate 38 An 'Enigma' cylinder escapement movement made by the Tavannes Watch Company (sometimes under the brand name Cyma). The case is blued steel

6 *The modern watch*

In the hundred years being considered in this chapter the rate of watch production increased dramatically. The new method of machine manufacture demanded full use of high capital cost machines and watches had to be made in a variety of styles and offered over a spectrum of prices to find and satisfy the potential customers. New techniques to sell watches were required in a competitive situation for which an increasing number of models were produced. To indicate the common variations available the list below is presented followed by a brief description of the more interesting points.[1]

WATCHES 1880–1980

1   Mechanical Movements

(a) Escapements: English lever escapement (Chapter 1, Fig 4b)
Swiss lever escapement (Chapter 1, Fig 4a)
Cylinder escapement (Chapter 1, Fig 3)
Pin lever escapement
Duplex escapement
Other escapements[1]

(b) Timekeeping: Terminal curves for balance springs
Compensated balances (Chapter 1, Fig 2)
Metallurgical balances and springs
Regulators
Free sprung watches
Tourbillon watches
Karrusel watches
Kew certificates

(c) Complications: Striking, alarm, repeating
Day, date, moon phase
Perpetual calendar
Stop watches and chronographs
Multiple complications
Key wind

	Automatic winding
	Button winding
	Eight-day watches
	Analogue and digital display
(d) Layout:	Fusee (rare) (Chapter 1, Fig 1)
	Going barrel (Chapter 1)
	Conventional calibres: full plate (Plate 5)

Conventional calibres: full plate (Plate 5)
                          barred or Lepine (Plate 2)
                          threequarter plate (Plate 9)
                          split plate (Plate 48)
                          wrist watches (Plate 92)

Special calibres: Roskopf (Chapter 5, Fig 5)
                          Waterbury (Chapter 9, Fig 14)

(e) Finish: Jewelling
                    Gilt, nickel, skeleton, etc

2 Electric Movements (Chapter 12)

(a) Type: Electromechanical (Plate 153)
                    Electronic, analogue, LED, LCD (Plates 155, 158)

3 Cases

(a) Style: Pocket watches
                    Ladies' watches
                    Wrist watches
                    Open face (Plate 40)
                    Half hunter (Plate 50)
                    Hunter (Plate 83)
                    Dress, formal, sporting, etc

(b) Material: Gold, silver, nickel, titanium, plated or blued
                    base metal, etc

(c) Decoration: Engine turning
                    Engraving, chasing, chiselling (Plate 88)
                    Enamel (Plate 85)
                    Niello (Plate 87)
                    Jewelled (Plate 94)

PIN LEVER ESCAPEMENT

The pin lever (pin pallet) escapement may have originated from one devised in 1798 and described in 1834 by Louis Perron.[2] An alternative ancestor may be a c1820 Ellicott lever watch which uses an escape wheel of appropriate form.[1] Chamberlain[2] illustrates a pin lever watch by Pichon, Geneva, made in about 1830 and Grossman[3], in his 1866 treatise on the detached lever escapement, describes a form used at Glashütte in Germany. However the escapement was not used in quantity until the

Fig 6 The pin lever escapement

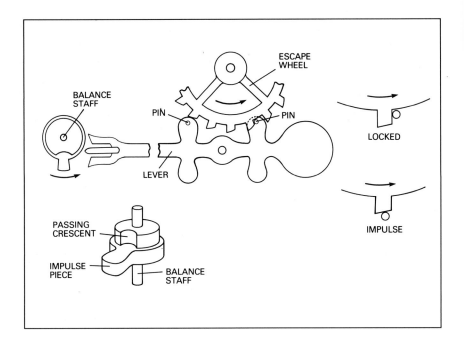

Fig 7 The duplex escapement

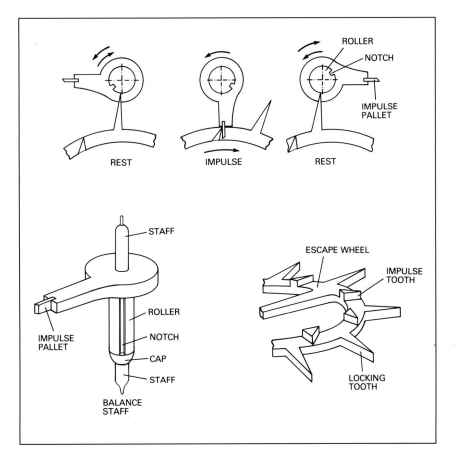

advent of cheap clocks and watches in the late nineteenth century in America, Germany, and Switzerland. It owes success to simple detached form which uses flat faces on the escape wheel teeth and cylindrical pins as lever pallets, the impulse being supplied by the sloping ramp on the escape wheel teeth. The lever fork arrangements are crude but have conventional impulse and safety arrangements (Fig 6). The simple form of the escapement parts enables them to be cheaply produced, mainly by stamping processes.

DUPLEX ESCAPEMENT

The duplex escapement was conceived by Dutertre in about 1720 but reinvented and patented by Thomas Tyrer in 1782 (UK patent 1,311). It was used as a high-quality alternative to the verge escapement until about 1850 and later revived in America as a *cheap* escapement. There are two sets of teeth on the escape wheel (Fig 7). An outer tooth locks the train by resting on the balance staff until it is allowed to slip through a vertical slit in the staff, permitting an inner tooth to strike the impulse piece on the balance roller and give impulse. The train is locked when the next outer tooth rests on the balance staff. On the return swing of the balance the outer tooth does not escape through the slit so that impulse only occurs once per vibration. This type of action is known as single beat. The duplex escapement is an unsatisfactory design because of the friction between locked tooth and balance staff.

TIMEKEEPING

In watches most of the problems of timekeeping are caused by:
(i)   friction in the escapement
(ii)   unequal arc of vibration (amplitude)
(iii) temperature changes
(iv)   position changes of the watch in the pocket, on the wrist, etc.

The problem of friction in the escapement was solved by the universal adoption of the detached lever escapement (page 12) and the problem of achieving constant vibration time for all amplitudes, known as isochronism, was solved by the use of special terminal curves on the balance spring. The action of a terminal curve is to ensure that the centre of inertia is always on the balance axis during the coiling and uncoiling of the balance spring. Although Arnold and Breguet solved this problem empirically (page 11) it was left to Edouard Phillips (1861) and L. Lossier (1890) to produce a justification.[4] In most modern watches the spiral balance spring is finished with a Breguet overcoil (Fig 8).

The effect of temperature change on timekeeping became apparent as soon as the balance spring was introduced and the ingenious solution of

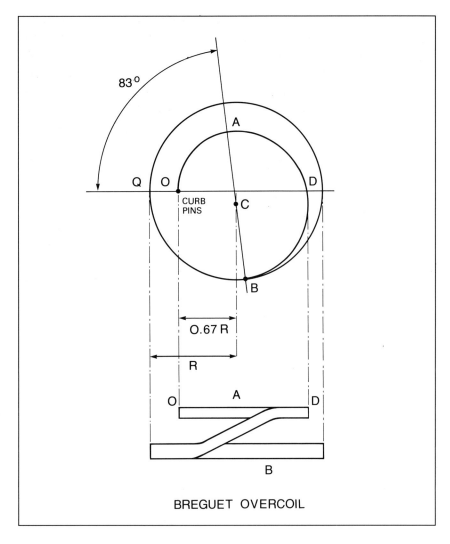

83°

A

Q O

CURB
PINS

C

D

0.67 R

R

B

O

A

D

B

BREGUET OVERCOIL

Fig 8 The overcoil used with a spiral balance spring to connect the spring to the cock. The overcoil is above the plane of the spring. Arc ADB is 180° of radius AC and arc OA is 83° of radius 0·67R struck from the centre

the compensated balance (page 10) sufficed for many years. Because the rate of change of spring elasticity with temperature is not exactly equal to the rate of change of balance inertia with temperature the compensation achieved was not perfect. By careful adjustment the errors can be eliminated at two temperatures but between (and beyond) these two there is always a middle temperature error. Charles Edouard Guillaume, a Swiss working in the early years of the twentieth century sought to perfect new materials to avoid these problems and for ordinary watches a material with negligible coefficient of expansion was developed for balances and Elinvar, a material with negligible variation of elasticity, was developed for balance springs. For the very best watches, however, a special Guillaume metal was used with brass in a cut compensated balance together with a *steel* balance spring and with this combination middle temperature error was virtually zero.

Regulators[2] had always been fitted to watches to alter the working length of the balance spring to enable the watch to be adjusted to keep good time. However with good materials and careful adjustment high-quality watches often omitted this crude device and were set up by the adjuster as 'free sprung' watches. This arrangement was well suited to gimballed chronometers and clocks but a watch, whether regulated or free sprung, would always suffer some positional error due to the change in inclination in pocket or on wrist. Tests clearly show that the performance of a watch changes if run dial up, dial down, pendant up or pendant down, etc. To minimise this error rotating escapements were used.

In the tourbillon, invented by Breguet in 1795, the escapement (balance, escape wheel, etc) is mounted on a carriage which carries a pinion driven by the third wheel. The fourth wheel is fixed and is concentric with the carriage shaft. The escape wheel pinion meshes with the fixed fourth wheel. Thus, as the carriage rotates, the escape wheel pinion will roll around the fixed fourth wheel which will cause the pinion to rotate and operate the escape wheel and balance in the normal way (Fig 9).

Plate 39 An alarm watch in a blued steel case which opens to stand up as a clock for use at night. It was made in c1925 and the alarm is set with the button on the right. It has two springs, the alarm spring is wound by pulling out the button and then winding. The watch is Swiss with a lever excapement and is still useful when travelling

In the karrusel by Bonniksen (UK patent 21,421 of 1892) the carriage is mounted on a karrusel wheel driven by the third wheel pinion. The fourth wheel staff passes through the centre of the karrusel bearing to allow the fourth wheel pinion to mesh with the third wheel and power is transmitted to the escapement in the normal way rather than through the carriage rotation as in the tourbillon. The rate of rotation of the karrusel is about once per hour compared with the tourbillon which may rotate once per minute. Both these designs require considerable skill to manufacture, and are only found in watches of high quality (Fig 9).

Fig 9 The tourbillon and the karrusel

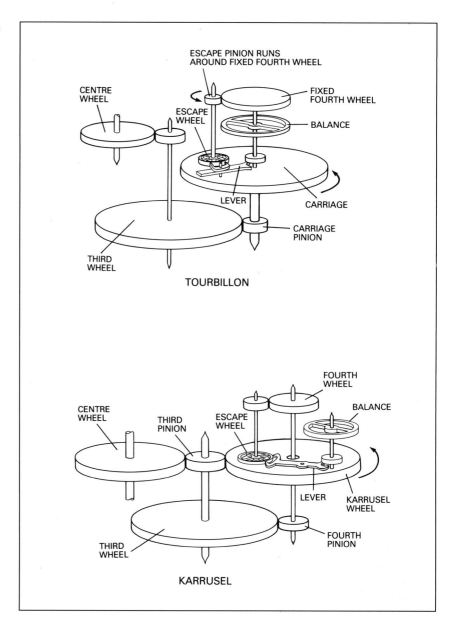

Timekeeping performance came into prominence towards the end of the nineteenth century and regular trials were conducted in Switzerland, America and England. Kew trials [5] started in 1884 (till 1951) and certificates of performance were issued based on the rate of the watch for variations in position and temperature.[6] The rate of a watch was chosen, for it was realised that none kept exact time but, provided a constant rate of loss or gain was known, the exact time could, if required, be calculated. The aim of the watch adjuster[7,8] was to produce a watch with a constant rate and the trials measured this parameter. In the early years of the twentieth century Kew trials were dominated by karrusel watches and from 1911 by Swiss watches. High-quality watches were sold with their certificate of performance. It should be realised that the quartz watch has set new standards which would be impossible to achieve and sustain in a mechanical watch.

COMPLICATIONS TO GIVE MORE INFORMATION[9]

From the earliest days watches have been made to give additional useful information. Striking watches tell the time in the dark at hourly intervals and an alarm watch is a striking watch operating at a preset chosen time (Plate 39). A separate spring and train are used (as in a clock) to avoid running the normal spring down. A repeating watch is an extension of the

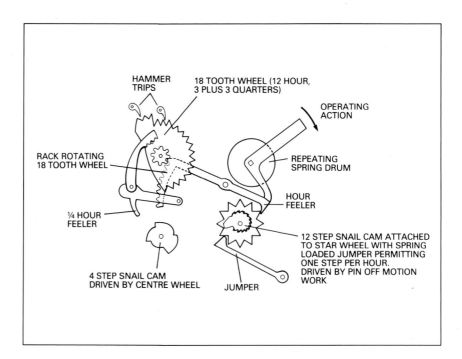

Fig 10 A quarter repeating mechanism

striking idea which enables the owner to demand an audible indication of time at any instant. The general principle of repeating work is to actuate a button or lever so that it performs two functions. Firstly, it winds a spring to turn the repeating mechanism and secondly it positions feelers on stepped snail cams that indicate the time to the repeating mechanism (Fig 10). A twelve-step cam for hours and a four-step cam for quarter hours is the most common quarter repeating form which enables time to be indicated on gongs to the nearest quarter of an hour when the button is released. (One ring for hours and two rings for quarters.) Some watches give time to the nearest seven and a half minutes, these are half quarter repeaters, others to the nearest five minutes and others to the nearest minute (Plate 40). The availability of electric light and luminous displays obviated the need for repeating watches.[10]

Day, date and moon phase indication can be achieved by pins attached to wheels which rotate notched wheels one step at the appropriate interval. As an example, date work (Fig 11) uses a 2 to 1 gear ratio to translate the rotation of the hour wheel to the rotation of a day wheel with a pin to move the date ring forward one notch every twenty-four hours. The date ring can operate a month indicator every thirty-first day and hand correction can be used to compensate for short months. Weekdays are based on the date pin operating a seven notch wheel and moonwork requiring a twenty-nine and a half day cycle uses a fifty-nine or one hundred and eighteen notch system. A perpetual calendar watch automatically allows for variable length months and leap years.[11]

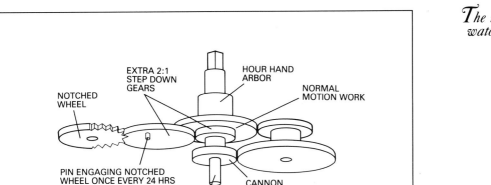

Within the figure:

EXTRA 2:1
STEP DOWN
GEARS

HOUR HAND
ARBOR

NORMAL
MOTION WORK

NOTCHED
WHEEL

PIN ENGAGING NOTCHED
WHEEL ONCE EVERY 24 HRS

CANNON
PINION

CENTRE WHEEL
SHAFT

Fig 11 Date indication mechanism driven by the motion work

STOP WATCHES AND CHRONOGRAPHS[12]

These terms are used to indicate a watch designed to measure the time taken to perform some function such as a race. It requires the ability to stop and start an indicator from zero at the command of the operator. The first such watches had a lever which stopped the watch completely by interference with the train. Other designs had two separate trains, one of which operated the normal watch and the other which could be stopped and restarted at will. This was an improvement but still lacked a resetting device so that time was not counted from zero nor was a minute counter fitted to enable elapsed times greater than sixty seconds to be recorded.

These two functions were both achieved in the mid-nineteenth century. In 1842, Adolphe Nicole patented a reset system for a seconds hand which could be independently stopped and started, and in 1862, the familiar three-press button system was also patented in which the starting and stopping is achieved quite simply by bringing a wheel into mesh with another wheel which rotates permanently with the main train of the watch. The engaging and disengaging is achieved by pushing the winding button or a special button which operates a spring controlled lever system. The lever ends not concerned with engaging or disengaging feel their way into, and out of, slots in a column wheel which rotates one step at each push of the button to control the stop, reset, start sequence. The third push of the button is used to reset the seconds hand which is achieved by a special heart-shaped cam pivoted in such a way that when the heel of a spring-loaded piece presses against it, the torque will bring the cam around to the starting position (Plate 41). Other watches were developed with two seconds hands each of which could be stopped and started independently which allowed the difference in two elapsed times to be observed directly (split seconds watch).

Plate 41 This watch, unlike those in **Plates 6, 7** and **37** is a proper chronograph or stop watch. The timing mechanism can be started, stopped and reset by pushing the winding button without stopping the whole watch so that the watch may tell the time however it is used. It has a Swiss lever escapement and is in a plain silver case

MULTIPLE COMPLICATIONS

Watches were made which included several of the features discussed above. In mechanical form these watches were exceedingly heavy and very expensive. However in a modern quartz watch complications are made available very cheaply.

WINDING MECHANISMS

From the convenience, dust and damage viewpoint the most annoying part of owning and operating a watch is winding and handsetting by key. The problems were long recognised and many makers produced solutions. One of the earliest ideas was the self-winding watch with a swinging weight which wound the spring by its motion. This was invented by Perrelet in 1770 and Recordon in 1780 and used by Breguet from about 1780. It did not become popular until wrist-watch days after Harwood had patented a design (Swiss patent 106,583 of 1924).[13] During the final years of the eighteenth century and the early years of the nineteenth century several makers patented keyless winding devices. Most of these were short lived but Thomas Prest's design (UK patent 4,501 of 1820) was a modern looking concept.

The first man to devise winding and hand setting with the button was the Swiss maker Louis Audemars in 1838. He was followed by other makers, notably Adolphe Nicole (UK patent 10,348 of 1844), Adrien Phillipe, Antoine Lecoultre and Gustavus Huguenin. Nicole's method was used by the English maker Dent from 1846 to 1862 as the 'sole

Fig 12 Four types of keyless winding mechanism

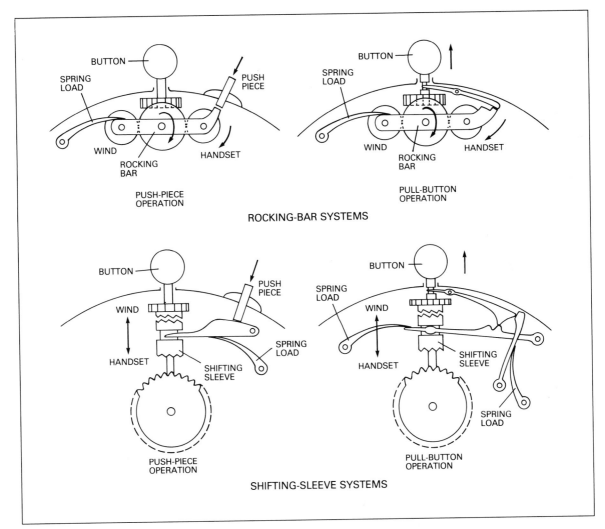

Licensee'. Phillipe was responsible for the shifting sleeve design which was eventually to become the final form of keyless winding (French patent 1,317 of 1845) and Lecoultre and Huguenin (UK patent 2,144 of 1855) for rocking bar designs. In some forms of these designs the change from wind to handset was achieved by means of a small push piece at the side of the winding button but this push piece was not required in designs in which pulling or pushing the winding button effected the change of mode.[14] Fig 12 shows four arrangements but over a thousand patents concerned with winding were registered between 1888 and 1914.

JEWELLING

Bearing surfaces in a watch are often jewelled for long life with less friction. The common smallest number of jewels used is seven which allows the escapement to be treated; the balance staff having four jewels (one at each pivot and a cap for each), the impulse jewel and two lever pallet jewels. The common larger number used is fifteen which additionally allows the lever, escape, fourth and third wheel staffs to have pivot jewels. Higher numbers of jewels are associated with higher quality or complex watches. Jewels are also used in the train of analogue display electronic watches.

The remaining variations shown in the list at the beginning of this chapter are either discussed elsewhere or clarified on examination of the illustrations.

7 English watchmaking

In this chapter consideration is given to the English firms which adopted the new system of machine manufacture of interchangeable parts. It would be expected that there would be plenty of documentation available but this has not proved to be the case and the story is built from fragmented evidence and is therefore incomplete. The shortfalls are due to company failures, takeovers, wartime bombing losses, etc. In this chapter 'Kelly' refers to *Kelly's Directory of the Watch, Clock and Jewellery Trades* (1872–1932)

ANGLO-AMERICAN WATCH COMPANY AND
ENGLISH WATCH COMPANY (Plates 42 and 43)

It is difficult to be certain of the first real user of machinery to produce watches in quantity in England but it was most probably Aaron Dennison. The way in which this came about is interesting. When Dennison finally left the American Watch Company in 1863 he came to Europe as agent for an American company making machinery for the iron trade. He settled in Birmingham, England. On a return trip to America in 1864 he was approached by A. O. Bigelow to help form a new watchmaking company in Tremont, USA. The idea behind this company was to make plates and barrels by machine in Tremont but to import wheels and escapements from Zurich, Switzerland. This was successful and the company then decided to move the whole operation to Melrose, USA, where a new factory would make the whole watch, producing 100 per week. The Melrose company failed in 1868 and Dennison was asked to find a buyer for the whole concern. (The company never succeeded in making all the parts, still importing from Zurich.) Dennison found no buyer in America, or Switzerland, but did in due course find one in England where the Anglo-American Watch Company was formed late in 1871 with Dennison as the manager who also owned rights in the machine tools.[1] The products were sent to America for sale but without success and late in 1874 the company was wound up and sold for £5,500 to William Bragge who called it the English Watch Company. The address was 45 Villa Street. Bragge ran the company until about 1883 after which his son Robert appears to have taken charge. Dennison was not part of the new company and he decided to make watch cases setting up the enterprise at 24 Villa Road, his home at the time. This company became an instant success obtaining a contract with Waltham for their watches late in 1874. Dennison was never to look back and the case-making company survived until 1967.

Although not a *watchmaking* firm the Dennison Watch Case Company (known by various names but this is the best known) was part of the English horological scene for almost 100 years. Its history is told from family papers by Priestley and Dennison[1] and for some years there was a house journal called 'Dial' (1920–27), some parts of which have been reproduced.[2] It is worth recording that the company not only supplied cases to Waltham, but in relatively small numbers to English companies including Rotherham, Smith's, Williamson and the Lancashire Watch Company. The failure of the company was due to the closure of Waltham and the final demise of the pocket watch in the post World War II era even though Dennison had diversified their products in the 1920–30 period. Dennison cases can often be recognised by their Assay Office mark AB, ALD, A. L. Dennison or AW or by their trademark for base metal plated cases ALD, Star, Moon or Sun.[3]

The English Watch Company at its foundation in 1874 had a set of machinery for making plates and barrels but it would appear that it was, for some time, still dependent on the import of parts. The earliest report found suggests that in 1878 the company was experimenting in using a microphone to listen to the watch action[4] and in 1880, it is reported that the machinery was little improved and that the escapement and much of

Plate 42 The two most common English Watch Company movement styles each of which was also available with opposite direction winding. Note the similarity between the movement on the right and the Tremont movement in **Plate 19**

the material still came from Switzerland.[5] In the same year Poole[6] suggests that 200 men were employed making a slightly more expensive but long-lasting watch for the least cost which included both full plate and threequarter plate design. Again in 1880, six complete watches and some parts were shown to British Horological Institute members[7] and in 1881 members of the Society of Arts were shown some keyless watches thought to be the most complete exhibition of the stages of machine making ever seen in England.[8] These may have been new models. It is quite probable that changes were slow, for the company secretary Robert Bragge said[9] that British workmen were conservative in their ways and difficult to emancipate from traditional methods, and the works manager, Charles Master, said new technical methods had to be introduced 'tactfully'. In 1881 the company was advertising in 'Jeweller and Metalworker' and in 1882 the company was registered at the Stock Exchange.[10] Progress was being made for in 1885 at the 4th Annual General Meeting[11] there is a report giving some definite idea of the state. It lists the death of the 'founder' William Bragge and records an expansion with an enlargement of the workshop accommodation costing £950 and the erection of a new and more powerful steam engine by which an increased production of 50 per cent could be obtained. It also records the purchase of a patent from Mr Douglas of Stourbridge for his double chronograph and his stock of finished and unfinished movements and materials.

The patent acquired was probably No 4,164 of 27 September 1881 which allows the fitting of a centre seconds hand and minute counter to a normal watch either on the conventional dial or a back dial. The chronograph part was operated by a three-push button. The English Watch Company proposed to produce a combined repeating and chronograph watch known as the 'Chrono-micrometer' and one was exhibited at the 1885 Inventions Exhibition in South Kensington. The watch was a minute repeater with the chronograph showing minutes, seconds and fifths. This was an ambitious project in a different class of watchmaking to those previously marketed.

In 1886 the company was reported to be very busy[12] and in 1890 Robert Bragge and the company took patent 2,856 for 'Improvements in Chronographic watches'. The ventures could not have been successful for the next record shows the firm went into voluntary liquidation on 11 February 1895. Kelly shows entries for the company from 1875 to 1901. Ehrhardt reports[13] that the English Watch Company had failed and the equipment dismantled in January 1897. If the equipment was dismantled this could be taken to mean that some other person had acquired it. One purely speculative possibility is that the plate-making machinery and trade name passed to H. Williamson who were expanding their watch business at this time. The justifications for this speculation being a Williamson watch fragment of about 1905 which is marked English Watch Co, London, a report that one of Williamson's factories only had

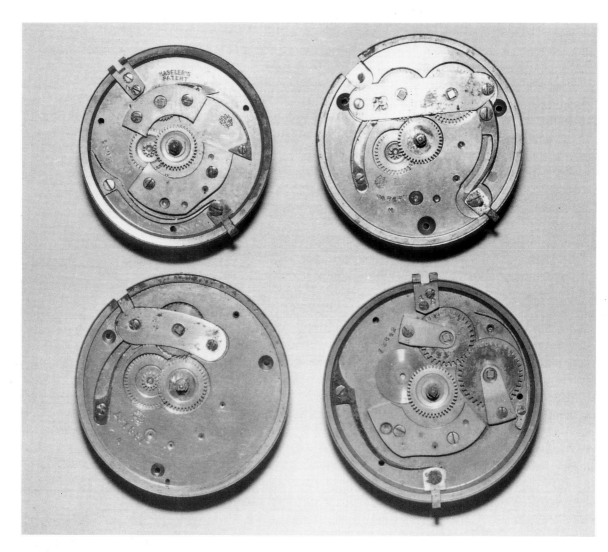

Plate 43 Four English Watch Company underdials, three of which bear the company trademark shown in Fig 13: *(top left)* a movement similar to the left-hand movement of Plate 42 but it has clockwise winding and is marked Haseler's patent (UK patent 646 of 1877) which is for a device to avoid leaving the fully wound spring in complete tension in watches without stopwork. Many EWC watches used this device; *(top right)* the underdial of the left-hand movement in **Plate 42** with an extra wheel in the winding train to allow anticlockwise, fusee style, winding. It has an English escape wheel; *(bottom left)* the underdial of the right-hand movement in Plate 42 and this winds in a clockwise direction; *(bottom right)* this movement may be an early product with the Tremont style, a Swiss escape wheel and American-style underdial support bridges. A similar movement has been seen with the company trademark and engraved Haseler's patent (some part is missing in this view)

machines for making the frame of the watch, Williamson's interest in a Swiss factory at Büren to make parts for him, and a report in 1916 of the continued existence of the Birmingham factory.[14]

What sort of watches did the English Watch Company make? The machinery was basically American and the watches it produced were made for the American market by Tremont, Melrose and the Anglo-American Company. They were not right for the English market for they were keywound in a clockwise direction since they used a going barrel rather than a fusee. The new company soon put an extra wheel in the winding system so that the winding was anticlockwise. In the later examples the escape wheel has English-style pointed teeth but Swiss-style teeth were originally used. The new company also used pins in the pillars rather than screws for fixing the top plate and changed the shape of the barrel bridge on some models. Those with the original bridge shape look very much like Tremont-Melrose movements. The company registered trademarks on 19 May, 1876 (trademarking commenced 1 January 1876) and a mark is stamped on the plate under the dial which allows movement identification (Fig 13). Not all movements were necessarily marked and the barrel bridge and dial would have the retailer's name on them. Full plate and threequarter plate movements were made in different grades. A 'chrono-micrometer' was seen but not examined. It is therefore difficult to estimate production with any certainty. The 14, 16 and 18 size movements suggest a total of perhaps 250,000 if the numbering sequence starts at 1 and is continuous. Most watches have a letter as well as a number. With 200 men this total represents 300 watches per week for fifteen years.

Fig 13 Some English watchmaking trademarks *(top, left to right)* English Watch Company, Ehrhardt, Ehrhardt, Rotherham; *(bottom, left to right)* Coventry Cooperative Watch Manufacturing Society, Nicole Nielson, Guye

Plate 44 A typical Ehrhardt watch in a silver case hallmarked 1915. Similar watches were made throughout the firm's existence and the cases are often marked WE. It is an antiquated style for 1915 but was obviously in demand for many such watches can be found

WILLIAM EHRHARDT (Plates 44 to 48 and 72)

William Ehrhardt (1831–97) was an unwitting rival to Dennison to be the first person to employ machinery for the mass production of watches in England. Like Dennison he was not British, being born and serving his apprenticeship in watchmaking in Germany. He came to England in the Exhibition year, 1851.[15] During his stay he worked with Upjohn and Bright and attended classes at the Royal School of Mines. Even at this early age he wished to establish his own business but not in a traditional watchmaking area so that he could apply his own ideas without resistance. He chose Birmingham, England, in 1856, well before Dennison. Although he had his own ideas the business was small and it was not easy to recruit workmen until the American Civil War caused some job losses in the export trades. Since he did not want traditional watchmaking workers they would have come from other industries. The addresses of his operations were 30 Paradise Street and 26 Augusta Street (wholesale) from 1856–63 and 72 Great Hampton Street from 1864 onwards.[16] In 1872 he advertised from his Hampton Street address that he had 'constructed machinery to make his PATENT KEYLESS MOVEMENTS on the Interchangeable system'. In 1874 he built a factory (Time Works, Barr Street) to improve his rate of production. Because Ehrhardt was well established and had probably already produced 200,000 watches his chance of success with this factory was much greater than Dennison's who was starting in England anew. This is evidenced by the fact that Ehrhardt's firm survived until about 1924,[17] the date of the last Kelly entry.

In 1880 Ehrhardt wrote a letter[6] stating that the greater part of the work was done by steam-powered machinery and that the machines were attended by *girls*. The watches produced were nearly as cheap as the equivalent grade from Waltham. In the same paper[6] it is said that a Coventry-made fusee watch could be obtained at the same price but this would not be true for long. Gannay[5] also mentions Ehrhardt as a machine user in 1880 but Rigg[8] says, whereas other makers supplied him with complete movements for a lecture illustration, Ehrhardt only supplied frames. In 1886 he is recorded as busy[12] and in 1889 unable to meet demand[18] but

Plate 45 The most common Ehrhardt movement of low quality. A similar higher-quality movement is fitted in the watch in **Plate 44** (jewelled train and compensated balance). The Ehrhardt trademark (Fig 13) can be seen on the underdial view. The winding is anticlockwise

Plate 46 Five Ehrhardt underdials: *(top left)* the movement shown at the top of **Plate 47** which has the 1911 tree trademark (Fig 13) on the dial together with the words 'British Watch Company Ltd, London'; *(bottom left)* a threequarter plate movement marked '1906 series' which is similar to that at the bottom of **Plate 47**; *(top centre)* is an incomplete, 1920 series, threequarter plate movement bearing the name 'British Watch Company' and the winged arrow Ehrhardt trademark; *(bottom centre)* one arrangement Ehrhardt used with full-plate watches with clockwise winding; *(right)* another arrangement for clockwise winding

making his own mainsprings. By this date Ehrhardt is probably close to making complete watches for Ehrhardt movements in silver cases with maker's initials WE are in evidence. This has been confirmed as Ehrhardt's mark,[19] first registered on 14 November 1867, the last entry being on 12 September 1923. At this stage Ehrhardt is classed with Rotherham, Nicole Nielson and the English Watch Company as a large producer making his own movements.[20] The word 'large' is misleading for the production rates of these firms was not large compared with American ideas of the same period. (Waltham were making about 8,000 watches per week by 1883.)

In 1890 a letter says Ehrhardt has had success in utilising, inventing and adapting tools and in visiting principal factories.[21] This could be taken to mean that Ehrhardt had visited America but there is no other report. At his death in 1897 the factory had 400 employees making 500 watches per week.[15] The business was carried on by two of his sons, William and Gustav Victor, after William (Senior) died and William (Junior) was made vice president of the Coventry Watch Trade Association in 1900. Production peaked at about this time and the firm also had success at the Kew watch trials coming 11th with watch 272,874 and 46th with watch 284,583 in 1899, 13th with watch 472,902/272,902, 28th with watch 284,560, 49th with 272,896 and 50th with 272,897 in 1900. All these watches had single roller lever escapements with a going barrel and single overcoil balance spring whereas virtually every other successful maker used a karrusel or tourbillon. The firm was also 2nd and 33rd in the Greenwich deck watch trials in 1900[22] and, using a karrusel themselves, 9th and 25th in the 1902 Kew trials.

Some information about the Ehrhardt factory in 1899–1900 can be obtained from the evidence of William Ehrhardt (Junior) during the case of REGINA vs WILLIAMSON LTD.[23] Ehrhardt said they employed 250 persons to make 600 to 700 watches per week and all the parts of the watch were English made except for balance springs for which the wire was made in England but coiling and setting done in Switzerland. Mainsprings were made in their own factory as were all the wheels but two or three years before some wheels were bought from English makers. Mr Ehrhardt said they did not use dummy winding wheels in their key-wind watches but used another method (wheels under the dial) to achieve anticlockwise winding. Their production of keywind watches was about half and half clockwise vs anticlockwise winding. He also said wheels were produced in one cutting. This is an interesting statement especially with regard to production rates and employees. The Ehrhardt (Senior) obituary said in 1897 that 400 persons made 500 watches per week.[15] One is incorrect or quite possibly when the father died the sons implemented a higher productivity system.

Soon after this period trading became more difficult and in 1905 there was an agreement between Ehrhardt, Williamson and the Lancashire

Watch Company to raise prices by one shilling. In spite of this the Lancashire Watch Company collapsed in 1910 and a representative of Ehrhardt attended the auction sale of equipment. Ehrhardt continued in business until the early 1920s but it was clear from movement numbers that production was falling and the firm's last appearance at the British Industries Fair in 1921 showed they were making three grades of 16 size watch; a high grade threequarter plate model and two lower grade split top plate watches. Ehrhardt is also clearly stating that the parts are *interchangeable* and can be obtained from the makers. This may be true of late watches but the early keywind models required some degree of fitting. Ehrhardt watches were standard size to fit any standard cases but they made many of their own cases for the English market. Uncased movements may have been for export and some products look quite American.[17] The general feeling at this 1921 fair was a lack of buyers, the only other watchmaking firms present being Rotherham and Williamson.

In 1921 a firm called The British Watch Company Ltd appears in the

Kelly Directory at Ehrhardt's London office address. Movements can be found with this name stamped underdial together with Ehrhardt's winged arrow trademark (Fig 13). These movements are dated '1920 series' (Plate 46). The winged arrow trademark was first registered on 4 February 1878 but changed form several times during the period in which it was used. There are also watches of an unusual calibre (Plate 47) which again bear the name British Watch Company but which carry a different trademark. This mark shows a tree and was registered on 4 August 1911 in the Ehrhardt name. The use of such a name may have been an attempt to persuade buyers to support British products. It is not clear when Ehrhardt ceased making watches nor what happened to the machinery. In 1926–7 the Barr Street address features in directories with Gustav Victor Ehrhardt as a watch *cleaner and repairer* not as a manufacturer and with G. V. Ehrhardt and Hereward Ltd as watch repairers from 1928.[16] The Kelly Directory shows the latter firm in 1932. It might well be that since Ehrhardt had produced about 700,000 watches, one of the sons continued to operate the spares and repairs department.

The watches Ehrhardt made in 1856 would be the conventional design. This is before Wycherley's standard frames were sold but it may well be that Ehrhardt eschewed Prescot ébauches and made as much as he could himself as a move towards breaking tradition. The early movements appear to be 8, 14 or 16 size full plate, keywind watches with going barrel and English lever escapements. Some wind clockwise and some anticlockwise. No fusee watches have been examined. All the top plates are held in place by pinned pillars. Some are engraved W. Ehrhardt but others have the name of the seller. The majority of balances seen are plain. All have the characteristic Ehrhardt shaped barrel bridge by which they can be recognised. There are also English lever threequarter plate, keywind watches made in size 2. Those examined have numbers between 56,000 and about 240,000 which might suggest an average rate of production from 1856 to 1874 of 200 per week. This would imply some mechanisation over that period, which would be in accord with Ehrhardt's ideas. Later watches are usually 16 or 18 size and the top plates are all screwed to the pillars. All the serial numbers are above 250,000 and a cased example 257,250 shows a hallmark for Birmingham 1876 with maker's mark WE. Most of these later movements have going barrel with anticlockwise winding, *Swiss* lever escape wheels and until about number 300,000 are full plate watches with keywind. The underdial winding work has a recognisable bridge shape. Ehrhardt was not ignoring keyless designs for in 1888 he took English patent 17,175 which was concerned with dustcaps for keyless watches. The earliest dated keyless example examined is 369,637 of 1906 which is a threequarter plate watch with right angle layout of balance lever and escape wheel. There are keyless examples with rocking bar push piece and shifting sleeve pull winder operation. In 1911 there is a very American-looking split plate design inscribed 'safety

Plate 47 *(top)* An interesting Ehrhardt calibre with an unconventional balance cock. This particular example is marked 'British Watch Company Ltd. London'; *(bottom)* a threequarter plate example of Ehrhardt's work clearly marked 'English Manufacture'. It has a Swiss lever escapement

pinion' with straight line layout of balance, lever and escape wheel. The better watches have compensated balances. The highest dated serial number sighted is 629,186 of c1920 but 713,389 has also appeared. Some 0 size keyless, threequarter plate watches were also made probably with a different series of numbers. The total number of factory-made watches appears to be about 500,000 over a fifty-year span, 1874–1924, just about 200 per week but production during the final years was probably small since the peak was around 600 per week. Towards the end not all exhibit the trademark but there are other recognisable features such as a 'British Watch Company Ltd' mark.

It is not easy to fit the Kew trial watches into this sequence with serial numbers 270,000 to 290,000 which represent 1876–8 dates. It is quite possible that these watches were made then and later prepared specially for the trials. Kew trials started in 1884, which is itself after the date indicated by the serial numbers, and were from 1894 onwards dominated by karrusel watches.[24]

Plate 48 A split plate, negative set Ehrhardt movement marked '16 size 1911, Handsworth, Staffs, Eng[d].' The movement has a Swiss escape wheel. It looks American and some may have been for export

Summary of Ehrhardt watch serial numbers

Serial Number	Type
1? to 250,000 made from 1856 to 1874	Full plate keywind watches with pinned pillars and English lever escapement made by semi-traditional method.
250,000? to 750,000 made from 1874 to 1924	Watches initially full plate keywind with screwed pillars and Swiss lever escapement later threequarter plate keywind or keyless wind.
–	'O' size keyless threequarter plate

ROTHERHAM AND SONS (Plates 49 to 52 and 72)

Rotherham of Coventry can trace their history to a firm started in 1747 by Samuel Vale which became Vale, Howlett and Carr from 1754 to 1790. Richard Kevitt Rotherham appears as a partner in Vale and Rotherham in 1790 but he had already served an apprenticeship within the firm.[25] From 1842 the firm is listed as Richard Kevitt Rotherham and Sons and Rotherham and Sons from 1850–80.[26] Rotherham and Sons appear in all Kelly Directories at 27 Spon Street (ie 1872–1932). In 1843 the company attempted to use some sort of factory system to make 6,000 watches per year but it was not a success. This was not machine based but a centrally organised system which was not an unrealistic proposal since the whole Spon Street area was a watch manufacturing enclave of traditional workers.[27] Rotherham also backed the Wycherley system (Chapter 4) and wrote a letter in 1867 describing a successful trial.[28] Many Rotherham

Plate 49 A typical Rotherham full plate keywind design. The trademark (Fig 13) is clearly visible

movements of this period bear the initials JW on the movement.

With this enterprising history it is not surprising that in about 1880 John Rotherham (1838–1905) sent Mr Gooding, the manager, to America to arrange the purchase of some machinery from the American Watch Tool Company[21] (Chapter 3). This would be similar to that at Waltham and one delegate at a meeting in 1890 at which pictures of this machinery were shown commented that he felt he was back at Waltham.[29] In reply Mr Gooding said that only 5 per cent of the machinery was American and 95 per cent their own (which they perhaps declined to show). Bailey[30] suggests that Rotherham produced the *first* English machine-made watch in 1880 but this is a dubious suggestion bearing in mind the English Watch Company and Ehrhardt. It is interesting to compare these three firms. Whereas the English Watch Company inherited the Tremont system and Ehrhardt introduced his own ideas, Rotherham sent Gooding to America to get a proven start and then developed the system to suit his firm.

Rigg[8] showed Rotherham machine-made parts to the Society of Arts in 1881 and also gave information (from Gooding) that 99 different machines were used in the manufacture of a watch movement, 13 for plates, 35 for wheels and pinions, 12 for steelwork, 22 for the escapement, 11 for jewelling and 6 for screws; Gooding also told Rigg that it took 30 hours to make a movement. This time would not include assembly else the production rate would be very high. Bailey suggests 100 movements per week with 400–500 workers in 1888. By 1887 Rotherham are reported to be busy with machine-made watches steadily making their way[31] and by 1889 unable to meet demand[18] as a large producer making their own movements.[20] Whatever the exact numbers it is clear that Rotherham steam-powered machinery made watches and cases in their factory in 1888[32] when they were visited by a delegation from the British Horological Institute, but they were still apparently making some watches by traditional methods. When the serial numbers of watches entered for Kew trials are examined and compared with those of ordinary watches it is possible that these special watches might give that sort of impression. Illustrations of some machines at the factory are given by Tripplin.[29] In the 1889 Paris Exhibition, Rotherham showed watches which made the Swiss stare[33] and report the exhibits as an incontestable demonstration of the awakening of English watchmaking from the state of decadence. This was overreaction for the total English production rate was small.

In 1894 Rotherham started to issue their own performance certificates free of charge with a first-grade equivalent to Kew A and second grade to Kew B.[34] They also started making keyless watches for ladies and in 1897 they marketed good watches to compete with better-class Swiss watches (possibly the elegant threequarter plate keyless style.[35]) (Plate 50.) Rotherham naturally gave evidence in the REGINA vs. WILLIAMSON LTD case[36] and we find Gooding had been with Rotherham since 1876 (he retired in 1915 and died in 1917 aged 77) and that they employed 500 persons (1899). He stated they used foreign material (mainsprings, balance springs, rough screws and jewel holes) in their ordinary watches but that the Swiss machines used for wheel cutting did not make watch wheels but wheels for their other products. Gooding also stated that until a few years ago hands were imported. If this was the state in 1899 then it is unlikely that they made a complete machine-made watch in 1880 but this tedious case was concerned with small quantities of foreign parts in English watches. One of the problems with the small scale of English production was that it was not economic sense to make some parts.

Rotherham entered watches in Kew trials in 1893 achieving 23rd (watch number 97,865), 24th (13,421), 27th (94,692), 31st (95,453), 32nd (13,414) and 34th (97,867) place, all with single roller, going barrel and single overcoil as were those of most other makers, for Bonniksen did not patent the karrusel which would later dominate the trials until 1892. Rotherham also came 1st, 2nd and 3rd in the chronograph class in 1893 (97,865, 97,867, 92,488) and 4th (13,405) in the non-magnetic class.[37] In 1899 they achieved 42nd (23,608) with a plain watch in a karrusel dominated result and second in the chronograph class (21,633) but in 1900 they did not appear; they may have decided not to compete against the karrusel.[22]

Rotherham were an astute firm for they had survived for a long time

Plates 50 and **51** A typical Rotherham watch in a silver half hunter case hallmarked 1907 with the casemaker's mark JR is shown in **Plate 50. Plate 51** shows the attractive, keyless, threequarter plate movement of good quality

and realised that mass-production machinery had other uses. Thus, at the turn of the century, they started to diversify into cycle parts and later into motor car parts which enabled them to continue as precision engineers when watchmaking ceased.[38] They kept abreast of developments evidenced by Gooding giving a lecture about Guillaume's metallurgical work to reduce temperature errors in watches.[39] In 1903 John Rotherham celebrated fifty years with the company during which time he and Gooding had moved them into a prominent position in English watchmaking.[40]

It is interesting to compare the report of the factory visit in 1888[32] with another in 1909, the latter including a visit to a Swiss factory.[41] The 1888 visit describes casemaking from silver including five press processes and lathe work for the back and the manufacture of band, bezel, bow, pendant, etc. Wheel making included shaving presswork and tooth cutting and polishing. Plate making processes included the information that the dial feet and pillar holes were used as a datum for the remaining processes. The escape wheel was cut by a multiple fly cutter as at Waltham but the pallets were made by a Rotherham machine. Little is said about assembly, balances, springs, jewels and hands but dials were made in the works. It notes the development of a 1 size watch and mentions keyless designs. The 1909 paper says processes at Rotherham have changed little

but emphasises the inspection during assembly and the use of gauges, verniers and micrometers. It also mentions the use of drawings to set the machines, some of which are *semi* automatic requiring hand feed of parts. Significantly it mentions Rotherham diversification into motors, fitments, electrical and gas lighting, artificial silk and watch bracelets. Rotherham watches of this period appear to have interchangeable parts with minimal fitting work. There is little information or comparison with the Swiss factory at Tavannes, the only significant point being that whereas Rotherham used 500 persons to make 100 watches per day, Tavannes used 950 persons to produce 2,500 watches per day, a rate thirteen times greater possibly due to the use of parts made elsewhere.

In 1911 a representative of Rotherham attended the Lancashire Watch Company auction and in 1912 Rotherham appear to have had a plan for extension but by 1916 problems were being discussed.[14] These were not only their own but for the whole trade and whereas many firms would collapse Rotherham survived because of their other work. Rotherham also made clocks and this eventually became their sole horological product. It is possible to trace their horological demise through British Industry Fair reports (BIF). Rotherham appear in 1920, 1921[17] showing a standard watch, a karrusel, a centre seconds watch, wrist watches from Coventry and cases for movements made in *their* Swiss factory. This could be the Rode Watch Company, La Chaux de Fonds, whose watches they marketed. At the British Empire Exhibition in 1924 Rotherham showed examples of all their models from the keywind capped full plate movement to the latest products.[42] In 1926 at BIF all types of watch and a few other mechanical products were shown.

In 1932 Rotherham became agents for Büren (Switzerland) following the collapse of H. Williamson, an agency they kept until the 1960s together with their agency for Ulysse Nardin, long after they ceased making watches at Coventry. At the 1934 BIF, Rotherham showed watches, clocks, escapements, barographs, time switches, etc and in that year they were the only English watchmakers on show. At the 1937 BIF, watches seemed less important than clocks and other products and it is doubtful if any watches were being made in Coventry.[43]

Plate 52 The underdial of a Rotherham keyless, threequarter plate movement clearly showing the trademark (Fig 13)

What sort of watches did Rotherham make during the period from 1880 to c1930? All their watches look of good quality including full plate keywind and threequarter plate keyless models in various sizes. Most are marked with their trademark (Fig 13). They also used other marks including 'Rotherhams, London' from 22 January 1886 and another complex mark number 15,543 of 22 October 1878. Examination of movements suggests two basic styles were made in various sizes. One style was a 14 or 18 size capped, keywind, full plate watch with going barrel and right-angle layout English lever escapement having a compensated balance with the spring above the wheel. Eleven jewels were fitted. A second style was a threequarter plate keyless watch with similar escapement in various sizes (0, 6 and 14) with 19 jewels, the earlier ones being screw fitted but the later ones pressed in. Handset was by push piece, rocking bar and pendant. All the watches used screws to hold the top plate to the pillars and many cases are marked JR at the Birmingham Assay Office, John Rotherham's mark.

Based on a sample of 35, the numbering sequence appears to indicate that up to 200,000 the products were mainly the keywind model and then to perhaps 450,000 mainly the keyless watch. Smaller size (0 and 6) threequarter plate models look similar but appear to have a different series of serial numbers. These were probably the post-1894 design. The production rate of 100 per day suggested by Tripplin[41] would probably be a peak value so that an estimate of 600,000 Coventry-made watches from both numbering sequences for the fifty-year period 1880–1930 would give an average rate of production of 200 per week. Here it is assumed that fully machine-made watches started at about number 50,000. This would give Rotherham a similar rate to the contemporary Birmingham companies. Full plate watches with serial numbers smaller than 50,000 can be found with fusees and machine-made ébauches which look similar in style but are obviously not made with the same tools as the later models.

COVENTRY COOPERATIVE WATCH MANUFACTURING SOCIETY LTD (Plate 53)

This group of traditional watchmakers were persuaded in 1876 to form a co-operative society presumably in the hope that the combined resources of a group would be able to cope better with American and Swiss competition. They were initially successful recording over a period of ten years to 1886, an average net profit of 15 per cent paying 7 per cent to capital, 5 per cent to workers and 2 per cent to customers.[44] The main persuader, Henry Gannay, had hoped that they would adopt machine tool methods but in 1890 he reported that they were not very interested in this approach but he had pointed out the error of their ways and they were now accumulating capital to invest. Gannay also states here that they had divided considerable sums amongst their workers and had 200 shares in the Coventry Watch Movement Company.[21] Records of the shareholders of this company show 20 shares to the Cooperative in 1889 so there may be an error here, as the maximum holding by anyone was also 20 at the time.

By 1895 Gannay reports that the Cooperative was crawling along making a few watches and dealing in foreign watches and clocks. He also suggests that they could obtain enough capital to rival Waltham or the Lancashire Watch Company but refused to look at machine tools even though he had a selection sent from Max Thum of Geneva for their inspection.[45] Gannay continues saying they atoned by taking 100 shares in the Watch Movement Company.

The Cooperative appears to have benefitted members but not been a machine-based manufacturer. There are few reports of their society in the literature surveyed after 1900 but Kelly recorded them from 1887 to 1917 by when it would seem their watch interests had ceased. The society registered a trademark on 21 November 1876 and it was regularly renewed until 1920. It consists of a Maltese cross with a monogram CCWMS entwined (Fig 13). This may not appear on all their products for some of their customers would prefer their own name to appear on watches they retailed. Thus there will be watches that cannot be identified as a Cooperative product. Kemp[46] suggests that there may be confusion between the products of the society and the Coventry Watch Movement Company but this seems unlikely in view of the clearly registered trademark. The few identified watches seen have this mark on the cock rather than under the dial (Plate 53) and all have a characteristic numbering system which, if enough could be examined, might be informative. All used JW (Wycherley) frames with going barrels.

One may speculate on how the Cooperative might operate. The group of makers would buy frames and wheels in batches from Wycherley and other parts from other suppliers for finishing. Since Wycherley frames were standard in size, cases could also be purchased in batches. The members would then complete the watches and the anonymous products would be numbered, trademarked and marketed by the Cooperative travelling salesman. The presumed advantage to the maker was that he did not have to worry about buying parts or marketing and he could concentrate on his skilled work. No attempt has been made to discover if each maker worked in his own premises or all makers worked under the same roof, but tradition would lead to the former mode of operation.

Plate 53 The trademark (Fig 13) on the cock of this movement clearly identifies it as a product of the Coventry Cooperative Watch Manufacturing Society Ltd. The 6 size movement has an English lever escapement, a going barrel winding clockwise and has no seconds hand. The ébauche is marked JW so that the movement was supplied to the co-operative for finishing, confirming that they were not a factory but a co-operative of traditional watchmakers hoping to survive in a changing world

When the Lancashire Watch Company and the Coventry Watch Movement Company were formed it may well have signalled the end of the Cooperative since the traditional supply of Prescot ébauches would have ceased unless, in the early days of these ventures, the new companies chose to supply the Cooperative. However the nature of the work would have changed in that the new machine-made movements would not require the same finishing treatment.

Plate 54 The most common Lancashire Watch Company movement which shows the company mark in the *right-hand* picture. The underdial should be compared with those in **Plate 55** and a common styling may be identified. This movement has an oversprung balance and a Swiss lever escapement

THE LANCASHIRE WATCH COMPANY LTD
(Plates 54 to 58 and 72)

The Lancashire Watch Company (1888–1910) of Prescot has been discussed in a publication [47] consisting of three parts; an essay, a reprinted catalogue and some articles about machinery and manufacture reprinted from the *American Jeweller* of 1893. An important part of this publication is the contemporary pictures of the workshops. The company is also featured at Prescot Museum where examples of some machines are displayed with relevant products and paperwork. The discussions below are not based on these well-known items but on consulting original sources and this enhances the information already published.

An outline history can be obtained from a report of the opening[48] and a

Plate 55 Lancashire Watch Company movements: *(left)* the *upper* underdial has a different winding mechanism bridge to that of the *lower* movement which has a bridge like that in the left-hand movement of **Plate 54.** Otherwise these two movements seem similar, both having the lever on the 'wrong' side of the escape wheel; *(right)* the *upper* is the underdial of a threequarter plate movement which uses a similar winding mechanism bridge to the *top left* movement. The *lower* (right) movement is very interesting. With a serial number 4,687 it is an early product with an undersprung balance and an English lever escapement. The underdial is like that in **Plate 54** and is stamped L W C° Ltd. It seems possible that this was made before all the departments were in full production and was finished with bought out escapement parts by traditional methods. This could have been done within the company since their workforce had these skills, or the movement could have been sold as an ébauche to another 'maker'

report on the proposed sale of the assets.[49] Prescot was a traditional watchmaking centre supplying rough movements to be finished elsewhere. In Prescot John Wycherley made an early English attempt at interchangeability (Chapter 4). In 1882 he sold his business to T. P. Hewitt to form John Wycherley, Hewitt and Company. Hewitt was progressive in thought and could see what Ehrhardt and Rotherham were doing so that in 1887 it was proposed to form the British Watch Company. Hewitt went with a businessman to America to examine their methods. It is reported that Mr Byam, an American with experience at the Trenton Watch Company was to manage the Prescot factory but this did not materialise.[50] The Lancashire Watch Company was registered at the Stock Exchange[10] in December 1888 with £50,000 capital and was reconstructed in 1897 with authorised capital of £200,000 in shares of £10, half 6 per cent preference and half ordinary. Not all the shares were taken up and no dividends were paid after 1897 but prior to this reorganisation there were payments. Later more capital was needed and three interest-bearing debenture issues A, B and C totalled £134,000. By 1904 the debit balance was £32,293 and the 'A' debenture holders took possession of the assets in 1906 to continue the business. Receivers were appointed on behalf of the 'B' debenture holders in 1908. The notice of sale to take place on Tuesday 21 June 1910 gives more information[49] by which it appears a competitor (Williamson, Ehrhardt or Rotherham?) had an option to buy the business but declined in view of the state of the trade and the final nine-day auction sale of tools etc took place from 22 March to 3 April 1911. The company was struck off the Stock Exchange Register in 1914. Effectively therefore we have a twenty-year working span from 1890–1910. Kelly shows them from 1892 to 1909.

It has been suggested that the personnel of the company, who were often employed after selling their own small business to the company for cash or shares, were never really in sympathy with the aims and that this may have led to the failure.[47] However the balance sheet for 1891 shows a profit of £4,832 on sales of £22,664 with capitalisation of £69,410 and it was reported that by 1893 three hundred thousand movements had been made and sold at an average profit of 15 per cent on the turnover.[51] This hardly suggests failure due to such a cause. Similarly in 1894 at the 6th AGM a profit of £8,375 and a dividend of 6 per cent is recorded together with the information that cases were now being made.[52] It would therefore appear that the start was successful, producing on average 500 watches per week. In 1897 with six months of orders in hand some movement makers were laid off for a few weeks because casemaking and assembly could not keep up.[53] At this stage there is no doubt that problems were beginning to appear in the whole English watch industry and the reconstruction with more capital was achieved. Firms like Rotherham and the Coventry Watch Movement Company were at this time thinking about diversifying their interests. The Merchandise Marks

Act case, REGINA vs WILLIAMSON LTD, was symptomatic of these problems and the Lancashire Watch Company evidence shows that, in 1899, they used 1,587 machines to make 2,000 watches per week employing nearly 1,000 persons. They did not make glasses, mainsprings or balance springs.[36] This is quite a large production rate for an English firm and would require good marketing. To this end they had arranged an agency for the Coventry Watch Movement Company in 1891 and opened an office in Birmingham in 1900. Possibly due to marketing problems the company decided to make a larger variety of models which created more problems, for unless the sales were large enough the cost of tooling up could exceed the return. This is evidenced later by their decision to produce the John Bull pin lever watch for which they tooled up to make 2,000 per week but actually sold a total of 5,000 between 1909 and 1911.[49] The

Plate 56 A Lancashire
Watch Company 'Prescot'
watch with a Vigil movement
in a plated case

sales records[49] for 1899 to 1902 show 80,086; 77,145; 90,115, and 84,746 which averages 1,650 per week less than they said they were making in their evidence in the Williamson case. However in 1903 they achieved a trading profit but no dividends were paid except to the debenture holders.[54] Later in the same year Joseph Chamberlain, as part of his tariff reform campaign, spoke about the problems at Prescot caused by foreign import duties. By 1903 production was 500 watches per day with 750 employees which is well in excess of sales[55] and it is no surprise to find losses in 1904.[56]

The adoption of keyless winding by the company whilst continuing to make keywind models meant that by 1905 they appeared to be making at least eleven different sizes (within the range 0 to 22) in various qualities.

The 1905 catalogue shows nine different watches varying in price from 52 shillings to £25 and the trademark register for 1904 shows these nine models (Druid, Curfew, Tally Ho, Wizard, Feudal, Vigilant, Witch, Elf and Monitor) plus another nine (Lodestar, Diva, Puritan, Sprite, Epicure, Halcyon, Compeer, Sentinel and Doomsday). These models embrace full plate, split plate, thick and thin calibres, straight-line levers, right-angle levers, etc. A short time later a threequarter plate, keyless model, the Vigil, was planned for a production rate of 1,000 per week.[49] It must be assumed that the full plate model was to be phased out and some eventual rationalisation with fewer models which would include Vigil and John Bull was planned. However this will never be known. Contemporary with these watches, 0 size 19-jewel threequarter plate ladies' watches can be found and some limited production of wall clocks and other mechanical devices was started.

A Waltham regulator clock was used at Prescot for timing watches and Kew trials show a Lancashire success in 1893 with 14th position (watch number 979 with single roller, going barrel and single overcoil balance spring). They do not appear in later results (1899, 1900 and 1901) which were karrusel dominated. The watches made at Prescot have been discussed above and consisted initially of full plate, keywind models (winding anticlockwise) fitted with a reversing pinion and oversprung balance, right-angle Swiss lever escapements, in sizes 14 to 22. An early serial number 4,687 has an English lever escapement and undersprung balance and examples with the lever placed on the unconventional side of the

Plate 57 *(left)* A 7-jewel Vigil movement which was an attempt by the Lancashire Watch Company to rationalise production of threequarter plate watches late in their history; *(right)* another attempt to come to terms with the needs of the twentieth-century customer by mass producing an inexpensive pin lever escapement watch known as the 'John Bull'. The movement is marked 'British made by British labour'. Only 5,000 were reputed to have been made (see **Plate 58**)

escape wheel can be found. Other calibres winding in a clockwise direction were also made. Later there were smaller numbers of threequarter plate or split plate keyless designs with straight-line Swiss lever escapements in sizes 0 to 18. Quality varied from 7 to 23 jewels. The only exception to this was the ill-fated John Bull watch. It has been suggested that they made over fifty models and this is easily believed if an effort is made to examine them in detail. Some models were equipped with a fusee to special order. The parts of identical models appear to be interchangeable from about 1895 on. The total quantity made, based on what seems to be a continuous series of numbering, is about 900,000 over about twenty years representing 900 per week. The highest serial number seen is 873,205. Watches carrying the company mark (Plate 54) seem to have been made before the 1897 reconstruction but there are other marks registered on 23 March 1892 and many movements are stamped 'L.W. Co. Ltd.' under the dial. Watches can be dated by cases, those made by the company bearing the maker's mark TPH. There is also a very valuable workbook at Prescot Museum in which each watch is listed with the features, invoice date and purchaser. Purchasers are in the trade and many are to big retail firms such as Samuel, Graves or Fattorini as well as small local traders. There was also a lively trade in the Colonies. The watches were solid looking, slightly old fashioned for the time and not as elegant as the Rotherham products. The company also sold a considerable number of movements, which may well have been unfinished, to the Coventry Watch Movement Company, who from 1891 acted as their sales agent.

Because of the surviving machinery at Prescot Museum and the articles in the *Engineer*[51] and the *American Jeweller*[47] there is more information of the processes used at Prescot than for any other contemporary English firm. C. J. Hewitt, the works manager (brother of T.P.), was an innovative man who developed and improved the original machinery, some of which came from the USA and some from England. Sources in the USA included the American Watch Tool Company (Webster) and Sloane & Chase, Newark NJ and in England the Anglo-American Tool Company and William Muir & Company. The small turret lathe in Plate 143 is from Sloane & Chase and is also stamped LWCo.Ltd. It is used for making plates. A similar lathe designed by C. Hewitt is illustrated in the *American Jeweller*.[47] Hewitt also patented a four-spindle screw-cutting machine which increased the rate of production by performing four different but *concurrent* operations on each spindle so that if these four spindles are set on the periphery of a drum each screw can have its four operations in sequence as the drum is turned, one complete drum revolution making four screws in the time that a single spindle machine would make one (UK patent 14,756 of 1894).[57] He also developed a similar machine for pinion cutting. Some of his machines are shown in Richard.[58]

The Lancashire Watch Company was an enterprise which failed not, in the author's view, due to lack of enthusiasm of the workforce but due to a lack of business acumen on the part of the management associated with the wide range of models and marketing problems. The year 1890 was too late for easy sales, Waltham recognised this problem in 1883 and appointed a salesman (Fitch) as manager. Other American firms suffered and only those who had the skill to relate their product to the market demand survived. The use of machine-manufacturing methods was not in itself the key to survival, business sense was also required. The company is interesting because of the surviving information but ultimately it was a waste of time, effort and money. Indeed, the impact of the company on the ailing English watch industry was probably traumatic for previously, part-finished movements had come from Prescot. The factory must have shut off this supply and closed many small firms in other parts of the country which just might have found some means of survival.

Plate 58 A John Bull watch (the winding button and staff are missing). The enamel dial is of good quality, this and the gilded brass case probably contributed considerably to the cost of the watch

THE COVENTRY WATCH MOVEMENT COMPANY
(Plates 59, 60 and 73)

The proposals leading to the formation of the Lancashire Watch Company in December 1888 caused a reaction in the Coventry watch trade. The small Coventry makers had been dependent on a supply of Prescot movements to finish which would no longer be available. Although there was the Cooperative Society (see page 95), it was decided to establish a new company to manufacture movements in a factory to supply the local (and other) makers and prevent a Prescot monopoly. Rotherham did not anticipate problems as they were established self-sufficient complete watchmakers.

The Coventry Watch Movement Company was founded in February 1889 with S. Yeomans as Chairman. C. H. Errington attended an early meeting, presumably as a shareholder; he was a local watchmaker before becoming part of H. Williamson Ltd, and spoke of 'breaking the back of the Lancashire Watch Company'.[59] The Coventry Cooperative Watch Manufacturing Society also held shares. The new company had so little capital that it was not able to set up a proper machine-manufacturing system and a poor compromise was made by purchasing the tools, equipment and goodwill of Edward Scarisbrick, a Prescot maker, for £1,000. The agreement also made Scarisbrick's brother, Charles, manager.[60]

Plate 59 A Coventry Watch Movement Company 14 size movement. This should be compared with the similar movement shown in **Plate 54**. The Coventry Company had an agency agreement with the Lancashire Watch Company and may have used some parts during their early years. However, as **Plate 60** shows, they did not use LWC underdial work. This watch has a fusee and English lever escapement but this would cause no problems as LWC parts allowed for a dummy fusee to give anticlockwise winding. The common LWC-CWMC price list of 1891 lists 14 fusee models, presumably Coventry products

Effectively for £1,000 they transferred a small Prescot watch movement business to Coventry including some workmen. After occupying temporary premises the enterprise was set up in a new factory in Spon Street which cost £1,190.[61] It was soon found that this method of manufacture was unsuccessful and losses of £511 were made within two years.[62] At this stage fusee movements were still made. Realising their error the company began afresh on correct lines by purchasing machine tools and hiring engineers to make proper watchmaking machinery giving higher output with no increase in costs. Scarisbrick's contract was terminated; however, most of their capital was consumed and in 1891 there was a recapitalisation by the offer of £5,000 of 6 per cent preference shares[59] but only £3,645 was taken up by 1900 by which time there had also been a debenture issue.[63]

During this period of reconstruction the company made a price and agency agreement with the Lancashire Watch Company and purchased a considerable number of movements presumably to enable them to supply customers in spite of their own limited output. By this means and the debenture issue the company survived with Yeomans as Chairman showing profits of £583 in 1900 with a 2½ per cent dividend.[63] Demand was steady but in small batches and it is clear that not all local makers gave them their support.[64] By 1903 the company was again in difficulty, Yeomans had retired and his successor R. Waddington was unwell so that S. T. Newsome stood in to report the worst year of trade in his experience with a profit of £101 and no dividend. The problems were the buyers' orders in batches of twenty to forty which did not suit machine production. Five hundred was suggested as the minimum possible and to this end new 16 size threequarter plate and 18 size keyless, centre seconds movements were being produced and were being ordered in this quantity. It is clear from Newsome's statement that *unfinished movements were sold* in the traditional way for finishing. Newsome also highlights the need to keep the machinery fully used to be profitable and the company were therefore looking for any 'small light metal repetition work', in particular electrical and cycle requirements.[65] This indeed was the clue to the future of the company.

By 1907 the profit was still only £151[66] but the progress to activities other than movement making was in hand and the company purchased suitable automatic machinery. By 1912 watches were only one third of the trade, the rest being cycle, motor and electrical. In view of the production of watches at Rotherham, Williamson and Ehrhardt it seems very unlikely that any movements were made after 1915 for their factory would be needed for other wartime products, for example aircraft parts. The war years set them up and increased their profits and in 1919 they joined the Cycle and Motor Cycle Manufacturers Trade Association. The company appear in Kelly from 1892 to 1917 but continued as the Coventry Movement Company from 1913 to 1972.

Plate 60 *(top right)* The underdial of the movement in **Plate 59.** The CWMC mark in the diamond is assumed to be that of the Coventry Watch Movement Company (no trademark has been found); *(bottom left and right)* watch fragments on which this mark also appears; *(top left)* this fragment marked 'Newsome' is also considered to be a CWMC product supplied to Newsome for finishing. The bridge fits other movements of the same size

What sort of movements did they make? This is difficult to answer because they were often supplied to finishers in small batches and would not bear the company name. A combined Coventry and Lancashire Company price list shows 50 models including 14 with fusees which were probably Coventry made. The complete watch movement shown in Plate 59 bears a diamond mark containing the letters CWMC. The other view of the movement is shown in Plate 60. This movement and the other remnants shown in Plate 60 all used fusees. From this scanty evidence it is suggested that these movements are from the Coventry Watch Movement Company. They may have been made with the Scarisbrick machines or they may have been supplied *unfinished* by the Lancashire Watch Company as the complete specimen shows great similarity with products from that company. Bear in mind the agreement and common price list of these

two companies. It is also possible that the diamond mark was used at this stage to distinguish Coventry-finished movements from those of Lancashire, many of which at this time used a diamond mark with LWCoLdP contained within it. A further scrap of evidence is that the watch plate with a bridge, also shown in Plate 60, is marked 'Newsome' and this bridge fits the same size CWMC plates. This suggests machine manufacture and there are other similar plates of different size marked 'Yeomans' or 'Newsome' (both of whom were closely associated with the Coventry company), suggesting that batches of part-finished movements were being supplied to finishers.

In the Kew trials[22] no company successes are shown but there are many from Coventry makers including Yeomans and Waddington. It would appear that no company trademark was registered between 1888 and 1920 (unless in the name of some official) so that identification of later going barrel watches has not proved possible. One field which could yield information should be 18 size, keyless centre seconds watches and 16 size threequarter plate watches of the period 1903–14 for which orders in batches of 500 were received. Plate 73 shows *possible* examples because these have not been identified.

It is not really possible to estimate the total production from this sparse information but it seems unlikely to exceed 150,000. Interestingly, after an indifferent start, diversification into the cycle, electrical, motor cycle and car parts industry enabled the company to survive for over eighty years.

P & A GUYE (Plate 74, *lower left*)

Auguste Guye (1835–93) came to London from his native Switzerland in 1856 and started watchmaking in Northampton Square with his younger brother Fritz who became responsible for the business aspects of the firm.[67] Philippe (1828–94), the elder brother, remained in Switzerland to form the company Ph. Guye & Cie, Geneva, making balance springs, but he became a partner in the English firm.[68] The address of P & A Guye is given as 8a Guildford Street (1861–4), 13 Northampton Square (1867–75)[25] and is shown in Kelly as 77 Farringdon Road from 1872 to 1905 but from 1909–32 Kelly shows P & A Guye at 26a Harrison Street. The factory is also recorded at St Brides Street in 1875 and later at 77 Farringdon Road[69] where it had a comprehensive plant for advanced watch manufacture including the production of plates for movements. There is a report about this factory which says the parts made are interchangeable,[70] a claim also made in a Guye advertisement in Kelly 1872, 'all pieces being so adjusted that they can be forwarded to be replaced . . . on receipt of the number of the watch'. The factory report says that holes in plates are placed to within 0.00011in when care is taken or for less important work to within 0.0004in. It gives details of the twenty-four operations to make a balance cock and emphasises the importance of keeping machines work-ing all the time, using a capacity of 500 watches per day as an example but not claiming to make this large number, rather suggesting 1,100 in three months of one model.

Other processes are also described including the manufacture of balance staffs. It is clear that the work in the factory is precise and to achieve interchangeability much attention is focussed on measurement, cutting-tool quality and careful and punctual resetting. Auguste Guye could therefore be considered an important contributor to the develop-ment of the principles of machine manufacture in England. His machines were his own design and not bought out or copies of existing American machines. It may be significant that his background was Swiss and that Philippe was still in Switzerland, but Auguste was obviously a competent horologist *and* engineer. This talent is recognised in another factory report of 1890 which features lever and pallet manufacture and polishing of pinions.[69] There is no record of the power source for the machines.

Information about the products is sparse. In 1880 it is possible that they are the firm making keywind going barrel movements in Clerken-well.[71] In 1881 they allowed Rigg to display keyless watches with machine-made escapements[8] and in 1884 they are reported to be making 500 movements a month and to supply firms like Benson.[47] By 1889 they were unable to keep up with orders[18] and classed with Rotherham, Ehrhardt, the English Watch Company and Nicole Nielson as large pro-ducers making their own movements.[20] In 1890 they made smaller keyless gold watches in 0 and 6 size for ladies[21] which were probably threequarter plate models with right-angle, English lever layout which was their usual pattern.[69] No information about the type of escape wheel teeth has been found. Auguste died in 1893 and the business was run by Fritz and Auguste's son. They registered a trademark on 5 June, 1894 (Fig 13) and 'in response to demand' started to make full plate capped watches with a patent balance spring stud and a new method of holding the cap in place by a disc under the cap which, when rotated, engaged a slit in the balance cock.[68,72] This might be used to identify a Guye full plate capped watch. In 1897 factory improvements and the production of complicated watches[73] were announced. No records of success in Kew trials are shown for 1894 and 1899–1901 but they were 11th in the 1901 Greenwich deck watch trials[22] with watch number 12,647.

Like other companies Guye appeared to have problems at the begin-ning of the twentieth century but the story is not clear. Advertisements for keyless and keywind, threequarter plate lever watches in the 1892 Kelly clearly state Guye's sole agent for the United Kingdom to be H. William-son of 81 Farringdon Road. In March 1903 Guye report trade as satisfac-tory for the preceding year[54] and in November 1904 it is reported that both Williamson and Guye have had the enterprise to construct a machine-made keyless watch with *pendant* handset which implies their previous watches had the push piece and pendant system.[74] A Williamson advertisement in the 1901 Kelly shows such push piece watches, however it is not clear whether the Williamson watches were made by Guye or whether there are different watches. The 1901 watch advert shows 17 jewels and different plates to the threequarter plate, 7 jewel lever model which was made later by Williamson in Coventry (Errington factory). In May 1905, J. Evans, the secretary of P & A Guye Ltd, writes that a report has been circulated among the trade that the business of this company has been taken over by another wholesale house but that there is not any foundation for such a statement.[75] The Kelly entry for 1905 shows *P & A Guy* in Harrison Street and the address of Williamson at 81 Farringdon Road does in due course change to include 77, 79 and 81. It seems possible that Guye (Guy) ceased making many watches from this time but carried on until at least 1932 in some other activity connected with the trade. They may have supplied parts or repaired watches. One possible reason for the end of production by Guye in about 1905 might have been the introduction of full-scale production by Williamson in Coventry. They may previously have used Guye watches which they no longer required, leaving Guye with insufficient marketing strength in a competitive situation.

Regrettably it has not proved possible to identify any Guye watches so that little can be said about them. If they produced 500 per month from 1880–1900 there should be a total of 120,000 in various sizes both full and threequarter plate with keywind and keyless operation using right-angle, English lever layout. The quality appears to be good by reports and Benson has been mentioned as a customer. Mercer lists of Frodsham watches show no Guye entries.[76]

NICOLE, NIELSON & COMPANY LTD

Adolphe Nicole came to London from Switzerland in 1840 and opened a watchmaking business with Henry Capt at 80B Dean Street, Soho, presumably similar to that which they had in Geneva.[76] Nicole patented a keyless winding method in 1844 (UK patent 10,348) which was used by Dent[77] under licence from 1846–62. Nicole also held patents for chronograph work and an escapement (UK patents 1,461 of 1862, 905 of 1870). The Dean Street address was used until 1858 after which the firm moved to 14 Soho Square.[25] Henry Capt was replaced by Jules Capt in 1843 and when he died in 1876 (Sophus) Emil Nielson, Nicole's son-in-law, became a partner, the firm becoming Nicole, Nielson & Company. In 1888 the firm was purchased from Nielson by a Mr North, possibly on Nicole's death,[76] but Nielson continued as joint managing director. The firm became Nicole, Nielson & Company Ltd in 1888 and North and Sons Ltd in 1917. North was also associated with Frodsham, one of their customers, becoming a director and Chairman in 1922. Nielson was also a Frodsham director until 1898, one year before he died.

In 1904 Nicole, Nielson & Company began to diversify its products to include vehicle speedometers which they sold to S. Smith and Sons[76] and during the profitable war years they made aircraft magnetos. After the war as North and Sons Ltd they made clocks for cars and other buyers but were never profitable and were liquidated in 1932. Nicole Nielson appears in Kelly from 1882 to 1913.

Nielson had experience at the Waltham factory in America[21] and in 1880 was not overenthusiastic in his comments,[7] however his obituary[78] says that as head of the firm he saw the machine system of manufacture introduced. This was a late development, for in 1884 a report on the factory[70] indicates that their power source was foot lathes and suggests that as a firm they wished to cling to the idea that their products were not machine made, as their customers were of a 'select and aristo-cratic character'. They made the whole movement except for the escape-ment on an interchangeable basis and also produced gold cases. By 1889 they had changed and they are described as a large producer[20] (possibly optimistically) and a factory visit records an Otto gas engine for power and describes some of the machines and processes.[79] As with other pro-ducers the dial feet holes in the plate were used to locate other holes. Gold casemaking was still pursued. The movement-making processes were different to other factories because they made small batches for different customers who did not appreciate uniformity with their competitors. They preferred that their own wares should be as distinct as possible and it was therefore a rule that a particular type of watch designed for one customer should be reserved for him. The machines and tools had to be very adaptable to suit this policy.

All this means identification of Nicole Nielson watches is unlikely to be easy and estimates of production impossible without documents. They had a trademark (Fig 13) registered on 23 May 1879 and one customer was Frodsham. Mercer gives lists of Frodsham watches attributable to Nicole Nielson.[76] Kew trials[22] for 1899–1901 show no entries for Nicole Nielson but some successes for Frodsham and other makers which may be Nicole Nielson watches. Benson also used Nicole Nielson movements for complicated watches[80] which could be another means of identifying Nicole Nielson products, however it seems possible that some of the parts used by Nicole Nielson in complicated movements came from Switzer-land which might lead to confusion in identification of unmarked watches. It can also be seen that S. Smith and Sons used Nicole Nielson watches in their complicated 'products' for Mercer shows a watch 12,246 involved with both Frodsham and Smith.[76] One particular design of watch made by Nicole Nielson and sold by Frodsham from 1895 was a 60 seconds duration chronograph for timing aircraft flights or other short duration events.

Plate 61 Benson movements: *(top left)* a 'Ludgate' keywind movement possibly made before the factory at Belle Sauvage Yard was opened; *(top right)* keywind movement made after the factory opened with under-dial similar, but not identical to, the former; *(bottom left and right)* similarly the keyless 'Bank' models were made at the factory. All are good quality, threequarter plate, jewelled lever movements with English escape wheels, cut compensated balances and going barrels. The underdial layout depends on whether the watch is destined for open face or hunter-style cases, similarly the balance cock may be to the right or left of the movement

Benson history starts in 1749 but little is known until about 1840 when small numbers of watches were produced in Cornhill, London under the name S. S. and J. W. Benson.[25,80] Some time after this the name changed to J. W. (James William) Benson and the firm moved to Ludgate Hill, originally number 33, later 58 and 60. Benson watches built in the 1860s were expensive and obtained Royal patronage in 1879, a fact clearly stated on their subsequent watch plates. Despite their price Benson watches were popular and the firm moved to bigger premises at 62 and 64 Ludgate Hill in 1879. Kelly shows these Ludgate Hill addresses from 1872 on and later, premises at Royal Exchange and Bond Street. In 1892 a steam-powered factory was opened at Belle Sauvage Yard (in Ludgate Hill) at which their well-finished, elegant threequarter plate pocket

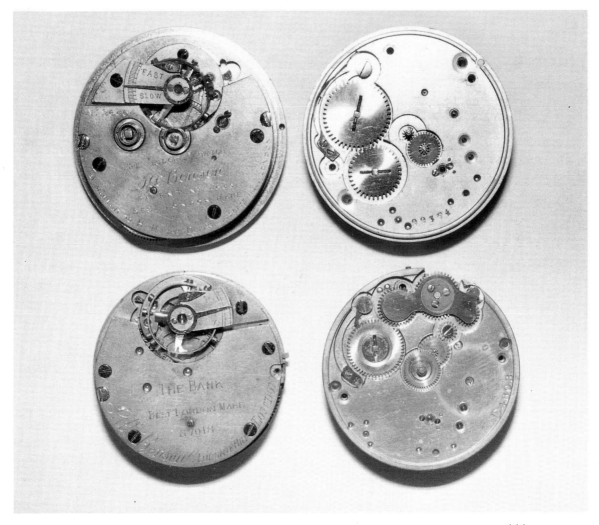

watches were produced in considerable numbers until 1941 when the factory was destroyed by bombs. Three grades of watch were produced, The Field, The Bank and The Ludgate which were initially keywind, later becoming keyless with rocking bar and push piece handsetting. They were produced for about fifty years with single roller, right-angle, English lever escapement, compensated balances, Venetian dials and English cases with maker's mark JWB. The factory was visited in 1935[81] and it is clear that the parts were interchangeable and that they were made with great care to maintain the firm's record for high quality and service.

Even after the bombing the service department was maintained but Benson never made watches again for the market was different after the war. Benson's are now a non-trading company in the Sears plc. Benson's were not primarily watchmakers. They were retail jewellers and sold clocks (Loomes records Benson as clockmakers, 1857–87) and watches from other sources. J. W. Benson himself[82] illustrates Swiss bar movement cylinder and lever watches and English full plate and threequarter plate fusee watches in a book of 1875, all the watches being engraved J. W. Benson, London.

Benson bought watches or movements from Guye,[47] Nicole Nielson, Williamson and other makers or Clerkenwell outworkers to supply orders which they were not able to fulfil with their own production. It is probable that the Benson Railway Guard watch was made by this method[80] but if not Benson sold movements to other retailers for whom identical products can be found. There are also keyless English-made 0 size threequarter plate watches made before the death of Queen Victoria which may not be Benson products.

From this fragmentary evidence it is difficult to estimate the production at Belle Sauvage Yard. Aked[83] suggests they *sold* tens of thousands of first-class quality English lever watches in Queen Victoria's reign but they may not have *made* all these. The numbering system used is not helpful using a letter and a four figure number on Field and Bank models and a continuous sequence (not necessarily starting from 1) on the Ludgate models but including 92,257 and 129,302, the latter probably made in c1903 as it is engraved 'late Queen' compared with 117,911 which is engraved 'Queen'. Railway watches, 0 size watches and three Victorian fusee watches (two with Wycherley movements) bear different incompatible numbers. The only Benson watch to feature in Kew trials[22] of 1899–1902, a minute repeating chronograph, number 2,324 of 1899, does not match any of the other numbers.

The bombing report[80] says that 12,000 watches in stock were destroyed (these may have included stored Swiss products as well as Benson) but a total Benson *factory* production of at least 100,000 sounds possible. It is interesting to note that the Rotherham manager from 1876 (Mr Gooding) worked for Benson before Rotherham; perhaps he wanted Benson to move towards factory production sixteen years earlier than they did.

H. WILLIAMSON LTD (Plates 62 to 66 and 72)

Williamson were wholesalers in clocks, watches, rolled gold ware and silver plateware. They made or had made for them all these items in various places and at various times and the exact story of the beginning is not clear. There are Williamsons in the Clerkenwell area of London in the mid to late nineteenth century,[25,26] notably Charles 1851–63, Henry 1844–81 and James 1861–71. There is also a William Williamson in London in 1858 and in Coventry in 1880. All these are possible family connections. Kelly shows Henry Williamson, dialmaker in Coventry in 1872 and Henry Williamson, 81 Farringdon Road, London, in 1892 and in this year an advertisement appears showing H. Williamson as the sole agent for P. & A. Guye watches in the United Kingdom. In 1901 a Kelly advertisement shows H. Williamson Ltd marketing from the English Watch Factory in Coventry, the new 'Empire' threequarter plate keyless watch and a keywind full plate watch. The full plate watch can be identified as a Williamson product but a threequarter plate model has not been examined. In 1901 it is unlikely that Williamson were acting for Guye since by this time supplies of watches came from Coventry or Switzerland. Williamson had developed his firm fairly rapidly from about 1890 onwards in both clock and watchmaking and the story can be traced.

In 1885 William Burden, a clockmaker from Quarley in Hampshire, opened a shop in Salisbury called the City Clock Factory. By 1897 the business had expanded and Mr Burden passed it to his sons who marked their product 'Burden Bros'. They built a steam-powered factory called the Steam Clock Factory but in 1900 moved the work to another site in Southampton Road. After a successful two years the brothers decided to make agricultural machinery and in 1902 sold out to Herbert Williamson (son of Henry?) and William Tucker from London who changed the name to the English Clock Factory and re-equipped it to produce different clocks. The factory is clearly shown in the 1901 OS map and appears in the local Kelly Directory for 1901.[84] In 1902 Mr Bley came to manage the Salisbury factory from Germany, where he had worked with automatic machinery in both the clock and watch industry, including the Hamburg-America Clock Company and Thiel, the watch firm.[84] Bley probably helped with the introduction of automatic machinery at Salisbury for clockmaking and may later have advised on the modernisation of the watchmaking business (Errington) which Williamson acquired in Coventry. He was also responsible for the introduction of a car speedometer designed and manufactured at Salisbury but this venture was discontinued because S. Smith and Sons claimed patent infringements. Williamson were supplying Smiths with a large number of watches and they could not afford to risk losing this customer.[85] Bley remained at Salisbury until the clock factory burned down in May 1909 and William-

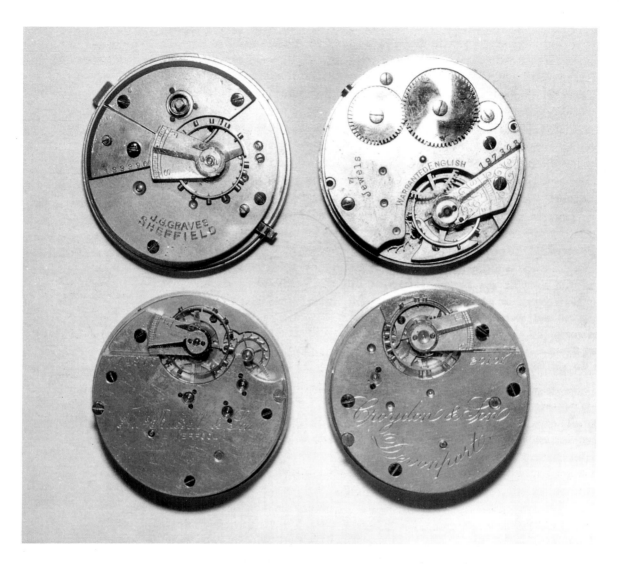

son transferred clockmaking to Coventry[86] (Bley returned to the Hamburg-America Clock Company). Advertisements for Salisbury-made dial clocks with *interchangeable* parts appear in 1908 and for the first new Coventry-made clocks in 1910.

An important report for Williamson history records the launch of a public company in 1898 (H. Williamson Ltd) whose shares previously had been held by the principal and the employees.[87] This report states that the private company had existed for less than five years and therefore sets the date of formation as 1893–4. Thus the 1892 Guye advertisement may have been Williamson as an individual. The Stock Exchange Register confirms this date.[10]

The watchmaking arm of Williamson derives from the small factory of Charles H. Errington. Williamson must have bought up Errington (possibly with shares) in about 1896. Errington remained manager of the factory at Holyhead Road, Coventry, until his retirement in 1910 and was largely responsible, just before retirement, for re-establishing the clockmaking in Coventry after the Salisbury fire.[88] Errington had been in Coventry for some years and held several patents. (UK numbers 1,433 of 1881, 5,636 of 1881, 6,617 of 1891, 10,356 of 1892 and 18,766 of 1892.) The latter two give some help for 18,766 appears on a machine-made watch movement number 15,851 which is almost identical to others stamped 'Williamson' and both 10,356 and 18,766 appear on a similar but not identical earlier movement number 12,058 (10,356 is linked with case bolts and 18,766 with barrel design). Prior to joining Williamson, Errington is shown in Kelly in 1875 and 1887 as a watch case engraver and in 1892 as a movement maker. He took rough movements from James Berry of Prescot to finish and market[89] (Berry movements are sometimes marked M.M. supposedly for 'Machine Made') so that Errington would not have owned *plate-making machinery* nor much other machinery suited to the large-scale production that Williamson envisaged. Errington offered skills, a factory and workforce and Williamson could start an expansion programme.

Earlier (p81) it was speculatively suggested that Williamson could have acquired plate-making machinery from the failed English Watch Company in 1896–7 and it would then seem probable that he imported Swiss parts *temporarily* to enable him to produce full plate, keywind watches[89] until he was able to enlarge his factory[91] to take a proposed 1,000 workers to produce new keyless, threequarter plate watches of his own. Williamson advertisements over the next decade and examination of identifiable watches show several threequarter plate designs using English parts different to the 'Empire' trademark model of 1901. This interpretation is backed by the defence evidence of William Tucker in the REGINA vs H. WILLIAMSON Merchandise Marks Act case of 1899–90 in which it was admitted that for the full plate keywind watch, Swiss barrel arbors, cap studs, centre, third and fourth wheels and pinions, pallets, pallet staffs, balance cocks, mainsprings, balance and barrels were used[89] whereas the threequarter plate keyless watches used English *outworker* parts. The Swiss parts were made at the Williamson factory in Büren[92] which Williamson had acquired specifically for this purpose in 1898.

After losing the Merchandise Marks Act prosecution the Coventry factory extension was completed[91] and machinery, some of which was automatic, was installed to make these parts. This would appear to be the first record of flat bed Swiss automatic lathe use in England.[90] The Büren factory then produced watches clearly marked 'Swiss made' for sale in England and elsewhere. Two of the better known watches made for the English market were the Acme lever and the Sphinx, the latter being a Williamson trademark from 1895. When Williamson failed, Rotherham took on a Büren agency.[43] The new mass-produced threequarter plate, keyless, 7-jewel movement from Coventry was for 16 size pocket watches

Plate 62 Williamson movements: (*top left*) an early full plate model. This example has an English lever escapement but Swiss examples are also found, indeed this is probably the style of watch which used parts made at the Büren Factory (**Plate 65**) and featured in the Merchandise Marks Act case; (*top right*) the 1905, 16 size, threequarter plate keyless model made after the legal case, clearly marked 'Warranted English'; (*bottom left and right*) two other threequarter plate Williamson movements. Both have double roller, straight line Swiss lever escapements but are not of such high quality as they at first look

Plate 63 Underdials of the four Williamson movements shown in **Plate 62**. They are arranged in the same positions. The *top left* is marked 'H. Williamson, Ltd, Coventry' and the remainder 'Errington Watch Factory'

and was introduced in 1905. By 1908–9 it was also made 0 size for ladies' and wrist watches.[93] In 1910 another keyless, threequarter plate model, the Astral, was introduced with damascened plates, advertised in two sizes and forty-nine styles. Each watch was sold with a two-position timing certificate. Casemaking, which had taken place in Birmingham, where presumably Williamson had acquired an existing business (possibly the English Watch Case Manufacturing Company of 24 Spencer Street), was also transferred to the new factory[91] and the Birmingham works continued to make the silver plateware mentioned earlier. The Reliance brand gold plated products were possibly made in the Goswell Road, London works of King and Sons which became part of Williamson.[94]

Williamson had new ideas about marketing which caused criticism in the same way as his use of Swiss parts had been an 'illegal' method of manufacture. He loaned money to retailers at 5 per cent interest to enable them to buy his products taking debenture shares of the retailing business as security. For this action he was accused of retailing watches.[95] However he overcame all these problems and in 1912 his Coventry factory was visited by members of the British Horological Institute.[96] Here the visitors saw automatic lathes in action for both clockmaking and watchmaking. Watches mentioned were the Astral 7-jewel model and 16- and 21-jewel hand-finished models. The watch shop had 260 machines and 270 workers and it would appear that the whole watch movement including hands and dials but possibly excluding springs was made. Casing but not casemaking was also mentioned. Williamson watches in hallmarked cases with maker's mark CHE exist but perhaps these were only made in small numbers for them to be omitted from the tour description. Unfortunately no production rate is given but in the later war years this factory made about a thousand watches a week for the government.[85] The number of workers is small but it depends on the amount of automatic machinery used. No real changes occurred in the products over the remainder of the life of the company and the reports of the annual general meetings[97] suffice to outline the rest of the Williamson story until the receiver was appointed in 1931.

Plate 64 A watch in an open-faced gold case hallmarked 1910. The movement is the better quality Williamson 16-jewel model of the type shown on the top right of **Plate 62.** It is marked 'Errington Watch Factory' under the dial

AGM (Year of pub')	Profit	Ordinary share dividend	Summary
3 (1901)	£38,430	10%	(Preference share dividends 5% unless passed.)
1902			Debenture issue £100,000 at 4½%.
5 (1903)	£44,421	10%	Total workforce 1,800 (Switzerland and UK) Swiss output 4,000 per week.
1905			Price agreement with Ehrhardt, Lancashire Watch Company.
7 (1906)			New model introduced in 1905 (7 jewel?).
9 (1907)	£30,044	5%	H.W. to Chairman. Joint MDs, C. H. Williamson (son) and W. E. Tucker. Demand good.
10 (1908)	£27,190	5%	Largest production ever. Purchase of John Troup and Sons of Hatton Garden.
11 (1909)	£21,237	2%	'0' size ladies' watch.
12 (1910)	£25,762	2½%	Fire losses of £10,000. More retailing complaints.
13 (1911)		2%	Strike at Büren, cost of clock factory transfer, Astral watch introduced in 1910, Errington retires, Fleming replaces. Business of Gay, Lamaille and West purchased: optical work in Manchester. Less profit due to this activity.
14–16 (1912–14)	£84,785 In 1913	2%, 2%, 2%	Losses due to retailers' advances (1914). H.W. dies (1914).
17 (1915)	£12,043	0%	War effects, imports down, opportunity to make cheap clocks but no time or money. Silver plate bad. Büren stopped, workforce temporarily in Swiss army. Büren lost German trade.
18 (1916)	£103,835	?	Best year but not war profits. Swiss problems, new clock, one soldier in four wears wrist watches. Sales of cheaper watches up.
19 (1917)	£46,836	5%	Gross profit more but property purchased. Coventry factory making government watches. Büren selling US market.

AGM (Year of pub')	Profit	Ordinary share dividend	Summary
20 (1918)	£67,066	5%	New clock, Büren not imported into UK – duties heavy.
21 (1919)	£105,463	5%	Excess profits tax, Treasury doing better than investors!
22 (1920)	£150,000	10%	English Clocks and Gramophones Ltd at Huntingdon floated. Williamson to take 1,000,000 clocks per year.
23 (1921)	£32,086	5%	English Clocks and Gramophones voluntary liquidation[98] (see also Stock Exchange list). Severe slump has set in, factories now reorganised ready for a recovery.
24 (1922)	£54,093 loss	0%	English Clock and Watch Manufacture Ltd set up at Holyhead Road, Coventry (Coventry factory traded under this name from 1922–34 with general manager H. N. Walford[99]). Partner in venture was Grimshaw Baxter and J. J. Elliot the clockmaking firm.[85]
25 (1923)	£25,035	0% pref passed	Investment in English Clock and Watch Manufacture Ltd £58,255. £5 shares now trading at £1. Profits retained.
26 (1924)	£18,633 loss	0% pref passed	Balance forward £452-8s-4d.
27 (1925)	£14,164 loss	0% pref passed	Repeal of wartime McKenna duties of $33^{1}/_{3}$ per cent on imports. (American assessment of potential UK market.[100])
28 (1926)	£2,612 loss	0% pref passed	McKenna duty reimposed but advance notice caused dumping. Büren doing well, five years of depression in UK.
29 (1927)	£11,942 loss	0% pref passed	Worse than before, exports up, home down. Factories in UK not working full time. Büren satisfactory.
31 (1929)	£29,938 loss	0% pref passed	Capital reorganisation proposed, all preference passed dividends cancelled.
33 (1931)			Receiver appointed 4 August, 1931, (A. E. Tilley of Singleton, Fabian & Co).

The problems for the receiver were the complex structure of Williamson which involved their own activities, Grimshaw, Baxter and J. J. Elliot in English Clock and Watch Manufacturers Ltd and a Swiss company, Büren. The English horological industry thought that clockmaking was viable and eventually S. Smith and Sons acquired the *clock* department.[101] A short time before this Charles Tucker and George Nunn, both ex-Williamson, had set up as clock wholesalers using products from the new Enfield Clock factory[85] and when Smith acquired the Williamson interests they invited Tucker and Nunn to join them as part of the Smith Group to be called Tucker, Nunn and Williamson. In 1939 this became Richard and Tucker, Nunn Ltd, as more of the clockmaking industry came under Smith control. Watches however had ceased to be made in England in any quantity from about 1930 and it is reasonable to assume that the receiver had no problems in disposing of the successful Büren factory in Switzerland.

A similar story is echoed in the BIF exhibitions between 1924 and 1937[42,43] when the name Williamson gradually disappeared, the last appearance being in 1934 under the presumably temporary title Williamson Clock Company (before Tucker, Nunn and Williamson) on the single stand for Smiths English Clocks Ltd, Williamson Clock Co Ltd and Richard and Co Ltd which displayed only clocks. Some trademarks passed from Williamson to Smith including 'Astral' and 'Empire' which were to appear again on Smith post-1945 watches.

Confirming information can be gathered elsewhere for the Stock Exchange Register[10] shows that the debenture holders received 6s 4½d in the pound after all the assets were sold and Williamson were struck off in 1944. Similarly, Kelly lists Williamson in Farringdon Road, London,

Plate 65 An advertisement in a Swiss journal of c1910 for the Williamson factory in Büren. The advert also shows some Büren watch movements and indicates the production rate

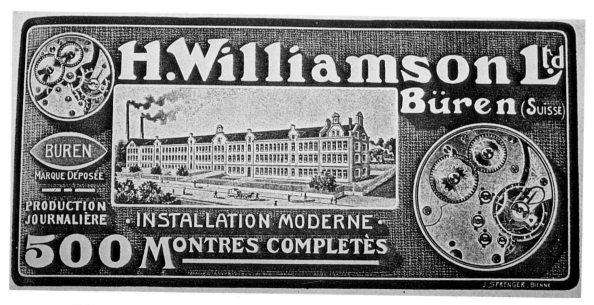

Spencer Street, Birmingham and Holyhead Road, Coventry from 1901–24 but English Clock and Watch Manufacturers afterwards. There was also a house journal called *Astral News* at Williamson but no copies have been traced to supplement the information.

Williamson had a special department where *handmade* (finished?) pocket watches and deck watches were made.[85] Some of these were karrusel watches and were sent for Kew trials[22] recording successes in 1900 with 56,019 (46th) and 56,020 (47th) and in 1901 they were first and second with 56,365 and 56,371 and 31st with 55,935. The other watches they made consist, as described above, of early full plate keywind models then a series of threequarter plate keyless models of various qualities, the main product being the 7-jewel quality in 16 and 0 size. At some stage a split top plate design was also produced and was sold by various retailers including J. W. Benson. The numbering sequence is not absolutely clear. There was a series for the full plate design which might be sequential with that of the threequarter plate 16 size watches but there was certainly a separate sequence for the 0 size watches. Full plate watches have several similar but different underdial styles (Plate 63) and serial numbers between 12,000 and 187,000 have been seen. Threequarter plate watch numbers between 61,000 and 430,000 have been seen and 0 size between 2,500 and 25,000 which suggests a total production including the wartime government watches of about 750,000. Since Williamson were producing watches from about 1898 to 1928 this represents an average rate of production of 460 per week for the 600,000 watches made in the non-war years. With manpower recorded as 400 in 1899 and 270 in 1912 this represents a reasonable rate. The figure includes watches made when trading under the name English Clock and Watch Manufacturers but excludes Büren products.

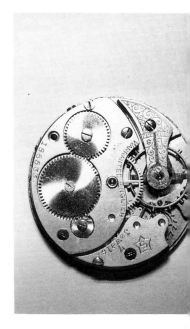

Plate 66 The 1910 Williamson split plate 'Astral' model. The star mark appears to identify this model. It appears in contemporary advertisements

SMITH AND SONS LTD (Plates 67 to 70)

This firm which still exists today as Smiths Industries PLC probably originated in about 1830[102] although Mr Barrett, one time Managing Director of Smiths Clock and Watch division suggests 1851.[103] Loomes[26] shows a Smith & Son, London, 1881 which could be an early record and the Stock Exchange Register[10] shows Smith S. and Sons Ltd registered in 1899, in voluntary liquidation on 31 March 1930 when a portion of the business was acquired by S. Smith and Sons (Motor Accessories) Ltd, later S. Smith and Sons (England) Ltd, later Smiths Industries Ltd (1966). In 1900 Smiths described themselves as Watch and Clock makers, Diamond Merchants, Jewellers and Silversmiths at 9 Strand, London, with factories in Clerkenwell, London and Bienne, Switzerland.[102] Kelly shows Smith, Samuel, Newington Causeway from 1872 and Smiths, Samuel and Son from 1887 in the Strand and Samuel & Son Ltd (1905–27) between formation and liquidation. At this stage they were mainly retailers[104] and their range of watches can be seen in a facsimile illustrated catalogue.[102] At their Clerkenwell factory they were finishers of watch movements or assemblers of watch parts obtained from local Clerkenwell makers or Switzerland. It is possible some came from Nicole Nielson.[76] They also sold watches made by other English factories such as Williamson.[85] Although they offered watches in various grades they were best known at this period for their high-quality watches, often with complications, which they supplied to officials, governments and expeditions as well as the public. Their display of watches at the 1900 Paris Exhibition received a bronze medal.

Clearly Smiths felt that the new motor car industry offered scope and they purchased speedometers from Nicole Nielson until 1909 when they designed and sold their own model[76] which provoked patent discussions with Williamson. This new venture succeeded and overshadowed the jewellery part of the firm and a new company, S. Smith and Sons (Motor Accessories) Ltd, was founded in 1913.

World War I caused demand for their products and they made instruments for aircraft and later, at a new factory in Cricklewood, they made fuses. After the war their main business became motor car and aircraft instruments and they acquired the firm of Jaeger (Chronos works) in 1920. Smiths then started to make an 'All-British' car clock using Swiss escapements but this contravened the Merchandise Marks Act[85] so that in 1928, they formed the All British Escapement Company to make the necessary parts in England.[105] Soon they were making clocks for other purposes and with the acquisition of the Williamson remains they became a large clockmaking concern. The voluntary liquidation of the original company in 1930 had signalled the end of their watchmaking interests and indeed there were virtually no watches being made in England from 1930 onwards although Smiths were still retailers in the Strand. This is confirmed by the British Industries Fairs of 1934 and 1937 at which Smiths only show clocks.[43] Clearly this was not in the national interest and in the years just before World War II, Smiths, with the encouragement of the government, set about reviving watch manufacture. This was not easy for the necessary machinery and materials came from Switzerland who were reluctant suppliers for fear of damaging their own export-based industry; indeed England was soon stockpiling Swiss watches for the impending war.

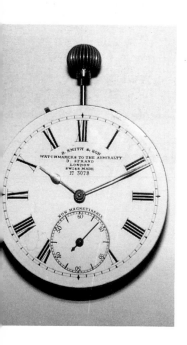

Plate 67 A movement from a Smiths' watch of c1920. It is clearly identified as Swiss and has 15 jewels and a straight line lever escapement. Smiths *made* very few watches at this stage of their history but relied on imports which were clearly marked

There was success in manufacturing clocks and large watches at Cheltenham for aircraft use and also with pocket and stop watches of which about 150,000 were made.[110] Wrist-watch manufacture was not really successful, only small numbers being produced. Some parts were obtained from Switzerland.[85]

After the war the government decided to revive the watchmaking industry and Smiths, Ingersoll, Vickers-Armstrong and Newmark were involved in the project to mass-produce various grades of watch. Smiths were encouraged to produce jewelled lever pocket and wrist watches at Cheltenham[110] and a new factory for the new Anglo-Celtic Watch Company opened on 15 March 1947. This was sited at Ystradgynlais in Wales and pin lever escapement watches were made by a consortium of Smiths, Ingersoll and Vickers. However Vickers withdrew in 1948 and Ingersoll in 1969. Smiths' progress in the venture is recorded in the 32nd AGM report of S. Smith and Sons (England) Ltd on 20 December 1947.[106] This stated that one of the Cheltenham factories was producing high-grade jewelled lever watches with quality and quantity constantly improving. However the new factory for the production of pin lever watches was not yet operating due to delays in the delivery of machinery. Production was expected to begin in the spring of the next year.

Plate 68 A 19 ligne model PY Smiths' Empire pocket watch which used a movement based on the Ingersoll 'Crown' which was made in London from 1905 till 1922 (from American parts at first). The modern watch was also sold under the name Ingersoll and Services. It has a pin lever escapement and was sold from 1947 until 1980

A visit to the Cheltenham wrist-watch factory in 1956 describes the manufacture of watches in sizes from 5¼ ligne to 12 ligne and stop watches.[107] The processes used in the manufacture of a 15-jewel man's wrist watch at this factory are discussed in detail in a paper[108] in which it is clear from the correspondence from Colonel Rothschild of Newmark that Swiss machinery was now being used in English factories but that due to the design success during the war Britain was no longer *dependent* on machinery imports. It was however economic to import due to the small market available to British machine tool makers. The machinery was purchased by the government and initially hired to the companies with a later option to purchase.[109] Smiths continued to make jewelled watches at Cheltenham for many years but after production ceased the factory was used for other products.[117] Pin lever watches continued to be made in South Wales until 1980 when the factory closed.[109] Mechanical movements were imported from Japan in 1975 for 'Astral' watches.

Smiths sold electronic watches from 1976 to 1983 which were imported from Germany and Japan. During the period from 1979 to 1981 Smiths developed their own 'Quasar' electronic watch at Cheltenham. When the Cheltenham factory closed in 1981 development continued elsewhere and limited production started in 1983. Only about 500 Quasar movements were made and these were not marketed.[117] This was the end of the last British attempt to manufacture watches in quantity.

Although Smiths did not actually make all their pre-1930 watches but only assembled or finished them it is worth recording that those shown in the catalogue[102] were good-quality, keyless pocket watches with smaller models for ladies and a selection of more expensive complicated watches. Over 200 examples are shown, from plain open faced, silver cased, lever escapement, gentlemen's pocket watches at thirty shillings to a striking, repeating, perpetual calendar, minute and seconds chronograph with split seconds and moon phase for £250 with Swiss ébauche or £450 with English ébauche. There are also cylinder escapement watches for children and ladies, and lever escapement watches for ladies. Apart from the complicated or karrusel watches which can be seen in museums, few Smiths' watches appear today compared with Benson or Frodsham models which would be competitors, from which one might assume that the total number sold between 1890 and 1920 was quite small. Their brand name was the 'Strand' watch selling at prices between £5 5s 0d and £26. Many Smiths' watches had Kew certificates and many were successful in Kew trials[22,37] including 101-1892 and 13,131 in 1893; tourbillon 238-99 was *first* in 1899 and 1899-1 was 13th; karrusels 229-309, 192B10, 229-308 and 192A2 were 16th, 31st, 36th and 37th (these numbers identify the watches in the catalogue). Other 1899 successes included 148-90, 13,159, 153-4, 153-5 and 192C225. In 1900 karrusel 191-227 and 172-351 a plain watch feature, also deck watches 193-391, 193-387, 193-389 and in 1901 tourbillons 1901–22, 1900–4 and karrussels 193-387, 1900-A and 193-399 appear. This impressive list illustrates Smiths' policies for sales in this period.

In the post-World War II period the story was different. Smiths certainly *made* watches at Cheltenham and Ystradgynlais. At Cheltenham they made a 15-jewel, 19 ligne lever pocket watch derived directly from the watch produced for the services during the war, a jewelled stop watch and a 12 ligne, 15-jewel model RG, Astral and de luxe lever wrist watch described by Robinson.[111] The watch was also chosen for the services in 1967 and 1968 and also sold in this form, the GS4701.[112] Later an 11¾ ligne, 19-jewel, shockproof, antimagnetic 'Imperial' model with provision for selfwinding was made for gentlemen, and for ladies an 8¾ ligne, 15-jewel model KG, Astral and de luxe, a 5¾ by 8¾ ligne, 17-jewel watch

Plate 69 Two Smiths' pin lever escapement wrist watches: *(left)* the 13 ligne model RY, first made in 1948; *(right)* the 8¾ ligne model LY for ladies, first made in 1954. These watches were also sold under the Ingersoll and Services labels

Plate 70 Three Smiths' pin lever escapement wrist watch movements: *(top left)* the 13 ligne model RY; *(top right)* the 8¾ ligne model LY; *(bottom)* the 1956 10½ ligne model TY, then considered a preferable size to the original RY

calibre 200 de luxe and a 5½ ligne, 15-jewel Astral model.[113] Smiths also supplied jewelled movements or parts to Benson, Frodsham and other firms to market as their own.[76]

In Wales, Smiths (Ingersoll) made Empire pin lever watches including a 19 ligne pocket size from 1947–80 (model PY) based on the Ingersoll Crown full-plate watch first introduced by the American Ingersoll company when they opened their London office in 1905. A short while later the 13 ligne wrist watch (model RY) of which 2.65 million were produced, was introduced but this 5-jewel Roskopf layout watch was replaced in 1956 by the 10½ ligne, 4 wheel train, model TY. This watch is analysed by Pike as a boy's watch[114] but Boult, for some time the MD of Anglo-Celtic suggests that by 1958 the 13 ligne model was too large and needed replacement.[109] For ladies there was, from 1954, an 8¾ ligne model LY followed in 1972 by the 6¾ ligne model. All these wrist watches are split plate designs built up on a solid dial plate. Most of the watches were available in various styles and prices, with and without seconds hand, with centre seconds hand, etc, and in a variety of cases. The pin lever pocket watch was also arranged with special dials printed for referees, yachtsmen, etc. A 10½ ligne, 7-jewelled lever watch known as the 'slim-line' model was also made at Ystradgynlais, the only product of a planned range, and is described in Ingersoll form by Pike.[115] All the watches appeared with Smith or Ingersoll on the dial and also with the name 'Services', a wholesaling firm who before the war had used German pin lever movements. A total of 28.3 million watches was produced in Wales of which 17.3 million were made in the fourteen years from 1954. This represents a production rate of 25,000 a week and during this time involved up to 1,450 employees. Later the number of employees fell to around 400 before closure in 1980.[109] The start of the fall in demand in 1967–8 was probably caused by increasing affluence causing a bigger need for jewelled watches.

The production rate above from one factory is very significant when compared to the figures achieved in the 1890–1920 era of British watch production which averaged something less than 4,000 a week from all sources. Smiths' marketing during this period was to wholesalers, the biggest of which was Richard and Tucker, Nunn who were themselves part of the Smiths group of companies. Each wholesaler advertised independently and Smiths themselves also advertised extensively, one particular advertisement showed sketches of all their factories. After Ingersoll withdrew from the production side in 1969 they continued to sell the same watches buying from Smiths but later they used Swiss movements in their wrist watches. Because of the volume of pin lever watches produced it is easy to forget that Smiths' jewelled lever watches were of good quality and they supplied to the government, the Everest expedition of 1953 and the Fuchs Antarctic crossing of 1957–8. More information about Smiths' activities should be available, if copies can be found, in their house journal called *Timecraft* until 1938, *Smiths Times* until 1953 and again *Timecraft* from 1953 onwards.[116]

Although the production of pin lever watches is known and has been discussed the total production of lever watches is not known.[117]

INGERSOLL LTD (Plates 68 to 70, 120, 128 and 129)

The Ingersoll Watch Company Ltd was formed in 1915 by the American parent company although there had been a London branch office from 1905. At first Ingersoll marketed the 'Crown' pocket watch for five shillings adding the 'Midget', a smaller watch for ladies, in 1910. This size watch was also sold in wrist form. From 1911 American parts were assembled in England at a rate which eventually reached 3,000 a day. In 1922, the parent company in America went into liquidation and was acquired by the Waterbury Clock Company who continued to make (Ingersoll) watches until 1944. In 1930 the London operation was purchased by E. J. Daniels, W. M. Manning and P. J. Morren and a new British company, Ingersoll Ltd, formed. This company acquired a factory in Clerkenwell and continued to assemble American parts but also diversified using German and Swiss movements in its pre-war products which were basically pin lever watches although some jewelled versions were sold.[118,119] Pre-war advertisements show their price range to be from five shillings to four guineas. During the war, Ingersoll continued to assemble watches at High Wycombe but later turned to instrument production.

After the war Ingersoll became part of the government plan to re-establish the English watch industry and joined Smiths and Vickers-

Armstrong in the Anglo-Celtic factory at Ystradgynlais in South Wales.[115] They withdrew from this venture in 1969 but continued to buy movements from Smiths. Ingersoll could be considered watch manufacturers during this 1947–69 period.

In 1964 Ingersoll had purchased Andrew and Company, watch and clock importers, and by 1969 they had acquired other companies and had diversified their interests as the Ingersoll Group. They continued to sell watches, including electronic models, mainly imported from Switzerland, successively being taken over by the Heron Group and then Steven Strauss & Co Ltd.[119] Ingersoll handled a large volume of watches in their capacity as importers, makers, assemblers, etc totalling 51 million between 1905 and 1956. The Ingersoll name is still used on watches containing Swiss analogue quartz movements.

LOUIS NEWMARK (Plate 71)

The Newmark family appear in Kelly from 1875 onwards at various addresses. Originally they are shown as Geneva watch importers but later they imported German clocks and watches. In particular they sold the 'Torpedo' brand of pin lever pocket watch. (Torpedo is the trademark of Gustav Hausler, registered in 1905, and it is possible that he was the German supplier.) In 1914 this supply ceased and Newmark returned to Switzerland for their supplies, continuing to do so until 1939 when Louis Newmark were the largest importer of Swiss watches.[120]

In 1947, in common with Smiths, Ingersoll and Vickers-Armstrong, Newmark co-operated with the government to set up a *watchmaking* factory in Croydon. The first watch was marketed in 1950 and by 1954 the output was a million a year,[121] manufacture ceasing in 1960 when Newmark again concentrated on the import of Swiss watches including the brand names Avia, Corvette, Cyma, Breitling, Ulysse Nardin, Inventic, Kered and Golay. Newmark are still UK agents for Avia watches as well as Swatch (ETA) and other makers. As importers they introduced the first Swiss electric watches and the first LCD quartz crystal watch to Britain.

As a British manufacturer of pin lever watches Newmark first produced a 13 ligne, unjewelled Roskopf wrist watch in four styles with or without seconds hand for the lower price-range customer (2 to 3 guineas). To give good value for money effort was concentrated on the finish of bearing surfaces, pivots, pallet pins, etc rather than on elaborate plate work. The factory was equipped with new Swiss machines and considerable attention was placed on quality control and inspection.[121] All watches were tested in four positions for a total of three days after two full twenty-four-hour trials to set them up. The mainsprings, balance springs, dials and hands were not made at Croydon nor, at first, were watch cases but all bought out parts were made in Britain. A six-month guarantee was given.

Plate 71 The original 13 ligne Newmark pin lever watch first available in 1950

By 1955 the range of watches produced included a four-wheel train, split plate 10½ ligne model which was cased for both ladies and gentlemen and the new design had 5 jewels (6 for the centre seconds layout). Newmark movements were presented in a wide variety of styles to meet the demand for attractive watches and included a waterproof model, a skeleton model and a 13 ligne 'Phantom' with an invisible seconds 'hand' which was a transparent disc with arrow mark on the circumference. The price range was from 52s 6d. to 92s 6d.[121]

It is not clear why the government decided to support the establishment of two factories to produce pin lever watches; probably it was to satisfy demand without the need for imports or to widen the UK horological base, but whatever the reason Newmark were a successful British manufacturer for a decade producing 7,000,000 watches in the period 1950–60 which represents an average of 14,000 per week and gave employment for up to 850 workers.[122] Tastes change and it was clear that by 1960 demand was for different watches and the relaxation of import duties made Newmark decide to cease manufacture and re-establish themselves as important Swiss watch importers.

MULTINATIONAL COMPANY WATCHMAKING IN BRITAIN

The American-owned Timex and Westclox companies both had factories in Scotland where watches were produced. Timex[123,124] operated from c1960 to 1987 making pin lever watches and later quartz watches with imported movements. Westclox[124,125] made pin lever watches from 1959 to c1975 and still make clocks. Multinational companies are discussed in Chapter 10.

Plate 72 The main English watchmaking companies also produced ladies' watches. *(Top left)* A threequarter plate keyless Rotherham movement; *(top right)* a threequarter plate keywind Ehrhardt movement; *(bottom left)* a threequarter plate keyless Williamson movement; *(bottom right)* a threequarter plate keyless Lancashire Watch Company movement

In this chapter we have examined several watchmaking companies and the general conclusion must be that the British contribution to the development of the modern watch is small. The table below shows the changes in populations and production from 1800 to 1925. It would also seem that any attempt at initiative was stifled, the Merchandise Marks Act prosecutions producing results which were not conducive to the enterprising manufacturer.

YEAR	POPULATION (MILLIONS)				WATCH PRODUCTION ESTIMATE (MILLIONS)			
	UK	SWISS	EUROPE	USA	UK	SWISS	USA	WORLD
1800	16	–	–	5	0.2	0.2	0	0.4
1850	27	2.5	250	23	0.2	2.0	0	2.5
1900	42	3.2	400	93	0.2	8.0	4.0	13.1
1925	46	3.8	460	120	0	17.0	9.0	26.3

It is interesting to comment on the changing methods by which watches were sold in Britain. Before 1880 there were local shops selling a few watches each year who purchased from travellers such as Samuel Smith which was described in Chapter 1. As mass-produced, machine-

Plate 73 It has not proved possible to identify all machine-made English threequarter plate watch movements. This picture shows six such movements with similar underdial work which is shown in the bottom right movement of Plate 74. Since all these movements are machine made and are similar underdial they probably come from one maker. There are several makers in the text for which watches have not been found but because of the quantity discovered it is felt that they are the later products of the Coventry Watch Movement Company. This view is helped by the fact that two are finished with Newsome's name and one is a centre seconds model which they certainly produced

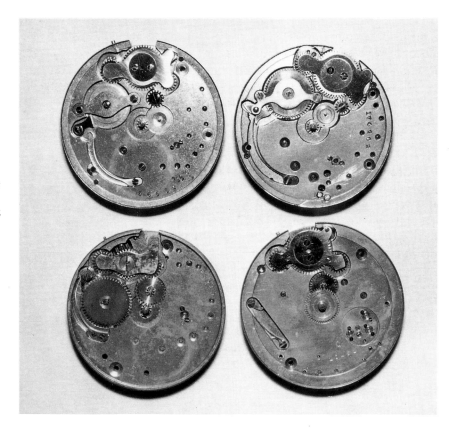

Plate 74 Four underdial views of unidentified threequarter plate watch movements: *(top left and right)* these are probably Lancashire Watch Company products because of their winding mechanism bridges; *(bottom left)* this is almost identical with Benson 'Railway Guard' watches which are believed to have been made by outside suppliers such as Guye or Williamson, thus this movement may be from one of these makers; *(bottom right)* the underdial style of the six movements in **Plate 73** in which it is suggested that the maker is probably the Coventry Watch Movement Company

made cheaper watches became available new types of outlet occurred to augment traditional methods of sale. These were convenient for the manufacturer who needed to dispose of large volumes of his product and included wholesalers who dealt with the retail trade and larger retailers who had branches in many towns. Three examples of the latter were Fattorini, Samuel and Graves who can all be found in Kelly Directories at the end of the nineteenth century. It is therefore common to find identical watches from such firms at Ehrhardt, Williamson and the Lancashire Watch Company sold with these retail house names on the dial and movement. Some of these firms still survive and these methods are now common in all types of retail trading.

Pre-1940 machine watchmaking in England, estimated dates and total production

Anglo-American Watch Company	1871–4	few
English Watch Company	1874–95	250,000
William Ehrhardt	1874–1924	500,000
Rotherham and Sons	1880–1930	600,000
P. & A. Guye	1880–1900	120,000
Nicole, Nielson & Company	1887–1914	50,000

Lancashire Watch Company	1888–1910	900,000
Coventry Watch Movement Company	1892–1914	150,000
J. W. Benson	1892–1941	100,000
H. Williamson	1897–1931	750,000

Post-1940 machine watchmaking in Britain, estimated dates

S. Smith & Sons	1940–80
Ingersoll	1947–69
Louis Newmark	1947–60
Westclox	1959–75
Timex	1960–80

Endnote

This chapter has been concerned with factory-made watches. No consideration has been given to English going barrel watch movements or ébauches made by small makers using methods of small batch production.[126]

8 Swiss watchmaking

In the period from 1870 to 1914 populations were increasing, more people used railways and working life became factory, office and shop based with fixed working hours. Thus more people became aware of the benefits of watch ownership especially those who were forced by their employment or wished to participate in the increasingly time-dominated pattern of modern life. Literacy also increased so that the audience for advertising was greater. Although watches were increasingly being made by machinery and the larger production rates meant unit costs were falling, a large percentage of potential customers could not afford the conventional lever or cylinder watch even when fitted with the minimum number of jewels. Roskopf had considered the problems of cost when he designed his 'Montre de prolétaire' but because of his concept of quality his price was too high (Chapter 5). In America where marketing skills were more developed the need for cheaper watches was realised by several companies, the best known being the Waterbury Watch Company (1880) and Robert H. Ingersoll and Bro (1892). Ingersoll started to sell small pin lever clocks cased up to resemble button wind watches and these products soon evolved to become proper 'dollar watches'. These watches and those of other makers were mass produced by machinery and export markets were required to absorb the production (Chapter 9). Ingersoll opened a London office in 1905 and started to assemble watches from imported parts in 1911. It is doubtful if there was any threat to the Swiss home market nor to the existing higher-grade export markets but there is no doubt that the Swiss industry did not have a cheap enough watch to compete with the new concept. The Swiss outlook may have been more influenced by the fact that a new German industry to make cheap pin lever watches was started at the end of the nineteenth century (Chapter 10).

The Swiss reaction was to cheapen and adapt their Roskopf watch which had a pin lever escapement. This was a continuous process and by examination it is possible to see the steadily decreasing quality. The separate escapement was abandoned, plates became thinner with flimsy bridge structures, finish was minimal with crudely pressed parts, dials

were printed, etc. This happened over a period of time because the manufacturer needed a different mental outlook but by the 1930–40 period an enormous quantity of cheap pin lever pocket and wrist watches were made for export. Before World War I much of the cheap watch market in Europe (Britain in particular) was supplied by Germany and America but after the war the German watches were less in favour and in 1922 the Ingersoll company ran into difficulties so that the Swiss were able to achieve greater penetration of the market. The presentation of the watches was in a variety of styles. Many were labelled 'Railway watch' with printed locomotives on the paper or thin metal dials. Similar emblems were stamped on the cases, cars and aeroplanes were also featured. Watches in dress style, with sweep seconds hands on imitation chronographs, with decorated cases, indeed anything that would sell in an impoverished, unemployment-ridden decade was made (Plates 75–8).

Repair of most of these watches was not envisaged but a short-term guarantee for replacement was given. Subsequent failures were consigned to the dustbin! It is however interesting to note that experiment shows that some of the parts in these watches are interchangeable (Chapter 11) and it is possible to repair such a watch by taking parts from a similar calibre. The cost of repair at the time would have exceeded the cost of a new watch and the throw-away ethic was established. This tenet is still true for cheap electronic watches. Thus the Roskopf watchmakers were

Plates 75 and **76 Plate 75** shows an Oris pin lever watch using the Roskopf calibre with the brand name Siro, c1925. The movement is shown in **Plate 76** and is an 'exécution économique' product. The back of the case has a cartouche with a railway engine and the words 'Railway Regulator, Swiss made'

Plate 77 Roskopf calibre watch with a pin lever escapement. Although labelled 'Chronograph de Sport' the watch cannot be stopped, c1930

Plate 78 A dress-style Roskopf watch of c1930

probably the first Swiss firms to achieve mass interchangeability by machine manufacture not, as we see, from a repair viewpoint but for the certainty of assembly without adjustment which was essential for cheapness. This is emphasised in an article[1] produced by the ébauche factory of A. S. Schildt in 1971.

> Except for Roskopf and pin lever watches [meaning pin lever watches not using the Roskopf calibre], it was still customary fifteen or twenty years ago, for a single watchmaker to assemble the movement blank as far as the stage at which the movement was in working condition . . . He was also able to make certain small corrections . . . any occasional imperfections could be remedied at the assembly stage.

Because of the marked difference in assembly methods the new Roskopf industry seemed to engender a slight feeling of shame in Switzerland and little has been written about the pre-1939 Roskopf industry. After World War II (1939–45) a measure of recognition and respectability was achieved and indeed all over the world the greater significance of the pin lever watch was recognised (Smiths, England; Timex, America; etc). Production was now mainly centred on smaller wrist-watch calibres because the day of the pocket watch was over. The improved manufacturing techniques enabled better-quality pin lever watches to be produced and many new calibres with a centre wheel were produced which were officially defined in Switzerland[2] as 'watches of Roskopf type'. It also became clear that if so desired the pin lever watch could achieve satisfactory results when prepared for trial at a Swiss 'Official testing station'. The Oris Watch Company started entering in 1945 and although, as is often the case in trials they only entered small numbers, by 1962 they had 2,579 certificates with mention, 225 certificates, 109 failures and no withdrawals.[2] A very interesting result showing that with attention the pin lever watch was a good watch and the quality produced was to satisfy the market. Public demand now was for a cheap watch which would last several years, look good on the wrist and keep satisfactory time to enable life to be lived in the modern style. By 1972 Ebauches Bettlach, who made nine million pin lever movements a year, point out that nearly half of Switzerland's watch exports (by number not value) are pin lever watches and emphasise the importance of correct quality.[3] (Plates 94–7.)

Statistics can be chosen to demonstrate almost anything and the viewpoint above can be demonstrated in this way. However in extracting these figures it would be less than honest not to say that there might be some overlap between watches, movements and unassembled movements.

Plates 79 and **80 Plate 79** shows an ordinary quality Swiss lever watch in a silver case of c1925. It has not been identified as made by a particular firm but many of this type can be found. **Plate 80** shows the movement which has a dust cap

Roskopf watch production[4]

In 1970, 98 per cent of production was for export representing 46 per cent by number of Swiss watch exports. Destinations are shown in the table below.

Place	Number in millions	
	1962	1970
Europe	3.07	7.03
Africa	1.20	1.87
Near East	0.88	0.84
SE Asia	1.57	8.62
North America	7.67	11.81
Central and South America	2.18	2.30
Australia and Oceania	0.23	0.11
Total	16.80	32.58

Proportions of Swiss watch production[5,6]

Year	Number in millions			
	Lever	Roskopf	Electronic	Total
1980	29.9	41.1	12.7 (15.1%)	83.7
1981	26.1	30.5	16.2 (22.2%)	72.8
1982	12.7	14.0	17.3 (39.3%)	44.0
1985	5.8	6.0	47.2 (80%)	59.0

Production of watches (millions) in various countries

Year	Swiss	Japanese	American	Russian	Hong Kong
1951	34	0.9	11	3	–
1962	46	10	12	18	–
1974	87 (peak)	22	24	29	–
1978	63	50	27	30	50
1985	59	180	12	37	325*

*mainly assembled from parts made elsewhere in Asia

Three points emerge from these figures. The importance of the new Roskopf industry to Swiss watchmaking, the appearance of new manufacturing nations and the impact of electronic watches on the traditional manufacturing industry. It is also interesting to see how many Swiss watches were exported to North America.

Having traced the importance of the pin lever watch it is time to examine the Swiss cylinder and lever industry which dominated the market for these models and exported seventeen million watches a year by 1913. The cylinder escapement watch which was the traditional cheaper Swiss product produced in barred Lepine and threequarter plate calibres continued to be made for pocket and wrist watches until World War II (Plates 91 and 94). The American industry had clearly shown that the jewelled lever escapement was the choice for the machine-made watch of the future by the time that Favre-Perret took one for examination in 1876. Thus the cylinder watch was bound to be replaced by the pin lever or the lower-priced models of the jewelled lever range (Plates 79 and 80). One problem of the period was to produce small, moderately priced machine-made calibres with lever escapement for wrist watches but this was achieved by the 1930s (Plates 92–4). The jewelled lever escapement continued to reign supreme in the quality products and indeed held over 50 per cent of the export market in numbers and perhaps 80 per cent in value in 1970 (Plates 81, 82, 85, 87, 88, 90, and 98). (By 1982 this was to be 46 per cent of the value as the electronic watch absorbed 47 per cent with the rest Roskopf.[5])

Plate 81 Rode movement with 17 jewels, whiplash regulator and 3 adjustments. Rotherham were the agents for these Swiss watches. This one is housed in a Dennison gold-plated case of moon quality which is numbered and suggests a date of c1920

Plate 82 Omega pocket-watch movement with 15 jewels in a Dennison gold case hallmarked 1921. This movement was first introduced in 1894 and was so successful that the company name was changed from Louis Brandt and Frère to the Omega Watch Company

Plates 83 and **84** A pocket chronometer of c1910 with a pivoted detent escapement and helical balance spring, going barrel and cut compensated balance. A hand-finished, high-quality Swiss product in an engine-turned gold hunter case. The movement, shown in **Plate 84**, was finished by Maurice Dreyfus of La Chaux de Fonds

This continued supremacy was not without problems caused not only by competition from new makers and new technology but also by tariffs, two world wars, a Russian revolution and world-wide slumps. When these setbacks occur countries often look toward restrictive trade practices or tariffs to preserve their industry and jobs and the Swiss horological industry has been particularly skilled at preserving its position by forming associations and cartels with government and financial backing. It remains to be seen if the problems caused by the latest electronic changes coupled to assembly in countries with cheap labour will be overcome. At the present time it appears that the situation is in control but the next decade will be decisive as the industry has suffered a change in which a rival producer can now make a very accurate digital electronic watch for one tenth of the cost of the cheapest lever watch or analogue electronic watch. This sort of change is equivalent to asking a car manufacturer to survive the challenge of a rival producing an adequate vehicle for £600 instead of £6,000!

The ups and downs of Swiss trade can be seen in export figures; the slumps and the impact of World War II are clear, as is the impact of competition.

1899 distribution[7] of Swiss exports
Value million Francs

Germany	28.9
Britain	21.4
Russia	12.2
Austria	10.4
Italy	6.1
France	4.6
USA	3.8
Spain	3.7
Rest	8.3
	——
Total	99.4
	——

Swiss production
Total millions of watches

1900	7
1913	17
1921	8
1929	21
1932	8
1937	24
1944	12
1947	24 (60% of world production)

Watches and Movements[6]

1974	96
1976	74
1980	88

Impact of Far East nations[6]

1985 Market volume excluding 'planned economy' countries

Switzerland	10%
Europe and USA	5%
Japan	35%
Hong Kong	45%
Rest of Asia	5%

1985 'Planned Economy' countries, millions watches[6]

Russia	37
East Germany	6
China	35

Employment in the Swiss watch industry

1970	89,500
1975	62,600
1980	47,000
1985	32,000 (37% of 1970 total)

The progress in the organisation of the Swiss watchmaking industry started in 1890 with the formation of the Chambre suisse d'horlogerie, a consultative body to represent the economic view of the industry from a national standpoint. It was not until 1922, as the table above shows, that further action was needed. In 1924 the Fédération suisse des Associations de Fabricants d'horlogerie (FH) was formed to organise prices, conditions of sale, etc for all makers and sellers.[8] The FH was designed to eliminate unfair competition. In quick succession the movement makers

formed Ebauches SA in 1926 and the component part makers (dials, escapements, hands, etc) formed the Union des Branches Annexes de l'horlogerie (UBAH) in 1927. There was also an Association d'industriels suisses de la montre Roskopf. In 1928, these groups agreed to restrict the export of component parts, tools and machines and only allow complete movements or watches to be sold abroad. In due course, prompted by the slump apparent in the production table in 1932, the government decided to support a combined holding company Allgemeine Schweizerische Uhrenindustrie AG (ASUAG) with money to purchase shares in Ebauches SA and an interest-free loan to finance the industry. By 1934 the new cartel's rules became law controlling output, prices, export of parts and tools, formation of new firms, etc. It is important to realise that ASUAG was not nationalisation, control of the industry was by itself and it worked. This situation remained until 1952 when relaxations were made in export licensing for complete watches which were now needed in a post-war, watch-starved world. Most of the other restrictions were retained in a less rigorous form.[9,10]

The next crisis to face the Swiss was international competition caused by the marketing of Timex watches (Chapter 10). In America modern

Plate 85 Small ladies' watch (10 ligne) in pendant form with a gold case and matching brooch decorated with coloured enamel iris. This is dated 1910

Plate 86 An Omega 24 ligne chronograph designed in 1930 and used in the Olympic Games from 1932 until quartz technology took over. This particular example is a skeletonised version with considerable hand finishing made to commemorate fifty years of Olympic timing

production techniques produced pin lever watches which were then sold in any available outlet rather than solely by jewellers. The watches were better value than earlier pin lever products due to superior materials, superior machining accuracy and increased production rates. Soon the product was moved to Europe and factories were opened in England, Germany and France where again the aggressive marketing was successful. At the same time the Japanese and the Russians were beginning to export watches in large numbers. The latter countries were new exporters who had not been pre-war competitors. Between 1974 and 1975 Swiss exports fell by 20 per cent. The Swiss would probably have come to terms with these problems for they had the necessary skills and resources.[1,11] Indeed between 1948 and 1978 the number of Swiss manufacturers fell from 1,000 to 500. The number of basic calibres produced was halved between 1946 and 1968 and between 1966 and 1976 production per capita doubled. The Swiss remained the world's largest producer until about 1979. The Swiss did not in fact have a real chance to see if they could compete successfully for the electronic watch had been born during the early 1970s as a result of the effort put into miniature circuitry to produce quartz crystal timekeeping accuracy for navigation in space.

The electronic watch problem was entirely different; it offered vastly superior timekeeping compared to the ordinary mechanical watch (causing the cessation of wrist chronometer trials in 1968), it could be made in large quantities more cheaply than the mechanical watch and it needed no background in traditional horology. Anyone involved in the new electronic industry could make watches and, if the factory was placed where labour was cheap, could make them inexpensively. By 1982 competition had reduced Swiss production to 48 million, half the 1974 peak, and 40 per cent of these were electronic. A dramatic reorganisation was needed. This was achieved in two parts. In 1982 the Chambre suisse d'horlogerie merged with FH to become the Fédération de l'industrie horlogère suisse (which is also now known as FH). This new organisation involved 90 per cent of the industry and in 1983, encouraged by the help of a Swiss banking organisation, ASUAG merged with Société Suisse pour l'industrie horlogère (SSIH).[12] SSIH was another grouping of companies including Omega and Tissot. The new ASUAG-SSIH was renamed in 1985 as Société suisse de microélectronique et d'horlogerie SA (SMH). Thus there were only two bodies to deal with the industry, one for national policy (FH) and one for the makers (SMH).

The resulting industry was different to that of the past but the change was recognised as vital.[13,14] Debts were paid off by bank loans, companies were sold off and movement manufacture for SMH was centralised into one firm, ETA.[12] There are still firms outside SMH such as Ronda SA who produce movements and there are specialist firms producing high-quality, expensive mechanical and electronic watches for a small market. These would include Patek Philippe, Girard Perregaux, International

Plate 87 A pocket watch in a gold case with niello decoration

Watch Company (IWC), etc. The majority of firms now use movements from SMH (ETA) to produce mechanical or quartz analogue watches in their own style suited to their own traditional price ranges. Figures for 1982 show that watch production fell by 32.7 per cent but in 1984 rose by 7.4 per cent on the lower total,[15] indicating some success due to reorganisation (Plates 99–103).

Looking ahead it is clear that in the short term the mechanical watch will probably cease to be made in quantity when the time comes to replace the machinery at present in use and that the Swiss will concentrate on trying to keep a viable proportion of the analogue electronic watch market. There will always be a small market for the specially made mechanical watch but it is unlikely that Switzerland would ever find it economical to compete in the cheap LCD field which will be dominated by the countries with the cheapest labour costs.

Plate 88 An Omega 'Art Deco' watch of 1927 with a 23.7mm diameter movement. It has a gold case with decoration matching the dial and covered in enamel

Plate 89 Two Tavannes Watch Company products. The size of the wrist watch can be judged relative to the pocket-watch movement which is 42mm in diameter. Both examples have Swiss lever escapements

Whilst these changes had been taking place (1920–80) the industry was slowly moving towards completely interchangeable replacement parts. Complete interchangeability was probably achieved in the early 1930s and the établisseur-based industry was slowly replaced by larger groupings. The arrival of interchangeability meant the organisation of a spare-part facility characterised by illustrated books of calibres from individual makers or published by the FH for the Ebauches SA group and other makers. There were also spare parts catalogues from other organisations such as Flume (Germany) and Bestfit (USA). Such publications enable the numbers of different calibres being offered to be calculated and the table below shows some data.[16] In this table the demise of the cylinder watch, the appearance of the Roskopf watch and the emergence of the wrist watch at the expense of the pocket watch are shown. The dominance of the Swiss industry is clear throughout but in the 1961 Bestfit catalogue the appearance of Japanese and Russian movements is a sign of the future.

		Lever		Pin lever		Cylinder		Total	Swiss	German	French
		Wrist	Pocket	Wrist	Pocket	Wrist	Pocket				
General Catalogues											
1938 Jobin (Swiss)	Round	343	407	Totals on left include all escapements				1,083	1,083	–	–
	Form	333	–								
1947 Flume	Round	402	236	50	44	87	43	1,253	1,153	87	13
	Form	330	–	21	–	40	–				
1949 Ebauches SA (FH)	Round	269	58	–	–	21	5	512	512	–	–
	Form	131	–	–	–	28	–				
1949 Swiss Lever (FH)		470	180	–	–	–	–	650	650	–	–
1961 Bestfit Vol 1*		1,736		170		23		1,929	1,800	60	20
Firms' Catalogues 1949 MST (Roamer, Medana)	Current	24	10	12	2	0	0	162	162	–	–
	Obsolete	36	21	5	–	39	13				

*Bestfit vol 1 includes 40 Japanese, 6 Russian, 3 UK but no Timex by name. US 'makers' fitting Swiss movements are in Swiss total, US 'production' in 1960 was 9.5 million, mainly Timex. A later supplement vol 2 includes more Japanese and Russian models.

The interchangeability achieved which demanded catalogues of spare parts was entirely due to the mechanisation of the industry. Although the earliest suitable machinery was apparently developed in America, so that by 1876 Favre-Perret was impressed, Switzerland did not copy the American designs. The Swiss developed their own better machinery so that they were able to surpass the Americans with their product. Uniquely they developed the sliding head automatic lathe which was such a fine production tool that it has since dominated the precision engineering industry. They also produced the pointing machine, which eventually developed to become the jig borer, another important precision engineering machine tool. (However a separate design was also produced in America.) Machine tools and processes are discussed in Chapter 11 but the interesting byproduct from the Swiss horological viewpoint is that because Switzerland designed and made the best machine tools for their watchmaking industry they were able, through the cartel organisation, to prevent exports of these machines and afford themselves a degree of protection. Theirs was the expertise and they kept it from 1910 until 1945 when protection was no longer realistically possible. After the war it was only a matter of time before mechanical watches from competitors appeared but Swiss experience in tool design kept them in command until the advent of the electronic watch which required skills they did not historically possess. The machine tool industry founded for horology is still very important in its own right as an exporter.

Plate 90 The first Omega wrist watch dated 1902. This particular example of a 15 ligne watch appears to have been customised for a person wearing the watch on the right wrist. Contemporary advertisements show both right- and left-hand versions. The watch was sold in Bath, England

In 1900 the Swiss watches being produced were pocket watches and smaller ladies' watches. The lever or cylinder escapement was used mainly with barred Lepine calibre layout but with a number of threequarter or split plate designs. There were also the new *well-made* Roskopf designs. Between 1895 and 1900 nine ligne size (21mm) watch movements, probably with cylinder escapement, were made to work and the way was clear for the wrist watch.[17] The first lever escapement wrist watch was marketed in 1905 by Hans Wilsdorf, the founder of Rolex. World War I provided the demand as it was inconvenient for the soldier to keep his watch on a chain in his pocket and thus the wrist watch started on its path to dominance. The cylinder escapement ceased to be used from about 1939 as is clear from the table extracted from catalogues and it can also be seen that by 1961 pocket-watch calibres were minimal.

During this fifty-year period (1910–60) the wrist watch developed. New smaller calibres were produced in a variety of shapes (Plates 92 and 93). Although it may appear simple to alter the layout of a watch it is not true in practice for it is essential to keep the parts as large as possible for strength and ease of manufacture. It was therefore many years before the wrist watch could achieve the accuracy of the pocket chronometer (Plates 83 and 84) and observatory certificates for wrist chronometers did not exist until about 1944. However notable performance was achieved by wrist watches in trials. For example, a Rolex gained a Kew A certificate in 1914, another Rolex 6¾ ligne wrist watch gained a Kew A certificate in 1927 with 85.6 marks and a further Rolex achieved 87.6 in 1936. At the same time pocket watches were achieving marks of the order 96 or 97 in Kew trials which were becoming dominated by Swiss entries from 1911 onwards.[24] The quest for accuracy in wrist watches was accelerated by the needs for air navigation in the faster World War II aircraft and one maker who produced a suitable watch was IWC.

All the complications fitted to pocket watches were fitted into mechanical wrist watches but like their pocket-watch predecessors they were initially expensive. However a study of catalogues shows that increasing numbers of automatic watches, chronographs and day, date watches were produced from the late 1950s at ever decreasing cost.

Examination of calibres shows distinct styles. Early wrist watches used barred or threequarter plate movements similar to those used in ladies' watches. In the intermediate stages from 1920 to 1960 the watches used bridges of a variety of shapes to suit the calibre and shape (Plate 92). In the latter days of mechanical watch production design changed to meet the demands of different manufacturing processes and some automatic assembly techniques so that the movements look less chunky with lighter bridgework (Plate 96). These last remarks apply to both pin lever and lever escapement models.

During the decade (1958–68) in which electro-mechanical watches were manufactured the Swiss industry monitored progress and Ebauches

SA produced the L4750 calibre with mechanical switching and the 9150 calibre with electronic switching (Plates 153 and 154). These watches are discussed in Chapter 12 and although interesting proved to be a transient phenomenon. The Swiss however had ensured that if they had become an important product they had the necessary technology to meet the demand.

Swiss quartz watches, after a short phase using the 'new' LED or LCD display, almost always use analogue display which requires a conventional mechanical gear train from the stepper motor drive to the hands (Chapter 12) together with a conventional dial. In some cheaper analogue watches the back of the case forms an integral part of the movement but the majority still use a plate to support both the mechanical and electronic components and the case is a separate unit. Indeed with most movements

Plate 91 Movement styles from 1920–50, six cylinder escapement wrist-watch movements from one maker: *(top, left to right)* AS 5¼ ligne calibre 555, AS calibre 740, AS 6¾ ligne by 11 ligne calibre 519; *(bottom, left to right)* AS calibre 749, AS calibre 960, AS calibre 200

Plate 93 Some interesting wrist watches: *(left to right)* a digital watch, c1930 with AS 748 4¼ ligne movement with a lever escapement, the case is steel with some decoration and plating but it is hard to read the time; a Hebdomas 8-day watch with a lever escapement; a BGF calibre 866,12 ligne pin lever movement in a metal case sold or given away as advertising material by the Bradley Time Corporation. This sounds an American firm but has not been traced

Plate 92 Movement styles from 1920–50, six lever movements which have not been identified

147

Plate 94 Changing styles of Swiss watches made between 1915 and 1930: *(left)* an ETA 213, 10½ ligne cylinder escapement movement in a rolled gold case c1915; *(top, centre left)* a silver watch dated 1917 with a cylinder escapement movement; *(top, centre right)* a silver watch c1925 with an AS 427 lever escapement movement; *(bottom, centre left)* a silver watch of 1920 with a Movado 9¾ ligne lever escapement movement with four adjustments; *(bottom, centre right)* a silver watch c1935 with a lever escapement movement; *(right)* a watch with an unidentified cylinder escapement movement in a silver case of 1928, engraved on the sides and decorated with marcasites or similar inexpensive jewels. Dial marked 'Tibet'

Plate 95 Movement styles 1930–50, pin lever watches and movements: *(top, left to right)* Brevo (Oris) watch and its calibre 91T movement; *(bottom, left to right)* BGF calibre 34, EB 13 ligne calibre 1229 and Brac calibre 20

being supplied by one maker, the only individual parts of a watch are the dial, hands, case and bracelet. Analogue designs are best suited to the elegant styles of traditional-looking watches at which the Swiss are experts (Plates 99–101). The export of movements which is now a substantial part of the Swiss trade is only viable if the movement is a unit free of the case so that integrated case designs have limited sales.

It is clear from opening a number of modern watchmakers' catalogues or looking in a mail order catalogue or peering into a jeweller's window that a bewildering range of models is offered which changes rapidly to establish a fashion. This is similar to the rapidly changing clothing market to which a watch can be considered an accessory. If watches are not too expensive a purchaser may well have several to suit the personal wardrobe, thus expanding sales. This a far cry from the earliest days of wider watch ownership about a hundred years ago when grandfather's watch was passed on to the next generation.

Typical mail order catalogue selection

Total	Japanese	Swiss	Timex	Russian
203	97	50	33	23

It is not possible to trace the development of many Swiss firms in a book of this length. In the 1901 Kelly Directory there is a list of 713 Swiss makers. A study of modern companies shows many have staff whose ancestors appear in this list. The 1937 Swiss Watch Fair at Basle had 32 well-known Swiss firms as exhibitors[18] and although the 1986 Swiss trade directory (section 231) lists 238 firms as watchmakers many only case movements and many are trading names within a group. The firms discussed below have been chosen on a basis of available information found in old journals[19,20,21] supplemented by correspondence or have been visited. Some firms have published their own history[22,23] and many firms' products are illustrated by Jaquet and Chapuis.[24]

OMEGA[19,25] (Plates 30, 33, 34, 35, 36, 82, 85, 86, 88, 90, 96, 98, 100 and 102)

The firm was founded in 1848 in La Chaux de Fonds by Louis Brandt to assemble keywind precision watches. Brandt's sons joined the firm in 1877 and they moved to Bienne in 1880 and started to make parts. In 1888 the Labrador lever watch was introduced and by 1889 production was 100,000 per year with 600 employees. In 1891 the firm was known as Louis Brandt and Frère and this name can be found in the 1901 Kelly. In 1894 the Omega 19 ligne calibre was introduced and was so successful that the name of the firm changed progressively from Louis Brandt and Frère – Omega Watch Company in 1903 to Omega Ltd in 1982.

Omega established a reputation for precision watches obtaining many rating certificates (33 per cent of all distributed in 1909) and quickly became involved in timing sporting events including the Olympic Games from 1932 to 1968 as Omega and from then on as part of 'Swiss Timing' in company with Longines. The Omega 'Speedmaster Professional' was chosen for space work by NASA and was involved in fifty missions including the 1969 moon landing and the 1970 Apollo XIII mission in which an explosion destroyed the normal timing instruments and the return rocket was fired using the 'Speedmaster'. Omega introduced their quartz watches in 1970 using the Ebauches SA Beta 21 calibre (Chapter 12) and used LED display in 1973. Currently Omega is producing a reproduction series of watches named after the founder Louis Brandt. Omega was part of the SSIH group of companies which amalgamated with ASUAG in 1983, now known as SMH. A measure of the changes occurring in the last decade can be seen by comparing the 1973 Omega catalogue with that of 1985. In 1973 112 mechanical and 21 quartz models were offered but in 1985 there were only 4 mechanical models in the 166 offered.

When visited in 1905 the host was Louis Brandt (son of founder) and the visitors saw both Labrador and Omega watches being made by up-to-date machines including automatic types. Some assembly machines were

Plate 96 This photograph illustrates movement construction in the period 1960–75. The movements should be compared to those in **Plates 91, 92** and **95**. Changing manufacturing and assembly techniques required differing structure: *(top left)* a 17-jewel Ronda RAX 1233 lever movement; *(top right)* Bettlach pin lever movement, calibre 8397-67; *(bottom left)* an Omega 'Seamaster' calibre 501 automatic winding movement with fine whiplash regulation; *(bottom right)* an Oris calibre 601 KIF automatic winding movement

149

being designed. The factory made both movement and cases but bought in springs, hands, jewels, glasses and gold cases. Cleanliness in the plant was emphasised with fines for spitting paid to the sick fund which operated on a contributory sick pay scheme. Unfortunately there is little detail about the plant but balance making is described in detail, the brass being cast into a hollow steel blank so that when the side and bottom of the blank are subsequently machined off a compensation balance rim is achieved. The 1949 Swiss lever catalogue (FH) illustrates twelve Omega calibres.

LONGINES[19,26] (Plates 29, 87, 97 and 99)

Longines trace their history to 1782 when Jonas Raiguel, living in St Imier, began trading in watches. In 1832 Auguste Agassiz became a partner in the firm with Jonas' son and one other person and by 1847 Agassiz was the sole owner. By this time he had established an American agency known as the Longines-Wittnauer Watch Co. Due to bereavement Agassiz gave up active participation in 1850 and the company was run by Ernest Francillon, his nephew. In 1867 Francillon built the first factory at St Imier and started to make watches by 'mechanical methods' in the building rather than by the homeworker and établisseur method. The 1901 Kelly shows Ernest Francillon and Co but the name changed progressively to Compagnie des montres Longines, Francillon SA by 1937. In 1971 it became mainly owned by ASUAG and Ebauches SA and with the ASUAG-SSIH merger it is now part of SMH.

Plate 97 Longines' first automatic winding calibre movement type 22A of 1945. Harwood's patent for automatic winding for wrist watches is dated 1924. Although Harwood was English he took his patent in Switzerland (No 106,583)

Like Omega, Longines has always been a quality watchmaking firm and made a number of innovative models. They became involved in timing events at the 1952 winter Olympics and in 1972 joined Omega in 'Swiss Timing'. In the same year collaboration between Ebauches SA and Texas Instruments enabled Longines to market an early LCD quartz watch (Plate 158).

There is a description of the Longines factory in 1885 (Chapter 5) so that when visited in 1905 Longines was already known in England. By 1905 the factory employed 750 persons but the buildings were being replaced. Power supply was by steam, electricity and water totalling 100 horsepower. A refrigeration plant was installed to test chronometers for expeditions including the intended journey to the North Pole by the Americans (presumably Peary) who for some reason were taking Swiss timekeepers! Electric lighting was used in the factory. Workshops were used to make most of the machines used and automatic types are mentioned including lathes and wheel cutters. Cases were made in the factory and at any one time 1,000kg of silver was being processed (if cases were 1oz this represents 40,000 cases of 800 grade silver). Punched-out plates and bridges were turned and pierced and in this workshop 100 machines had 80,000 movements in progress. A fairly long description gives a general impression of a highly mechanised plant producing 140,000 watches per year.

Plate 98 An Omega 'Speedmaster Professional' of the type chosen by NASA in 1953 for moon and space missions. It was made from 1946 to 1968 in calibre 321 and was updated in 1969. This particular model has a bezel scale for calculating hourly production rates or vehicle speed

SCHWOB BROS (TAVANNES WATCH COMPANY)[19,20]
(Plates 38 and 89)

The 1901 Kelly lists the Tavannes Watch Company and the factory was visited in 1905 and 1909. The factory was modern and equipped with machines which they also offered for sale. Schwob used many brand names including Cyma, Tavannes, Tonca, Alpha, etc. In 1905, 750 employees produced 450,000 watches a year which by 1909 had become 750,000 per year using 950 employees but the latter visit report felt that some bought parts were used. (This total was approximately four times the total UK production.) The surviving brand name is Cyma who feature in the 1949 Swiss lever catalogue (FH) with 8 calibres.

BÜREN WATCH COMPANY OF H. WILLIAMSON AND CO[19,21]

In 1905 this factory made 500 watches per day for the English firm, H. Williamson but some of these were sold in Germany and America. Cases were made in the factory and the latest machinery was used. A later visit in 1923 mentions that the Dixi pointing machine was enabling precision press work to replace some lathe processes so that production rates could be increased. At this stage Williamson was in financial difficulty and post-war import restriction in Britain had resulted in much of the production

Plate 99 Two electronic watches with both digital and analogue display by Longines. The digital display can give time, date, day, alarm, zone time and chronograph functions (see Plate 139). This design gives the pleasure of an analogue display with the convenience of digital functions

going to America. Soon after this the Büren factory must have become independent of Williamson because the agency in England was taken over by Rotherham in 1932. In the 1949 Swiss lever catalogue (FH) Büren feature 22 calibres.

REVUE-THOMMEN AG[27,28] (Plate 103)

In 1853 the construction of a railway tunnel effectively bypassed the small town of Waldenburg and caused loss of employment to the local people. Some forward-thinking citizens decided to start a watch assembly factory using bought out parts. As a first step seventeen young people, including five girls, were trained by apprentice masters attracted to the village by high pay. Although by 1856 150 workers were employed the business was not competitive enough and seemed doomed. However two men, Gedeon Thommen and Louis Tschopp, took over in 1859 and managed to survive. Tschopp however soon left leaving Thommen in sole charge.

In many ways the firm, which in 1908 became Revue-Thommen, reflects the pattern of life in a relatively small unit of the Swiss horological industry. Waldenburg is a single industry town in the Jura foothills 30km south of Basle and having established a way of life has been keen to retain it. Thus, following expansion including a second factory to produce wrist watches in 1917 and 'branches' in neighbouring villages in 1915 and 1919, it became clear in the inter-war years that reliance on watchmaking alone might be an error and in 1936 it was decided to diversify into instrument making and machinery manufacture. Indeed today, as part of a group which includes the Marvin and Vulcain & Studio companies, watchmaking at Waldenburg has ceased and Revue watches are assembled at the Vulcain & Studio works in La Chaux de Fonds using bought out electronic movements. At Waldenburg, instruments and thread-rolling machines are the products.

The horological history at Waldenburg started with assembly of bought out parts. It is not clear whether this was ébauche assembly or whether finished movements were supplied to the users. By 1860, 4,000 watches a year with cylinder escapements were being made in Thommen's works. By 1890, this had increased to 13,000 a year and both lever and cylinder escapements were used. Production was never large reaching a peak in 1953 of 200,000 a year with about 400 employees. This figure is misleading for right up to 1970 about 40 or 50 'homeworkers' were still used for assembly work. This enabled some flexibility in production rates depending on the amount of work put out. Production in 1974 was down to 120,000 watches.

Plate 100 An Omega 'Constellation' quartz chronometer giving time, day and date. The term 'chronometer' could be applied to any quartz crystal-controlled watch in the historic sense of the timekeeping capability of the instrument

One of the more interesting details in Thommen's history is that the early machinery was made in the factory and was so robust that two gear cutting machines made in about 1880 are still used today for small batch production of instrument gears. Interchangeable parts for their watches were claimed from the 1870–80 period but this must be interpreted in the meaning of interchangeability at that period and the capability of machines at that time. No doubt some fitting was required at assembly. Photographs in their centenary publication (1953) show most production processes including plates being drilled using templates and jigs, plate stamping, pivot burnishing, balance fitting and movement assembly in what must have been the last few years in which these methods would be employed. Within a decade such methods would be uneconomic except for expensive prestige makers.

Throughout their period of manufacture Revue watches (sold in England under the brand name 'Vertex') have been better than average quality products. They include some interesting models such as a digital display pocket watch of about 1890 and more recently a mechanical wrist watch with alarm, based on the 1947 Vulcain 'Cricket', and a 19 ligne mechanical chronograph. The 1938 Jobin illustrates 41 calibres including 23 wrist (10 form, 13 round), and 18 pocket, one eight-day, one with cylinder escapement and one with Roskopf layout, a considerable number of models for a firm with a small production. The economics of this are not clear but in 1947 it cost about 100,000 Swiss francs to introduce a new calibre for which the anticipated production was between ten and fifteen thousand.

When Gedeon Thommen died in 1890 the business passed to his four sons but only one, Alphonse, stayed in the firm. In 1932, H. Straumann, Alphonse's son-in-law, became Chairman and the Straumann family has remained prominent in the company to the present time. The 1901 Kelly shows Alphonse Thommen as the only watch manufacturer in Waldenburg. Kelly also lists A. Didisheim & Co, the predecessor of the Vulcain & Studio and Marvin part of the present group.

ZENITH[19,29,30]

In the 1905 visit one firm mentioned was that of G. Favres-Jacot at Le Locle who used the brand name 'Zenith'. The 1901 Kelly shows his name. The name Zenith is still used today for a high-quality mechanical chronograph watch and for quartz products but the company has passed through a number of owners. These include an American group and a Swiss consortium. Presently Zenith is part of the Dixi Group of companies owned by P. Castella and their interests include the manufacture of jig borers. This is significant for it was at Dixi in 1912 that an early pointing machine was developed. At this time Dixi produced a full range

Plate 101 A Girard Perregaux 'equation terre' electronic watch. This is an expensive, prestige product which gives time, date, moon phase, month, zodiac signs, seasons, solstices and equinoxes. It is one of a range of models giving information relevant to the earth, space, etc, this being the terre (earth) model

of horological tools (Chapter 11). Dixi itself is an offshoot of the watchmaking firm of Barbezat-Baillot who appear in the 1901 Kelly Directory at Le Locle. Their factory was called 'La Phare'. Unsatisfied with the accuracy they could achieve with existing machines they devised their own, choosing Dixi as a brand name for their 'machines de haute precision'. With the success of the pointing machine Dixi appear to have parted from the 'La Phare' watchmaking enterprise. This incomplete story is significant because it illustrates the relationship between Swiss watchmaking and horological toolmaking leading to the development of the important jig boring machine tool. Dixi today market borers, industrial refrigerators, mechanical fuses, automatic targets, watches (Zenith, Zodiac, Paul Buhre and Jean Perret brands) and Luxor clocks.

INTERNATIONAL WATCH COMPANY[31] (jacket photographs)

The International Watch Company at Schaffhausen was founded in 1868 by an American, Florence A. Jones, who set up a factory to build watches by machinery. By 1879 Jones was in financial difficulty and the firm was taken over by Johannes Rauschenbach and remained in family hands until 1978 when it became part of VDO, Adolf Schindling AG, a German firm with diverse interests including Porsche cars.

From the start IWC produced high-quality watches and has continued this tradition to the present day. Although machinery is used in the production of the parts, all mechanical watches are hand finished in the traditional way and production is in small batches. Records of all watches made are held in ledgers although the modern ledger is a computer. A full range of pocket and wrist models are made with skeleton plates, repeating mechanisms, moon phase, etc, using enamelled cases, niello decoration, etc. Quartz models are also made with equal attention to detail. Much attention is given to finish and assembly in an air-conditioned shop. Here traditional watchmakers continue to exercise their skills in poising balances, timing and adjusting in an unhurried atmosphere. This factory illustrates the area in which Switzerland intends to keep the world market. There are a number of other prestigious firms who sell their products to people who believe that such watches show their taste and refinement.

Plate 102 A pocket watch made in c1983 in traditional style by Omega to honour their founder Louis Brandt

156

ETA, GROUPE FABRIQUE D'EBAUCHES[32] (Plates 94 and 152)

This large factory in Grenchen is one of those making movements for the SMH group of firms. ETA itself has a history starting in 1856 when Anton Schild started to make ébauches. The various rearrangements of the Swiss industry meant that ETA became a part of Ebauches SA in 1932 whilst its sister company Eterna watches became part of ASUAG. Subsequent reorganisations to the current SMH have brought together virtually all Swiss firms and ETA produces movements for the whole group.

The factory is a complete contrast to that of IWC. Here automatic machinery (presses, lathes, etc) make parts. Rotary transfer machines finish them and part assemble them. Robots are also used so that the production of movements is achieved with a minimum number of staff.[11] In 1985 approximately 45 million movements were made of which 80 per cent were quartz. This total includes Swatch-style watches which have integrated case and movement, thirteen mechanical calibres and 27 quartz calibres enabling watches to be produced by their customers at various prices and with various complications. This is the new method of manufacture essential if Switzerland is to retain a hold on the high volume market rather than the specialist market typified by IWC.

ROSKOPF WATCH MANUFACTURE, ORIS[33] (Plates 75, 76, 95 and 96)

Although the 1905 visit[19] included a paragraph on M. Schmid's factory at Neuchâtel where original 'Roskopf' watches were made it really gives no information except that the factory make their own escapements. The 1901 Kelly shows Roskopf's son in Geneva. It is interesting therefore to consider a firm which was concerned with Roskopf and pin lever watches.

The village of Hölstein, 25km south of Basle, was a traditional ribbon-making centre. By the turn of the century this industry was almost extinct and the community decided to enter the expanding watchmaking industry. They founded their enterprise in 1904 but, presumably due to lack of experience, it failed. A second attempt was made again without success but finally, two men, M. Christian with watchmaking experience and M. Cattin with commercial experience, took over and the business became established. Illustrations of calibres made by 'Cattin et Christian' can be found in contemporary Swiss journals. Cattin resigned early in the company history but the Christian family continued to be in charge until 1971–2.

The company chose to work in the expanding Roskopf watch field and to do this they bought out machines but later made their own, including line assembly automatic transfer machines in the 1960s. The exact date of the adoption of the 'Oris' name is not known but it was their first brand name appearing as a telegraphic address in 1906 and being registered in 1918. Although they were successful with these watches, models with cylinder escapements were sold between 1920 and 1935 for which escapement parts may have been bought out. Oris also wished to make jewelled lever watches but the protective rules (discussed earlier) to limit competition would not permit this. Because of these restrictions Oris made considerable efforts to produce pin lever watches in various qualities to suit a wider sector of the market. Indeed, as mentioned earlier, after 1945 they entered watches for trial to establish that it was a chosen policy to make the cheaper variety and that with care it was possible to achieve certifiable performance with a pin lever escapement which was thought by many to be inferior in design. In spite of this proof Oris chose to enter the conventional jewelled lever market when the regulations were relaxed in 1961. The customer has the last word.

When the quartz watch entered the marketplace, Oris, together with a number of other firms became part of a group known as the General Watch Company (GWC) but after ten years the management bought them out of the group. Thus in 1982 'Oris SA' was formed which was a different company to the original 'Oris Watch Company SA'. This new company purchased some of the existing machines and materials, the brand name Oris, and in due course part of the factory, the remaining parts of the factory being used by other industries.

One interesting activity of Oris in the period from 1914–25 was the opening of assembly plants in Italy (Como), Germany (Rheinfelden) and France (Seppois), which explains the existence of watches which look Swiss but which are marked as made in France or Germany (Plate 126). These factories had to close after 1926 under the regulations prohibiting the export of parts.

Today Oris market electronic watches using bought out SMH movements and a few mechanical watches assembled from remaining stocks of parts. Their products of the past can be seen from an examination of their brochures. These show movements and complete watches in a variety of cases. The brochures also include illustrations of the factory departments and the text emphasises their close attention to quality control, metrology, interchangeability and the *availability of spare parts* to repair watches which many would regard as uneconomic to work on. Examination of these brochures enables the models on offer to be divided into five groups. Traditional Roskopf watches with heavy bridges (Plate 28), 'exécution économique' models (Plate 76) with thinner plates and bridges, made for the lower end of the market at a price to compete with the American and German products. It is this style of watch which gave the impression that all Roskopf watches are of poor quality. Several firms competed at this end of the market and there is no doubt that price dominated the quality.[2] The third and fourth groups are the cylinder watches and the later jewelled lever watches and the fifth group is alarm clocks mainly of 23 ligne calibre. There appear to have been over 200 movement styles between 1934 and 1981 and the 1961 Bestfit catalogue lists 62 types

including 59 wrist pin lever models. In the early days of the wrist watch Oris also used the cylinder escapement, indeed the change in taste may have forced them to make this choice since small size cylinder movements were well established whereas pin lever calibres needed development to suit the smallest wrist sizes.

Old Oris pin lever watches can be found in markets and they use a variety of brand names including Oris, Siro, Fides, Bentima, Brevo, Clymo, Fido, Fixor, Terma, Suizo, Novoris, etc. Cylinder watches use the brand names Rio, Virtus, Orisa, Inno, Valdoris, etc. In modern watches the name Oris has been used for the jewelled lever models.

Oris production figures for various years together with numbers of workers are shown below.

Years	Production in millions	Number of workers
1919–28	27.5	563 in 1928
1929–48	39.0	700 average (maximum 908)
1949–78	27.0	700 average

Plate 103 Possibly the last production model mechanical pocket chronograph that will be made. This elegant watch was produced by the MSR group which includes Revue-Thommen and Marvin brands, c1980

Endnote

This chapter is too short to do justice to all of the Swiss industry. Hopefully enough has been said to outline the success achieved in the context of the changing marketplace and technology.

It should be interesting to see over the next decade whether the mergers of 1980–85 succeed in allowing the Swiss to continue to make and sell ordinary watches or whether they will be forced to diminish to a small number of firms producing expensive handfinished prestige watches.

9 American watchmaking

The growing competition from new companies for the American domestic market was the closing scene in Chapter 3. The cheapest conventional watches being produced by various makers were still too expensive for many potential buyers and the same was true for the remaining imports of Swiss cylinder models. Harrold[1] reports a certain Jason R. Hopkins who in 1867 devised an inexpensive watch with a rotating movement, driven by a long mainspring with a detent escapement. The watch was shown to Benedict and Burnham, a company who stamped out brass parts for clocks, but they were not interested as their experience suggested that the use of a large gear in the design would cause problems (high pinion loads) and that the proposed layout was not suited to a cheap watch. The idea was however taken up by W. B. Fowle and the Auburndale Watch Company (1876–83) was founded. The product was not successful, only about 1,000 being made even though a lever escapement was used. Hopkins had several patents with this company notably US patent 161,573 of 1875.

Two of Hopkins' original associates, G. Merritt and E. Locke, apparently after seeing a miniature steam engine, approached Daniel A. A. Buck, the maker, to design a cheap watch. This he did using a full plate layout and a duplex escapement (US patents 204,000 and 203,999 of 1878) and again Benedict and Burnham were approached. This time it was felt that such a watch could be successful and production began in 1878. Buck took many more patents for his watches during the next five years involving dial design, case design, winders and special hands. These were improvements for the original design was based on sound principles for machine manufacture. Most of the watch was made by presswork at which Benedict and Burnham had considerable experience. The actual layout of the watch is interesting. The design had 58 parts eventually reduced to 54[2] and utilised a mainspring which was 3m (10ft) in length fitted in a large diameter barrel formed in the back of the case. This long spring needed about thirty winding turns and it drove the whole movement with minute hand round a fixed centre wheel once per hour. The motion work was arranged by having two wheels with slightly different numbers of teeth engaging the same pinion so that their rates of rotation

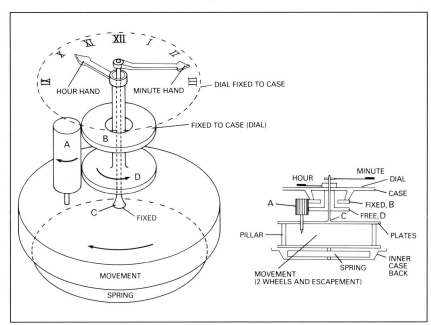

Plates 104 and **105 Plate 104** shows a Waterbury duplex watch, c1885, series C, which has a rotating movement and a paper dial. The movement can only be sighted by removing the case back (**Plate 105**) bearing in mind the long mainspring coiled below. The company lasted from 1878 to 1914 under various names

Fig 14 The Waterbury rotary movement watch; pinion A has 8 teeth, wheel B has 44 teeth and wheel D has 48 teeth so that one revolution of the movement complete with the minute hand will cause the hour hand to rotate one twelfth of a revolution

Plates 106 and **107 Plate 106** shows an early Ingersoll Yankee pocket watch made by the Waterbury Clock Company. It has a clock movement with a paper dial and although there appears to be a conventional winding button there is in fact conventional clock winding and handset in the case back (**Plate 107**). In 1896 such a watch cost one dollar and pin lever escapement watches became known as 'dollar watches' in America

were different (Fig 14). This is almost impossible to believe since all gears should have the same pitch. In effect the rotating watch was a crude form of tourbillon (Chapter 6), which Breguet had designed to combat positional error. The tourbillon needed very precise workmanship and was only fitted to very expensive watches. Buck's movement was designed for cheapness and the rotating action saved parts. It is doubtful if he was concerned with positional error.

Gannay[3] praises the escapement design as well suited to a cheap watch. The Benedict and Burnham watches were skeletonised and initially sold for $3.50, later at $3 they were not skeletonised. In 1880 the company became the Waterbury Watch Company and their watches are known as 'Waterbury watches'. These watches were made in series A to E with the long wind rotary movements but later series to W had more conventional layouts. In 1890 they changed their name to the New England Watch Company and in 1914 Ingersoll took over the factory to produce his own watches. Waterbury watches were never a dollar watch but they did establish the manufacture of cheap watches based on clockmaking technology. Production reached a maximum of 1,500 per week and a total of·12 million were made; certainly more than the total of conventional duplex watch production. Specimens purchased today appear to work quite satisfactorily (Plates 104 and 105).

The next designs of cheap watches used pin lever escapements and in this venture they were even closer to clock technology. In succession established companies such as the New Haven Clock Company (1880), Ingersoll by co-operation with the Waterbury Clock Company (1892), the Western Clock Company eventually Westclox (1899), the Ansonia Clock Company (1904) and a new company, the Bannatyne Watch Company, which became E. Ingraham (1905) entered the market and became successful watchmakers. There were also other short-lived ventures.[2] Today Ingersoll is probably the best remembered name. Some idea of the production of what are now known as 'dollar watches' is given by Townsend.[2] Ingersoll, 96 million; Ingraham, 80 million; New Haven, 40 million and Ansonia, 10 million. Harrold[1] shows that by 1930 the total US production had reached approximately 272 million of which 186 million (68 per cent) were dollar watches (Plates 106 to 114).

Since Ingersoll was so successful with his marketing techniques he had an impact on watchmaking both in America and Europe and this firm is chosen as an example of the group for discussion. Robert and Charles Ingersoll were brothers who were basically salesmen not watchmakers. Their first American watches (Ingersoll 'Universal') were made by the Waterbury Clock Company and sold wholesale to dealers to 1892. This watch was really a small clock put into a watch case about 3in in diameter and over 1in thick. Later that same year the Ingersolls produced a mail order catalogue and sold direct to the public and in 1893 marketed the Ingersoll 'Columbus' which was slightly smaller than the 'Universal' but still clock like. The Waterbury Clock Company also sold watches but the Ingersolls soon negotiated a sole agency agreement. In 1896 Ingersoll watches were reduced in price to one dollar and named the 'Yankee'.[4]

All these early clock watches used pin lever escapements and had paper dials with a seconds hand. The clock-like features included lantern pinions (which are made from wire rods held between two end discs), fold-away winding keys in the back connected directly to the open spring arbor and skeleton plates held together by nuts on threaded pillars. The Yankee had a false winding button fitted to make it look like a watch but it was still a small clock. Stem wind was introduced in Ingersoll watches in about 1896 and from about 1900 the Ingersoll brothers marketed machine-made full plate pin lever watches in conventional sizes with conventional winding and handset arrangements, paper dials being used. These were sold in America and Britain and eventually (1911) were also assembled in Britain. The early watches are marked with progressive lists

Plates 108 and **109 Plate 108** shows an Ansonia Clock Company pin lever escapement watch with a paper dial of c1910. It has conventional winding and handset but the back is still fixed to make the movement inaccessible (**Plate 109**). The back plate is engraved 'patented April 17th 1888'. The Ansonia Company was founded in 1850 and was sold to Russia in 1930

of patents indicating that detail improvements were being made but they all look similar. Many of the early watches also have their guarantee paper inside the back of the plated case. English watch warranties were similar but with English prices and address.

> This watch is GUARANTEED to keep good time for one year and if without misuse it fails to do so will be repaired by us FREE or (at our option) exchanged for a new one for 25c. Robt. H. Ingersoll and Bro., Makers, 315, 4th Ave, New York.

The insolvent Ingersoll brothers were bought out in 1922 for $1,500,000, creditors being estimated to receive 40 per cent.[5] The new owners were the Waterbury Clock Company who continued to use the Ingersoll name until in 1942–4 they were incorporated into a new company to be known as the United States Time Corporation formed to make Timex watches (Chapter 10). In 1930 the British Ingersoll Company became entirely separate from the American company[6] (Chapter 7).

Earlier we saw that by 1930, 68 per cent of the total American production was comprised of dollar watches. Of the remaining 32 per cent, Waltham and Elgin contributed 22½ per cent and the rest 9½ per cent.

Harrold[1] gives a list of companies which, if account is taken of name changes, etc, totals approximately 57. Many of these were short-lived ventures and only 16 of the 57 had made over a million watches by 1930 (Elgin, Waltham, Illinois, Hampden, Seth Thomas, New York Standard, Hamilton, Trenton, Columbus (South Bend), Rockford, Waterbury, and the dollar watch makers Ansonia, Ingraham, Ingersoll, Westclox, and New Haven). The remaining 41 companies appear to have made about 2 million watches between them and their products will be uncommon or rare (Plate 21). About 20 of the companies lasted less than ten years. Thus the history of American watchmaking is littered with unsuccessful ventures into what appeared a lucrative prospect. Many of the companies bought their machinery from failed enterprises as a short cut to getting into production. These new companies then failed either because the machines were inadequate for the product to be up to the high standards set by the successful companies or due to the unavoidable delay in achieving sufficient market penetration to get enough income to survive. The slump of the 1920–30 period closed many semi-successful companies and only seven survived beyond 1930 (Waltham, Elgin, New Haven, Hamilton, Ingersoll, Westclox, Ingraham). An outline history of American companies can be found in Appendix A in Harrold[1] and there are contemporary histories in Abbott[7] (1888), Crossman[8] (1885–7) and Milham[9] (1923). Here a summary of the history of Waltham from 1883 onwards is chosen as an example of one of the long-lived manufacturers.[10] The early history of this company is given in Chapter 3 when it was seen how it became established as a successful enterprise (Plates 115–17).

Plates 110 and **111 Plate 110** shows a Westclox pin lever escapement watch, c1920, with paper dial, conventional winding and handset. As can be seen in **Plate 111** the back can be opened to reveal the watch movement. All American pin lever watches had become conventional by this time. Westclox made watches from 1899 to the 1980s

Plate 112 *(top)* An Ingraham pin lever escapement pocket watch with a paper dial made in December 1918. This watch has conventional winding, handset and case; *(bottom left)* an Ingraham pin lever wrist-watch movement made in 1936; *(bottom right)* another Ingraham pin lever wrist-watch movement of the same period. The company made watches from 1912 to 1971

The remainder of the Waltham story is one of business ups and downs until failure in 1957. Ezra Fitch was appointed General Manager at Waltham in 1883 as a man who understood marketing. He became president in 1886. Under his leadership the number of grades of movement increased and the range of cases was enlarged so that more customers could be satisfied. At the same time, D. H. Church, who joined Waltham in 1882, made significant engineering contributions to the design of both movements and machinery. These men enabled Waltham to hold their market share in spite of labour and political problems. Trade cycles continued, for example the gold discoveries in Alaska in 1898 improved trade but profit was adversely affected by the need to 'dump' watches abroad at lower prices. Royal E. Robbins died in 1902 having been a leading shareholder and treasurer for forty-three years. In 1907 profits started to fall and continued to do so until the war years brought new business making fuses. Profits rose until 1921 when the world-wide depression (culminating in the 1929–30 stock market failure) began to cause problems. The General Manager became ill in 1921 and was replaced by the treasurer who, knowing little of the engineering problems, called in consultants to assess the Waltham problems. They diagnosed overmanning and poor organisation. There was also poor financial control as a legacy of Fitch's style of direction with high stocks and debts. Late in 1921 Waltham was taken over by the creditors (banks) and after an interim period they appointed F. C. Dumaine as president and treasurer and I. E. Boucher as General Manager. These two men embarked on a policy of small investment and cost cutting and efficiency which in due course brought the company to profitable operation. Due to a wage cut there was a four-month strike in 1924 and times were hard in the inter-war years but dividends were paid on preference stock from 1926–42 (except 1939) and on preferred and common stock from 1926–38. The war years helped the company to survive and Dumaine retired in 1944 in favour of Ira Guilden.

In the post-war years the lack of investment in machines and skilled men began to take its toll. This is illustrated by a visit to Waltham in 1954[11] which found the factory buildings and machines obsolete. Some production figures below illustrate the downward path,[10,13] in particular the relative fall of Waltham compared with Elgin, the major competitor.

Plates 113 and 114 **Plate 113** shows a New Haven Clock Company pin lever escapement watch with paper dial and conventional winding and handset. The front of the case is removed to show the small chapter ring with the numerals on the case as in a half hunter watch. The leather thong may be original as other watches of the 1940 period are similarly equipped. **Plate 114** shows the movement. The company made watches from 1880 until about 1956.

Year	Waltham pocket watches (millions)	Waltham wrist watches (millions)	Man days per watch
1922	–	–	1.7
1926	0.272	0.189	1.15
1931	0.034	0.083	–
1935	0.026	0.332	–

Years	Waltham (millions)	Elgin (millions	Total US jewelled watches (millions)
1930–35	1.3	2.2	4.0
1935–40	1.8	3.5	8.4
1940–45	1.7	4.0	8.0
1945–50	1.55	4.0	12.4
1950–53	0.26	3.0	–

In 1957, after producing a total of 35 million watches, Waltham ceased watchmaking and became the Waltham Precision Instrument Company. The Waltham Watch Company name was sold to the Hallmark Watch Company who imported movements to use with the name.[12]

Landes[13] (1983) compares Elgin and Waltham and concludes Elgin policies were better from the watchmaking viewpoint. Moore[10] (1945) assesses Waltham under Dumaine as a salvaged business. Although Elgin survived a few more years than Waltham the ultimate end would have been the same with the quartz revolution administering the *coup de grâce* in the 1980s. It came earlier because the traditional American watch was obsolete and the customer in the post-war years preferred the Swiss and Japanese products. With the exception of the multinational companies all American watchmaking was to cease. For a while some watch companies used imported movements[14] and there were some interesting innovative electro-magnetic and electrical developments including the Hamilton 500, Bulova Accutron and Hamilton Pulsar which are discussed in Chapter 12. In the electronic watch developments, the electronic industry, including firms such as Texas Instruments, supplied the timekeeping units and the watchmakers supplied the packaging in cases.

America is a big country and in order to develop its potential there was

Plate 115 (*left*) A Rockford Watch Company (1874–1915) movement of c1900; (*right*) a Waltham movement of c1897. The Rockford appears to be of better quality with 17 jewels and adjusted but the Waltham has a fine regulator. Both have interesting patterns on their nickel plates

Plate 116 An Illinois Watch Company (1869–1927) movement of c1907. Illinois were the third largest jewelled watch producer

a need for a transport system which was satisfied by building railways. Because of the large East to West distances involved in travel there was a longitude problem making noon in New York approximately 1 hour before noon in Chicago and 3 hours before noon in San Francisco. Cross-continental rail travel was possible from 1869 with the famous Union Pacific–Central Pacific link but, because individual railway companies tended to keep their own time, planning a journey involving connections could be difficult. An organised system was essential to make sense of time when travelling and to avoid accidents on communal single line tracks. A timetable convention held in 1872 was the first attempt to overcome problems and an international time-zone system was agreed at a conference in 1884. At this conference it was also agreed that longitude should be measured from Greenwich, England. Parallel with any system was a need for reliable, accurate watches and from about 1865 watch-making companies turned their attention to 'railroad watches' which had compensated balances, at least 15 jewels and which were adjusted for position. In order to avoid accidental hand movements the setting was achieved by pulling a lever from under the bezel to engage the handset gear and turning the winding button. The more conventional push or pull on the winding button to engage the handset gear was considered unreliable. In spite of the precautions taken an accident in 1891 made the railway companies approach Webb Ball to set up standards for railway watches and to establish a company to ensure that they were used.

These standards included[15] 16 or 18 size movements, a 17-jewel minimum design, open face watch, double roller lever escapement, over-coil balance spring with micrometer adjustment, 5 adjustments, lever handset, accurate to 30 seconds per week, dust tight case, undamaged clear glass, Arabic numerals with seconds hand and fortnightly inspections to be recorded on a log belonging to the watch. Annual cleaning was

Plate 117 *(left)* A New York Standard Watch Company (1885–1929) movement of c1910. The company made inexpensive watches, this example having 7 jewels; *(right)* a high-quality movement from the Hamilton Watch Company (1892–c1975). It is probably a 1940s example from a government watch for the services. It has 22 jewels and is adjusted for temperature and in six positions

Plate 118 A Ball railroad watch made by the Hamilton Watch Company in c1901. It has 23 jewels and is adjusted in five positions

Plate 119 A Hampden Watch Company railroad movement of c1910. It has 21 jewels and five position adjustments. The company had various names from 1875 to 1930 when it was sold to Russia (see also **Plate 130**)

also required. After Ball's standards had been set it was clear that because of the number of watches required and the consequent maintenance and repair load only American watches were suitable for which spare parts were readily available. Many companies made watches either with their own name, Ball's company name or some other indication of their 'railroad quality'. These watches are a significant American contribution to the development of the modern watch[1] (Plates 118 and 119).

The American watch industry produced many of the types listed in Chapter 6, exceptions being the cylinder escapement, karrusel and tourbillon watches and some other complications. It is possible that individual makers might have made occasional examples of these designs but they were certainly not produced by an industry arranged for the mass production of Swiss lever, pin lever or Waterbury duplex watches. Variety was achieved by increased jewelling, decoration or case choice. At first all the watches used a full plate design but threequarter plate and split plate layouts appeared by the end of the nineteenth century. Wrist watches were made when the machine-based industry became confident of the design and the demand. Some companies made high-quality specially finished watches as a prestige product but the total quantities produced were measured in hundreds or a few thousands rather than millions. Examples of this type of product include the 23-jewel Waltham Premier Maximus and the 23-jewel Hamilton Masterpiece (Plates 122 and 123). There were also some firms who made only cheaper 7-jewel watches and others who

120

121

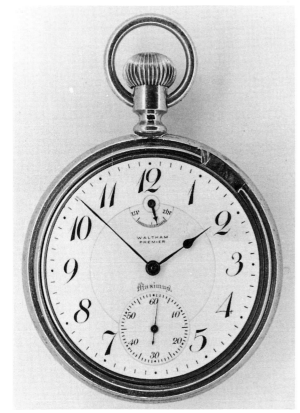

122

123

Plate 120 The Ingersoll company introduced pin lever escapement wrist watches, using their smaller movement for ladies' watches dating from 1906, in about 1914. They continued using the same movement for many years. *(left)* The 1914 style clearly adapted from the ladies' watch; *(right)* a 1933 example. Although the movements are the same the case style has changed to contemporary standards

Plate 121 Both Waltham and Elgin made wrist watches from c1914 and earlier they had made small ladies' models. *(left)* This high-quality movement of c1896 is from a Waltham ladies' hunting cased watch and has 17 jewels, fine regulation and adjustments; *(centre)* this watch in an engraved gold case has a 15-jewel Waltham 'Sapphire' movement of c1928; *(right)* this movement is from an Elgin wrist watch of c1919 (see also **Plate 130**)

Plates 122 and **123 Plate 122** shows a prestige Waltham 'Premier Maximus' of c1910. This model has 23 jewels, 6 of which are diamonds and the remainder rubies or sapphires. About 1,000 of these watches were made costing between $250 and $750 in 1908. Some were supplied with an A class Kew certificate. A movement is shown in **Plate 123**

produced very individual designs such as the three-wheel watch of D. J. Mozart and the New York Standard watch with worm wheel drive, both of which were unsuccessful.

America also had about twenty individual watchmakers, the best known being Charles Fasoldt (1818–98) and Albert H. Potter (1836–1908) who were high-class watchmakers. Potter eventually went to Switzerland in 1876 and besides producing about 600 high-quality watches produced a design for an inexpensive watch known as the Charmilles of which 10,000 to 15,000 were made between 1894 and 1896. Other individual makers include three mentioned before: Mozart, Hopkins and Reed (Chapter 3). American watches are in general relatively easy to date using serial numbers compiled from factory records.[2,12]

Most American watches seen in England seem to be pocket watches comprising mainly Elgin, Waltham and Ingersoll products. This does not mean that wrist watches were not sold but production figures show that the dominance of the pin lever watch kept the pocket design alive and the American rural population probably preferred traditional watches in the pre-World War II years (Plates 120 and 121).

	Year	Jewelled lever	Pin lever Pocket	Wrist
Watch	1936	1.4	7.5	3.5
production	1946	1.7	2.9	2.0
in millions	1955	1.9	3.0	3.6

The American watch industry was, if the successful multinationals Westclox and Timex are omitted, a hundred-year phenomenon which wounded the Swiss industry but did not kill it. Indeed the resilience of the Swiss coupled with the emergent Japanese finished what the depression and lack of investment had started, the defeat of the American industry. The survival of multinational companies is discussed in Chapter 10 but they illustrate an extension of the Ingersolls' early skills in matching the product to the market rather than trying to find a market for the product. Ingersoll eventually got the balance wrong and went out of business as did Waltham. This was probably due to over attention to marketing and not enough attention to product. Although America was the first country to achieve mass production by machinery in factories it is clear that after D. H. Church no great new machines were developed at Waltham. America lost its lead in horological machines to the Swiss and in fact copied some designs.[11] In a visit to some watch factories in America in 1952 including Elgin, Hamilton, Waltham, Ingraham and US Time (Timex), the reporter suggests the factories are obsolete in design and some machines were over fifty years old with many overhead belt drives.[11] This supports the lack of investment view of Landes[13] and the concentration on marketing. However the demands of a war may well have contributed to obsolescence.

10 Watchmaking in other countries

So far the demise of the English industry, the rise and fall of the American industry and the survival of the Swiss industry, albeit in a new role as a smaller producer in terms of world volume, have been observed. There have been and still are other watch-producing countries including France and Germany who were early makers and some newer makers including Russia, Japan, China and Hong Kong. There are also multinational watch-producing companies who may well stimulate manufacture in new situations. A brief outline of their contribution follows.

Watch and clockmaking have strategic importance, for timekeeping and fusemaking are important in wartime. Navigation depends on accurate timekeeping and it is easy to see why, with few exceptions, the countries listed above made sure that their horological base was sound before 1939. The advent of quartz timekeeping has made the need for an electronics industry equally vital in present times.

FRANCE (Plates 124 to 126)

Watches have been made in France from the earliest days. In Chapter 1, a watch of 1551, the French contribution to chronometer development and the significance of Breguet as a maker in Paris were mentioned. In Chapter 2 the contribution of Japy to machine production was discussed and France continued to support a moderate-sized industry making cylinder and lever watches concentrated around Besançon which is, not surprisingly, close to the Swiss border.[1] The 1901 Kelly lists 101 makers in this area. The pre-war industry made 2 million watches a year in 1938 and in 1948 this rose to 3 million.[2] At about this time Lip was considering pioneering manufacture of electromagnetic watches (Chapter 12).

An examination of the structure of the industry in 1960 shows many makers of parts and ébauches with numerous assemblers as in Switzerland[3] but in 1967 the industry was re-organised with one ébauche maker, France-Ebauches. This company is now setting up a factory in India to make 2 million watches a year for domestic consumption.

In 1984 France exported about 6 million watches to Europe and

Plates 124 and **125 Plate 124** shows a Japy cylinder watch of c1900 with a cylinder escapement movement. A typical inexpensive Japy product in a solid-looking and feeling nickel case. **Plate 125** shows the movement with the model name 'Le Fleuron'

Plate 126 A pin lever escapement with a cheap enamel dial which has a movement engraved 'Fabrication Française'. However it looks Swiss and parts may have been imported, indeed Oris had an assembly factory in France and it may well be that this is the origin of this watch. The blued steel case has an engraved back showing horses jumping in a steeplechase. The cuvette is marked 'Remontoir Perfectionne, Soignee'

America (3.5 million quartz analogue, 1.5 million Roskopf, 1 million lever) but more interestingly France exports parts to Switzerland, Hong Kong, Tunisia, Taiwan, the Philippine Islands and Mauritius,[4] identifying several new watch industries.

GERMANY (Plates 127 to 130)

Although the earliest surviving watch was probably made in Nuremburg (Chapter 1) German watchmaking was relatively sparse until the end of the nineteenth century. At this time there was a centre at Glashütte near Dresden where about 5,000 quality watches were made each year, the best known firm being A. Lange and Sohne.[5,6] In about 1890, at Ruhla, Thuringia, Thiel entered the market with a curious watch which had a backspring like the American Waterbury and a calibre with a large centre wheel driven directly by this spring, two further train wheels and a pin lever escapement with the lever fork having a combined safety and banking system which can also be found in American and German alarm clocks and later in many other German pin lever watches (Fig 15). The watch was held together by wedges and ran for about fourteen hours and it has been suggested it was a toy. There are at least three different plate forms and two sizes so that it must have been a success whether toy or watch. Some of those exported to England are marked 'Fearless'. Due to this success Thiel continued as a clock- and watchmaker and after World

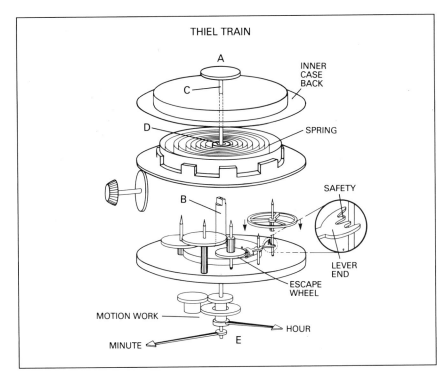

Fig 15 The Thiel pin lever escapement watch movement. The drive from the backspring collet D drives the large centre wheel staff B. The shaft CE is a friction fit inside B

THIEL TRAIN

A
C
INNER CASE BACK
D
SPRING
B
SAFETY
LEVER END
ESCAPE WHEEL
MOTION WORK
HOUR
MINUTE
E

Plate 127 A Thiel ladies'-size watch with backspring movement, pin lever escapement and a paper dial. The case is blued steel and the date is c1900. A larger size similar watch ran for only 14 hours and may have been considered a toy rather than a watch. This German firm is still in existence as part of the East German watch industry, VEB, Ruhla

Plate 129 British Ingersoll 'Defiance' watch made just before World War II. The movement is a German 20 ligne Junghans J 69 with pin lever escapement. Clearly marked 'Foreign' (see **Plate 128**)

War II when both Glashütte and Ruhla became part of East Germany they formed VEB, Uhrenfabrik, Ruhla, who today make quartz watches.

Whether the inspiration came from Thiel, America or both, a number of other German firms, some of whom already made clocks in the Baden – Württemberg, Black Forest area, started to make pin lever watches. These include[7] Thomas Haller (Schwenningen) who later became part of Kienzle, Junghans (Schramberg) and Muller-Schlenker (Schwenningen) and this industry enjoyed considerable success in the period until 1939 rivalling the American and Swiss cheap watch producers.

Plate 128 German pin lever wrist watches and movements: *(top and bottom, left)* Muller-Schlenker movement and watch of c1930; *(top and bottom, centre)* Thiel movement and dial with trademark; *(right)* Junghans of the type used in British Ingersoll watches during the inter-war years when German watches were marked 'Foreign' if imported to Britain (see also **Plate 129**)

A lever watchmaking enterprise developed around Pforzheim in the post-depression period, possibly for strategic reasons. Reconstruction after the war allowed the manufacture of watches to resume and details of the plant at Pforzheim are described by a visitor in 1954.[8] The firms include Deutsche Uhren-Rohwerke (Durowe) and Porta-Uhrenfabrik Wehner (now PUW) who presently make quartz movements. Like all countries Germany felt the effects of the Timex marketing methods and the electronic revolution.[9]

Production figures show a steady rise from 1945 so that by 1976 East Germany produced about 5 million watches and West Germany 9 million, a total of about 6 per cent of world production. As well as watches Germany had a well-developed spare parts industry for most calibres of watch including French, Swiss and German products. Two firms were involved, Rudolf Flume (Essen) and Georg Jacob (Leipzig), both of whom issued illustrated catalogues, and most English watchmakers used these catalogues to order their spare parts.

RUSSIA (Plates 130 to 132)

Russia was not a traditional watchmaking country although there were some craftsmen.[10] In pre-revolution days those who wanted watches bought Swiss imports and after the revolution some German clocks and watches were imported. Ingersoll is reputed to have been negotiating to open a factory in Petrograd in 1913 but war stopped the plans. In 1930 for good strategic reasons Russia purchased two bankrupt American companies, the Ansonia Clock Company who made clocks and pin lever watches and the Dueber-Hampden Watch Company who made jewelled lever watches. Not only did Russia transfer all the equipment but also hired 21 Dueber-Hampden staff to go to Moscow to supervise the setting up and to train new workers.[11] Tremayne[12] says that in 1937 the factory worked 3 shifts in a 24-hour day employing 3,000 workers and making

Plate 130 (*left*) A 1960s product from East Germany. It has a pin lever escapement and was made at the VEB factory at Ruhla, originally the home of Thiel watches; (*right*) a Hampden ladies' watch in a gold-plated hunter case made in 1910. The machinery used to make the movement of this watch may well have been part of that purchased by Russia in 1930

20,000 watches a month. With such a small rate of production it is doubtful if many watches reached 'civilian' customers for they would doubtless be needed for official purposes, but Flume (Chapter 8) shows two obsolete 19 ligne (16 size) watches from the 'Staatiche Uhrenfabrik Moscau' in his 1947 catalogue. The factories were extended to make aircraft watches and chronometers in 1934–5 and auxiliary plants were built. During the war the plants were moved east for safety.[13]

After the war the Russians set about establishing a modern watchmaking industry with vigour and published a book[14] in 1956 for use in technical colleges detailing the engineering processes required to make POBEDA and ZVEZDA brand wrist watches.

In due course watches were exported to gain foreign currency and this process can be followed in trade magazines. In 1956 Russian factories were visited by British horologists.[15,16] They reported that the two pre-war Moscow factories each employed about 5,000 persons producing a total of 3 to 4 million watches a year. These were 15- or 17-jewel watches, mainly wrist, but some pocket sizes were still made. A third factory 500 miles away employed 7,800 persons to make a further 3 1/2 million ladies' jewelled wrist watches a year. No pin lever watches were made. Russian machinery was being introduced but was not yet completely satisfactory requiring much product inspection. Several other distant factories were not visited. Considerable detail is given including insight into working conditions which seemed disciplined. It was noted that the 'bosses' wore Swiss watches! The general feeling was that Russia would become the largest producer of jewelled watches but this did not occur for Landes[17] reports production stagnation at about 17 million per year in the period

Plate 131 Two Russian watches made in 1986. Both have mechanical movements at a time when quartz watches were dominant but at this time Russia still produced mechanical movements relying on Hong Kong to produce quartz watches for them (see **Plate 132**). As can be seen from the dials both these mechanical watches have jewelled lever escapements

1959–67 during which time the Swiss output doubled to 72 million and the Japanese overtook the Russians. In 1956 there were a few exports to India, Siam, Indonesia, China, Poland and Czechoslovakia and in 1960 exports to Western Europe started.[18]

When the export watches were examined, quality had improved. All the models were initially 10½ ligne size with various amounts of jewelling but later other sizes were produced. Although the brand name 'Sekonda' was used there are several movement names including Poljot, Wostok, and Zarja.[19,20,21] The 1961 Bestfit lists those available in America as Pobeda, Kirovskie, Moskva, Sport, Start and Era.

Although quartz watches have now altered watchmaking technology, the 1986 (UK) Sekonda catalogue shows 54 mechanical styles and 80 electronic styles reflecting a higher percentage of mechanical models than most makers.[22] The reason for this distribution is probably due to a decision to continue manufacturing mechanical models for as long as possible and to use imported quartz components, movements or watches to maintain a position in the world market without the need of a traumatic change. This view is supported by the statement in a Sekonda publicity document stating 'These quartz watches are mostly put together in Hong Kong from parts made in Japan, Taiwan or Europe'.[22] Evidence is also temporarily available on the back of many Sekonda quartz watches which bear a sticky label stating that the watch was assembled in Hong Kong for Sekonda. At some stage a further decision will need to be made on this interim measure since the mechanical models will in due course be unable to find a market so that manufacture will be uneconomic and will not earn vital 'hard' currency.

Plate 132 Two quartz analogue watches made in 1986 and labelled 'Sekonda', the Russian mark used in export models. Note that they do not have USSR on the dial which the mechanical watches in **Plate 131** do. When new these watches have a sticky label on the back stating that the watch was assembled in Hong Kong for Sekonda. The parts would have come from other Far East countries. The watch on the *left* of the picture looks modern but that on the *right* is in the style of the 1930s

Japan had its own system of timekeeping which to Western eyes is unnecessarily complicated.[23] From about 1860 Swiss watches were imported and movements were cased locally[24] and in the latter part of the nineteenth century Japan decided to accept some Western ideas including the manufacture of conventional watches. With American help a factory was set up in Osaka in 1894 to make 16 and 18 size pocket watches. The machinery came from the defunct Otay Watch Company near San Diego, California, and the watches made appear identical to the American sire except for the name 'Osaka Watch Company'. A factory was built and about ten Americans from various watchmaking companies led by P. H. Wheeler from Otay had three-year contracts to set up the plant and train the Japanese.[25,26] Production started in 1895 and lasted until 1902 by which time about 19,000 watches had been made. Steam power was used and 170 types of machine were involved in the usual operations in an American watch factory. The enterprise was not profitable and after these few years during which the clockmaking side of the business (founded in 1889) supported the watch enterprise the company was dissolved.

Kintaro Hattori (1860–1934) had worked in the retail horological trade

Plates 133 and **134 Plate 133** shows the first Seiko watch known as the 'Timekeeper' which was produced from 1895 (not under the brand name Seiko which was not used until 1924). The movement in **Plate 134** shows Swiss rather than American influence. It has a cylinder escapement

since the age of thirteen and in 1881 he founded K. Hattori and Company in Tokyo. In 1892 he started to make his own wall clocks at a new Seikosha plant (Tokyo) and by 1895 success encouraged the production of pocket watches with the brand name 'Timekeeper'. This is the same year as the Osaka Company started production which might have been deliberate. Hattori watches however looked Swiss rather than American, probably reflecting the successful lines he had been importing. Hattori started to export his own products from 1895 and in 1913 started to produce a 12 ligne, 7-jewel, ladies' wrist watch under the brand name 'Laurel'. Tokyo suffered great earthquake damage in 1923 and the Seikosha plant was destroyed but reconstruction enabled a new 16-jewel wrist watch for men with the brand name 'Seiko' to be introduced in 1924.[27]

Before the 1941–5 war production reached a maximum of about $3\frac{1}{2}$ million in 1936 but then fell to a minimum in 1945 of about 50,000. Postwar recovery was steady, reaching $3\frac{1}{2}$ million in 1955–6, the same figure as in 1936, and continued steadily until 1969 (18 million) when Seiko introduced a quartz model 'Astron 35SQ' (Plates 155 and 156). Since that

Plates 135 and **136 Plate 135** shows the first Seiko wrist watch produced in 1913 and known as the 'Laurel'. **Plate 136** shows the 7-jewel, Swiss lever escapement movement. The photo size is misleading as it is a 12 ligne size for ladies' use as Japanese men preferred the pocket watch at this time; indeed in 1912 Seiko produced 60,000 pocket watches to supply 20 per cent of their market, the remaining 80 per cent being imported pocket models

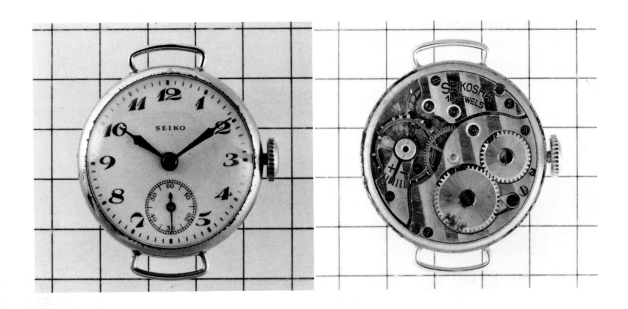

Plates 137 and **138** In September 1923 the Seiko plant was destroyed by an earthquake. It was rebuilt by 1924 and a new wrist watch was produced bearing the brand name 'Seiko'. The watch is shown in **Plate 137** and the 16-jewel movement with Swiss lever escapement in **Plate 138**. The photographs are larger than full size

date production has increased dramatically to reach 100 million in 1987. The company name was changed to Hattori-Seiko Co Ltd in 1983 and the Seiko brand name is used for the best-quality watches. Other brand names used are Lorus, Lassale and Pulsar. The products still include mechanical watches although quartz models represent most of the market.

The Citizen Watch Company was founded in 1918 as the Shokosha Watch Research Laboratory which six years later produced a 16 ligne pocket watch.[28] The name 'Citizen' was adopted in 1930 and watches were exported to SE Asia from 1936. Pre-war production figures are not clear, Tremayne[12] suggests 800,000 per year in 1929 for all Japan but Seiko figures would suggest this may be the Citizen total. An article featuring the Citizen factory in 1951 suggests a production of 30,000 a month.[29] Like Seiko, Citizen production has now risen showing a dramatic increase due to the electronic changes so that in 1984 Citizen produced about 55 million watches of which 66 per cent were quartz and 34 per cent jewelled lever. Of this total 45 million were exported.[4]

Japanese watches embrace the latest technology. Citizen-marketed electro-mechanical watches using both balance wheel and tuning fork oscillators (Fig 18)[30] and Seiko were early in the field with a quartz analogue watch in 1969 and an LCD digital watch in 1971–2.[27] Seiko have been recognised as rivals to the Swiss for timing sporting events following their debut at the 1964 Tokyo Olympic Games. The Japanese have worldwide branches to market and service their products and have achieved great success at all levels of price except for the exotic individual models which remain a Swiss monopoly. Although both the firms mentioned make mechanical, quartz analogue and some digital watches the latter type is now made by Casio who produce inexpensive watches with complications emphasising the big price advantage the quartz digital watch has over the mechanical design for this type of product. As a country Japan now holds about a third of the world market but must be conscious of the competition being offered by other Far Eastern countries.

HONG KONG (Plates 132 and 140)

Watchmaking in Hong Kong consists of the fitting of movements mainly imported from Japan, China, Thailand and Switzerland with locally made or imported dials and hands and placing them in cases imported from Japan, China and Taiwan or made in Hong Kong.[4,31] The output of this industry which employs 30,000 persons in 1,300 factories is 325 million watches and 52 million clocks. Thus an average factory employs 23 persons and produces 300,000 units a year. Viewed another way, a million units a day are made. The watch production of 1985 (325 million) represented an 8 per cent rise over 1984 and in 1986 there was a further 15 per cent rise. The breakdown of watches shows 20.5 million (6 per cent) mechanical, 54 million (16½ per cent) analogue electronic and 250.5 million digital electronic.

The assembly industry began in the 1950s using Russian movements but cases and dials had been made for export before this. The Hong Kong mechanical industry did not have a dramatic effect but in the 1970s the new quartz digital watch began a new era. Watches with LED then LCD display were assembled from 1974 and in 1978 Hong Kong exported 50 million watches to become the world's largest exporter (by numbers), a position which has not yet been lost. The value of exports is currently third behind Switzerland and Japan and this is reflected in the fact that in 1986 the value of the 67 million analogue electronic watch exports was over twice as much as that of the 283 million digital electronic exports. The rise in products for export from 50 million in 1974 to 375 million in 1986, most of which were cheaper digital watches, destroyed the European pin lever watch industry.

An interesting facet of the Hong Kong industry is the link with China which supplies about 30 per cent (by value) of the imported electronic movements and 7 per cent of the mechanical movements. Since Hong Kong will in due course become part of China one can expect this industry to be a major supplier of foreign currency.

CHINA

Swiss sources suggest China produced 35 million watches in 1985[32] but no other details are given. This figure is about equal to the total now made in Europe and America combined. There is little information about Chinese watchmaking but from the mid-eighteenth century until the be-

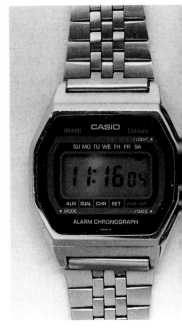

Plate 139 A Casio quartz digital watch of 1984 which apparently enables time and day to be seen. However by pushing various buttons on the case edge the watch will also give date, zone time, a chronograph facility with lap timer, an hourly bleep and an alarm. Because of the need for reflected light there is also a button for night use. The cost of such a watch in a plastic case was £8 ($12.50) in 1984

ginning of the twentieth century China imported limited numbers of watches from Europe. In 1957 a watch factory was reported to be under construction[33] and by 1960 it is reported that production had increased sixfold in the past six years with exports to Hong Kong.[34] Some Chinese watches (Seagull and Double Rhomb models) were sold in the UK in 1977–8. Since China had been involved in wars since the late 1930s it would seem that the industry was founded in the mid 1950s.

By 1981 China had become closely associated with the Hong Kong market,[35] being the fifth largest supplier of movements by volume (second in 1985 and 1986) and the third largest importer of Hong Kong watches (second in 1985 and 1986). Presently both electronic and mechanical movements are involved in this two-way trade but nothing has been discovered about the factories or their products. The close links with Hong Kong are strategically sensible.

MULTINATIONAL COMPANIES

In the modern world the cost of the product is all important. It is often necessary to open a factory to overcome trade barriers. It is also common to manufacture in developing countries which can offer cheap labour or in developed countries with unemployment problems who are prepared to offer suitable financial inducements. Thus the development of multi-national companies is encouraged and they then place their factories in the optimum country. Two such watchmaking companies are Timex and Westclox.

Timex Corporation (Plate 141)

Timex are historically related to the American Ingersoll Company which had been acquired in 1922 by the Waterbury Clock Company. In 1942 this ailing company was itself acquired by Joakim Lehmkuhl, a Norwegian refugee in America, and was successful during the war as a fusemaking company. After the war, as the United States Time Corporation, using new armalloy bearings and pallets for long life, Lemkuhl produced pin lever watches under the 'Timex' brand name and retailed them in *any* suitable situation breaking the jewellers' monopoly. The watches had completely interchangeable components but only from the assembly viewpoint. There was a limited repair system. The project was successful and by 1960, Timex were making 8 million watches a year in America and by 1962 had 33 per cent of the American market which increased to 45 per cent by 1973. In 1969 they became the Timex Corporation.[17]

Timex spread their operations abroad to Canada, Britain, South Africa, France and Germany and by 1972 were making 30 million watches a year employing 17,000 persons in twenty factories. In due course, as the market changed, Timex made watches with electro-mechanical movements and finally quartz movements with digital and

Plate 140 A watch made in Hong Kong which was given away with a five-litre can of automobile oil. It ran for about one year accurately indicating time with a button for date. After this period it ceased to function. Although this watch is the only Hong Kong watch illustrated as such, it should not be thought that this country does not produce better quality watches. Those in **Plate 132** are in the Russian section but are in fact Hong Kong products

analogue display. Many of these electronic watches are assembled from movements made in Far East countries such as Taiwan.

Westclox (Plates 110, 111 and 142)

Westclox history starts in 1884 when Charles Stahlberg came to Peru, Illinois, and designed a low-priced clock which was manufactured from 1885 to 1887 by the United Clock Company. When this company went bankrupt the Western Clock Company was formed who made watches from 1899 and used the name Westclox from 1906. In 1930, the General Time Corporation acquired the Western Clock Company and in 1936 renamed it Westclox. In turn, the General Time Corporation became part of Talley Industries in 1969 so that Westclox is at present part of this organisation.[36]

Westclox made pin lever watches in America and Canada and in 1959 they opened a factory in Scotland where they made an updated version of a mid-thirties-designed 9 by 11 ligne, pin lever, wrist watch with conical balance pivots.[37] This watch was discontinued as the electronic designs took the market but pocket watches were still made in America until about 1980.

The countries so far considered are by no means all those with an interest in watchmaking. Many other countries import movements or parts to assemble. They then complete the watch by further imports of cases, dials, bracelets, etc or manufacture these items themselves. The watches will either satisfy their home market or be exported to produce income. They have supplied essential employment for their population by this means. There is nothing new in this technique for the traditional maker (Chapter 1) gathered together all the parts to finish and market and the ébauche factory has been a feature of modern watchmaking. The location of these industries is new as developing countries seek ways of suiting their products to the modern world. A simple example of new locations was given earlier in the observation of French watch part exports to Tunisia, the Philippines, and Mauritius which are not countries which spring to mind as watchmakers. There will be many more of these in the future and indeed it is probable that the majority of assembly will take place away from the manufacturing centres. Hong Kong already has about 45 per cent of the world production of complete watches but most of the movements come from Japan, China, Thailand and Switzerland.

In such a system the 'watchmaker' contributes the design or style to suit the market. A poor design will not sell and the firm will fail. Design in the modern world must be in fashion. As with clothes, fashion watches constantly change. To the numerous young modern purchasers the movement of the watch is irrelevant. It is accepted that quartz watches are accurate and provided they last for the appropriate amount of time, probably without using up the battery, the watch is put aside and is replaced by

Plate 141 The Timex pin lever escapement watch illustrated was purchased in Germany in 1965. At this time Timex watches were being made in America, Canada, Britain, France, South Africa and Germany. If the quartz watch had not been produced it is likely that the Timex watch would today hold a large portion of the world watch market

the latest fashion. If a watch is changed every year there is no market for one to last longer. This is the new image which has boosted world production from 200 million to 500 million in ten years.

Production under these circumstances is not easy to determine for some countries produce watches from imported parts and others include exported movements in production. An estimate based on Swiss data would suggest that world production in 1985 was about 500 million watches distributed *roughly* as follows.[32] (Some 'watches' are also fitted into pens, etc.)

Traditional watchmakers	Switzerland	59 million	90 million
	America and Europe	31 million	
New Watchmakers	Hong Kong	325 million	410 million (difference
	Japan	180 million	due to assembly of
	China	35 million	watches from parts)[38]
	Russia	37 million	
	Asia	48 million	

Thus in a few pages this chapter has considered about 80 per cent of the world production which seems unbalanced. However the previous chapters have been concerned with a hundred and twenty years of development of the situation which has caused the dramatic changes of the last fifteen years. Indeed Europe was beginning to look over its shoulder at Russia, Japan and China in 1957[33] and 1960[34] and to consider a new cartel. This would not have succeeded for the electronic revolution was to sweep tradition aside.

Plate 142 Westclox, originally an American firm, became multinational in stages, operating in Canada early in the century and from 1959 in Scotland. Like all their watches, that shown has a pin lever escapement. This particular movement is machine assembled in such a way that it would have to be forcibly dismantled. It was clearly not designed to be repaired

11 Manufacturing principles

In the preceding chapters we have seen steady changes in the watch-making industry. These might be viewed as distinct phases.

1 The early European attempts at machine watchmaking which really came to nothing.
2 The developments in America starting in about 1850 resulting in a twenty-five-year lead in technology by 1876.
3 A progressive catching up and overtaking process in Switzerland to maintain a leading position in the world market. This process itself can be seen in sections.
   (a) pre-1900: when traditional watchmaking adopted some engineering assistance
   (b) 1900–50: watchmaking with an increasing production engineering contribution
   (c) 1950 on: production engineering applied to watchmaking.
4 The emergence of new manufacturing nations and new technology after 1970.

In a brief chapter it will not be possible to give much detail about manufacturing techniques but an outline of the principles should clarify the changes that have occurred in the 120-year span. The visible evidence of the change is of course the sheer number of watches produced due to the achievement of interchangeable parts.

Interchangeable parts are essential to large production rates since they can be assembled without additional processing. This statement does not preclude final adjustments necessary for correct timekeeping. Interchangeability enables the use of less skilled workers and allows predictable work rates and labour costs. It also enables an effective spare parts service to be available to the watch repairer who no longer has to make new parts by trial and error; an expensive process.

Interchangeable parts are not identical. The process of manufacture by machinery is continuous and often carried out by unattended automatic machines. Errors in the processes lead to variation in the size of the pro-

Plate 143 A small turret lathe used for repetitive production of parts by an operator working to preset stops. It was made by Sloane & Chase, Newark, New Jersey, USA and used by the Lancashire Watch Company (machine number 26,041) in about 1890. There are four positions of the turret on the right allowing four operations on the part held by the chuck in the centre which is rotated by belt drive from overhead power-driven shafting to the pulleys on the left

duct. These variations result from inaccurate tools, wear of tools, inconsistency in the raw material, deformation of the machine or tool, etc. The errors resulting from the various causes can be systematic or random. A systematic error may be constant for all parts in a particular batch (caused for example by a drill which is too large) or can steadily change due to tool wear. It is therefore possible to analyse systematic error and take appropriate preventive action by renewal of the tools at calculated intervals. In a complex machine tool the analysis may be difficult and statistical methods may be used. A random error is one which has no apparent consistency so that successive items produced by the same machine are of different size. Again statistical methods of analysis offer help.[1]

If a large enough batch of parts is measured the variation of size about the correct value should form a normal distribution curve. If it does not then further analysis would be needed. This curve has a characteristic shape but the width of the curve is defined by the standard deviation. Fig 16 shows that 99.7 per cent of the parts produced fall within a zone of ± 3 standard deviations of the nominal size. Thus the smaller the standard deviation the better the process, and it is possible to determine the quality of machine and tools required by the operator to make a part which is financially viable for the price to be charged for the watch. Different quality watches will have different economic accuracy levels (Chapter 8, pin lever watches). These calculations also enable the designer to set tolerances on the sizes of parts so that the range of sizes made will be within these tolerances and the watch can be assembled without problems. Some considerations for a pivot and its bearing hole in a plate are shown in Fig 16 indicating that with a small diameter pivot the large tolerances which would be needed with processes with large standard deviations would result in considerable variation in clearance between pivot and bearing hole. Since watch pivots are often of the order 0.1mm (0.004in) in diameter the variations allowed are exceedingly small and extremely high-calibre machine tools are required with very consistent material supplies. These considerations indicate why the Swiss had strict control over the export of their machinery in the years prior to 1950.

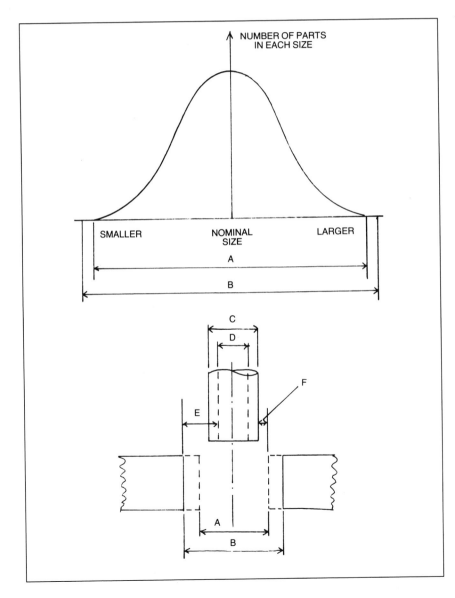

Fig 16 The *upper* diagram shows a normal distribution curve. The dimension A covering a span of six standard deviations (three either side of the nominal size) will contain 99.7 per cent of the parts made so that if the tolerance on the size of the part is dimension B there should be virtually no reject parts. The *lower* diagram indicates the problems caused by variation in size; dimensions A and B represent a minimum and maximum hole size and dimensions C and D represent the maximum and minimum size of the pivot to go into the hole. The radial clearance will therefore be a maximum of E = (B-D)/2 and a minimum of F = (A-C)/2

There is an additional design problem in a train of meshing wheels since each hole will not only have variation in size but also variation in position.

There are other interesting facets of engineering in watch manufacture which involve those which occur because not all parts are made on the same machine. Several machines may be making the same parts for one model so that they must all perform equally well. Some parts may require processing in two or more different machines before they are finished. There is also a problem of measurement of the small parts to sufficient accuracy to determine the data above and this is a separate field. All these pieces of information must be fed to the watch and machinery designer so that an organised system of drawing and communication is needed. These latter problems were not specific to the horological industry and were solved within the general manufacturing field but the measurement problem for watch-sized parts did require the development of special machines.

Drawing conventions are needed for the watch manufacturer and for the transmission of information to any subcontractor for parts. The drawing system evolved shows as many views as are needed to describe the part, dimensioned in such a way as to enable the part to be made to the carefully calculated, toleranced sizes for interchangeable assembly. From these drawings a planning engineer must decide which machines are needed for manufacture and in which order the operations have to be performed. His plan, together with the drawings, will, for mass production, pass to the skilled machine setter who will set the chosen automatic or semi-automatic machine (operated by a semi-skilled worker) so that it is making parts which satisfy the drawing requirements. For the automatic machine this involves fitting and phasing the existing cams, designed by a production engineer, to sequence the operations correctly. Once the setter is satisfied with the machine operation, parts can be mass produced with checking measurements made at predetermined intervals to ensure the part is still within the drawing tolerances. Thus a drawing system is vital in the industry.

Measurement or metrology is also a vital art and is performed with a variety of special instruments. In the very early days there were adequate instruments suited to slow rates of manufacture but with the introduction of mass production efficient, accurate and quickly useable instruments were required. Sets of ring gauges for pivot measurement or gear measurement and sets of plug gauges for hole sizes, each set consisting of gauges increasing in size by a small increment, were widely used. Micrometers of various forms with large visual displays were developed by 1900 and from about 1912 the coordinate measuring machines discussed later became available to determine the relative positions of holes in plates and bridges.[2] From about 1932 optical comparators were made which projected a large image of the part being inspected onto an enlarged drawing allowing rapid checking of size, depth of gear engagement, clearances,

etc. Increasingly in modern metrology computers are used to make comparative measurements automatically. It should be made clear that all measurement during production is to check manufacturing processes as a prototype watch is developed and tested before manufacture on a large scale is started.

Even with all the care and attention to design of watch calibres and machine tools there will be parts or batches of parts which will be unsuited for assembly without reprocessing or some selective processing. This statement would be especially true in the early days of machine manufacture and it shows the determination of the American pioneers, who must have been the first to discover the problems of size variation and machine tool quality, in that they persevered, succeeded and showed the Europeans the way forward. However it is interesting to see if it is possible as a layman to make interchangeability trials in old watch movements and determine whether progress can be detected. It is not easy to find pairs of movements which are intended to be interchangeable for the manufacturers made watches in various qualities which may look identical. The qualities in the early days may well have been based on selective

Plate 144 An early Swiss automatic lathe for making screws for watches. It was probably made in Solothurn by Müller and Schweizer in c1880. It has two cutting tools and a thread die and a transfer device to take the screw to the head slotting cutter at the top centre of the photograph. The camshaft at the left controls the thread cutting die, the transfer operation, the head brake and the rear cutting tool. The camshaft on the right controls the sliding head motion, the material feed and the cutting tool at the front. The machine base is 650mm×300mm

assembly techniques using the less well fitting parts for the lower quality watches and the better fitting parts for the higher quality watches which also had more jewelling and more adjustments made at assembly. This means that the conclusions below must be regarded with suspicion. Measurements of pivot diameter and arbor length were made with a micrometer which was checked to be accurate to 0.0005in (0.013mm). No measurements of hole diameters were attempted. It is also possible that the old movements were worn or had been repaired or rebushed without using the correct spare parts. In spite of these reservations it is clear that some selective fitting must have been used for pocket watches from the early days until perhaps 1900 and that escapements, bridges and cocks are often made unique to a watch by locating pins put in place during the assembly process. These statements are certainly not true in post-1945 watches and it would be fair to conclude that *complete* interchangeability was probably achieved in the 1930s. Lower quality pin lever watches appear to show easier interchangeability because price could only be kept down by certainty of assembly and it would be better not to complete a watch than spend time trying to make parts fit. Thus there may well have been a higher reject rate in this industry.

Plate 145 A pinion cutting machine of c1960 using one pass of each of two cutters to make one tooth space. The pinion is indexed round one space at a time by the slotted wheel on the left. The cutters are fixed to the rotating shaft protruding out over the chucks holding the pinion blank at the centre of the picture (there is no blank in position). This is a 'large' machine suited to carriage-clock-sized pinions

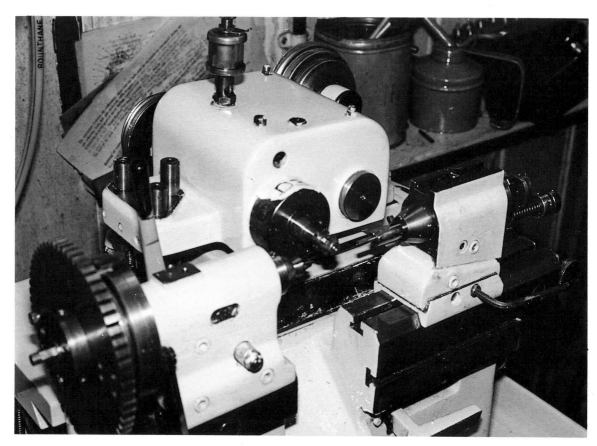

Results of interchangeability trials

Approx date	Maker	Model/escapement	Comment
1880	Ehrhardt (UK)	Full plate 16 size keywind Lever escapement	The parts were clearly not completely interchangeable. About half were including lever and balance to make two working movements. This is early in Ehrhardt's factory enterprise.
1883	Waltham (US)	Full plate 18 size, keywind Lever escapement	The trains were just about interchangeable, one movement had jewels and pivots on this model were slightly smaller. Balance cocks not interchangeable.
1891	Waltham (US)	Full plate 18 size, keywind. Lever escapement	Trains interchangeable except for escape wheels. Balance and cock were interchangeable.
1895	Rotherham (UK)	Full plate 14 size, keywind. Lever escapement	Appear to be completely interchangeable. An interesting result.
1900	Japy (France)	'Beaucourt' model pocket watch, keywind. Cylinder escapement	Only the train wheels were interchangeable. Plates were different thickness but compensated by pillar heights.
1901	Lancashire Watch Company (UK)	Full plate 16 size keywind Lever escapement	Seven 'similar' models tested; all were partly interchangeable but diameters tended to vary. Suggests much finishing, perhaps due to old-fashioned workforce. Disappointing.
1915–20	Büren (Swiss)	¾ plate, 19 ligne keywind, lever escapement	Watches appear to be completely interchangeable.
1925	Rotherham (UK)	¾ plate, 16 size, keyless, lever escapement	Completely interchangeable.
1910–40	Various	Swiss, German, American pocket watches; approx 19 ligne keyless, pin lever escapements	Eleven watches were 'repaired' by replacing respectively lever, balance, barrel, dial, balance, lever, second wheel, balance, barrel, plate, detent. Six watches did not interchange, these were mainly American with long production runs so that apparently similar models had different sized parts.
1930–40	AS (Swiss)	10½ ligne wrist watch, lever escapement, calibre 340	Two working movements were built with parts taken from eight broken movements.

Conclusions

1 Hole pitching in plates seems to cause little problem for train wheels due to good press work or because the intermittent train movements are less critical.

2 Pivot diameter and end shake appear the most crucial train dimensions.

3 The word 'interchangeability' in adverts from 1880 might assume that the watchmaker fits the part to the watch rather than expects it to be completely right.

4 These tests are minimal and there is scope for research here if it proves possible to collect enough 'similar' movements together.

In Chapter 3 it was seen that watch manufacture required four types of process (processes in lathes in which round parts were made using fixed tools and rotating work, processes in milling-style machines in which non-round parts were made using rotating cutters and fixed work, processes in presses in which parts were punched out and unspecified processes in special machines). At the outset the machines available for development were traditional hand-operated devices and machinery developed for other industries. The pioneering firms had to design and make their own machines and learn from their mistakes.

Lathes are used to make round parts in various sizes. In early factory watchmaking the larger lathes were used to process the pressed-out plate blanks.[3] The operations included facing the plates on both sides, turning the edges, drilling holes, cutting recesses, etc. These operations would each be performed on a separate lathe, each with its own face plate set up to hold the watch plate in a consistent position so that one operation could be repeatedly performed on each plate. The lathes had pre-set stops to ensure interchangeable parts. Later designs used collets to replace face plates and cams to replace the operator and provide automatic feed systems. As these machines developed they were no longer lathes but became special plate-finishing machines unsuited to any other use (Plate 143).

Smaller collet chuck lathes were used for staffs, arbors, etc and initially parts were roughed out on one lathe and finished (between centres for accuracy) on another. The progress was similar to the larger lathes from pre-set stops to automatic cam operation with automatic feed.[3] Multi-spindle designs were developed to enable sequences of operations to be performed on one lathe. The several spindles enabled all the cutting tools to work simultaneously which increased production but was not conducive to high accuracy in small watch parts. Large lathes of this design were used in general engineering.

In Switzerland, in 1872, Jacob Schweizer (1835–1913) invented a completely new design of automatic lathe for watchmaking. In order to achieve the required accuracy for watch parts the small diameter rotating work piece was fed by a sliding head past a cutting tool[4] (Fig 17). The

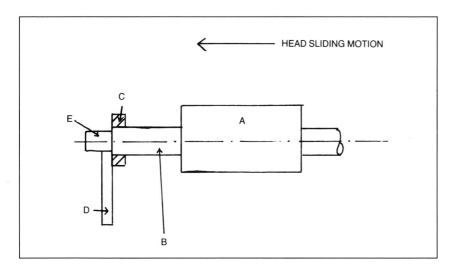

HEAD SLIDING MOTION

C
E
A
D
B

work piece was supported by a bush and cutting took place adjacent to the bush so that there was negligible deflection of the work piece (Plate 144). This led to exceptional accuracy and parts could be finished in a single machine. This design of lathe, known as the Swiss sliding head automatic, became dominant in the watchmaking industry and is one of the significant engineering contributions to come from watchmaking. Operation is completely automatic with pre-set sequenced cam feed of the long rod, from which a large number of identical parts are to be made, and of the multiple tools which were soon fitted to allow complex parts to be produced. (The original design only had two tools, one to turn and one to cut off.) Modern lathes of this style are still manufactured.[5]

Milling machines use fixed work with rotating cutters. In the watch-making industry this type of machine is used for various forms of gear cutting and for the shaping of many pieces which are not suited to lathe work such as pressed bridges. The most significant machines are those used for gear cutting. Early gear cutting machines worked with pressed-out gear wheel blanks arranged in a stack on an arbor. A shaped rotating fly cutter was passed vertically down the stack to cut one 'slit'. The cutter returned to the upper position and the wheel stack indexed one tooth pitch and the operation repeated. Indexing and cutter traverse were hand operated and this design is clearly based on the traditional wheel-cutting engine.[6] (Escape wheels needed several cutters to form the complex shape.) Clearly this process could be made automatic and could be rearranged to use a horizontal 'stack' of wheel blanks arranged below the cutter. Gears may also be cut by hobbing which is a later development based on allowing the teeth to be progressively formed by driving the gear stack round whilst the cutting hob passes overhead.

Pinions are much smaller than wheels, have less teeth and are made of steel rather than brass so that several cuts are needed to form a tooth. Pinions are cut one at a time from a pinion blank made in a lathe. Early

Fig 17 The turning process in a Swiss automatic lathe is arranged so that the sliding head A holding the rotating workpiece B is moved forward automatically by a cam. The workpiece is supported by bush C and the longitudinally fixed cutting tool D reduces the diameter of the workpiece E as it is moved forward by the sliding head. The tool can be moved laterally by a cam to produce shaped surfaces at E. For example, a steady outward motion of the tool as the work passes at a steady rate would produce a taper

Plate 146 An automatic transfer machine with 13 work stations and automatic feed at input. The machine is set up to perform a sequence of operations on plates, bridges or cases by automatically controlled tools at each work station

machines used three cutters arranged on a turret which rotated to allow each cutter to operate. The pinion was passed backwards and forwards under the cutter indexing at each pass. When the first cutter had machined all the teeth the turret rotated to allow the operations to repeat, finally the third cutter finished the tooth. Later designs arranged the cutters on one horizontal shaft which changed cutters by horizontal forward motion rather than turret rotation (Plate 145). Pinion teeth were polished on a self-indexing reciprocating 'wig-wag' machine. These pinion making machines were new (but obviously based on wheel-cutting processes) because traditionally pinion wire was drawn ready for use by the pinion maker who merely turned off the teeth to make the staff.

Automatic milling-style machines were also used to cut shaped recesses in plates in a more efficient way than the lathe method described earlier. A rotary cutter mounted in the vertical plane moves over the plates in a cam-controlled path to cut the recess shape desired. Different depths can also be achieved (Plate ·151).

In recent years, with the increased interest in cost cutting and high production by flexible machinery, the main milling-style machine used is the automatic rotary transfer machine. A series of work stations is arranged around the periphery of the circular table and the work (watch plate for example) is fed automatically around from station to station. At each station a different machining operation is performed. The efficiency of this machine stems from the fact that it is set up to do the work of several machines sequentially and avoids the time loss of moving the parts from machine to machine and resetting. They are flexible in their application to plates, cases, bridges, cocks, etc, performing horizontal milling, vertical milling, drilling, tapping, etc, and are also designed for assembly work with up to thirty-six stations per machine (Plate 146).[7,8]

Press tools for watch manufacture appear in the Frédéric Japy patent of 1899 (Chapter 2). These tools were for balance and wheel blanks. However the dies and punches would certainly only have allowed crude work and considerable finishing would have been required. The problem for early press toolmakers was to ensure that the male punch engaged correctly with the female die to avoid damage to the tool. Ingold was certainly aware of the problem for his 1843 patent (UK No 9,993) included 'a machine for stamping wheels and also polishing the inner edges of the arms of the wheels at the same time'. The patent shows four vertical pillars to guide the punch which was passed from above, down into the fixed die. It further suggests that after the first part of the pressing, which removed the unwanted metal leaving the spoked wheel form, the die was shaped to allow a second shaving cut on the inner surfaces to finish the wheel except for tooth cutting. Later, in 1854, Retor, a Geneva worker, designed a two-pillar die (Plate 147).

The machines used in these early days were fly presses in which rotation of a heavy flywheel or bar turned a robust screw thread to bear down on the punch and operate the press tool. The key to successful presswork is therefore the die rather than the press and the adoption of modern power-operated presses is of less significance except for their high production rates. Ingold's fly press might have made one or two wheel blanks a minute but modern watch presses can make up to 900 parts a minute. The rate depends on the finish required, a vibrating press to give very high-quality finish would make about 50 parts a minute.[9] In modern presses, the material feed is automatic, so that it is specially made in strip form (coiled up) so that it can be fed through the press tool between punch and die at a suitable rate. Parts made by this method include plates, wheels, bridges, cocks, cases, etc. Clearly the press is a most important tool for mass production so that the toolmaker who makes the punch and die is vital, but however skilled he was, he still needed a special measuring machine to enable him to succeed.

The precision necessary for tools to press out holes in plates is high and this was not a feasible operation in early mass-production factories. Watchmaking firms in both America and Switzerland were well aware of this problem of hole location both before fabrication and after when in-

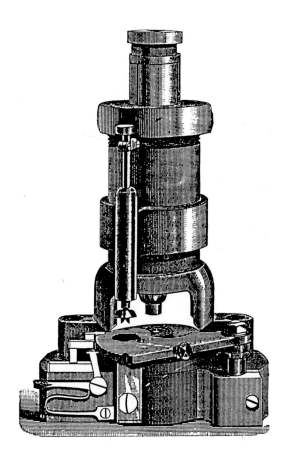

Plate 147 A press tool used at Rotherham of Coventry in about 1890 to shave wheel blanks. The assembly shown in the picture is placed in a press which pushes the male cutting punch down through the roughed-out wheel which is precisely placed on the female die. The rim and spokes are cleaned up in this final operation. The manufacture of such tools requires precise work and is essential to one of the most important forming processes used in watchmaking. The wheel teeth are cut later

spection of the finished product was required. In America Pratt and Whitney were involved and in Switzerland both the Société Genevoise d'Instruments de Physique (SIP) and Dixi produced machines to solve the problem. SIP was a measuring instrument firm founded in 1862. In 1865 they produced a linear dividing machine for producing scales and in 1881 an angular dividing machine.[10] With these established skills it is not surprising that the watchmakers asked SIP to solve the problem and in 1912 they produced a polar coordinate machine which combined their linear and rotary skills by locating a point precisely by its angular position and radius. The point located was marked by a punch and the device was called a pointing machine. At the same time Dixi produced an alternative design.

In about 1900 the watchmaking firm of Barbezat-Baillot started to make their own tools. These were so successful that they founded the 'Dixi' firm in 1904 to market their designs.[11] Contemporary catalogues show lathes, drills, grinders, polishers, etc together with micrometers and other measuring instruments.[11] Dixi were also aware of the problems of positioning holes and in 1912 they produced a pointing machine using rectangular coordinates (Plate 148). In this design, position is determined by distance from two axes at right angles (the way in which engineering drawings are normally dimensioned). The 'pointer' was moved by two micrometer screws and optical assistance was used for precision. The Dixi machine is fully described in contemporary literature.[2,12] The design was successful and SIP also adopted rectangular coordinates. Both Dixi and SIP later arranged for their machines to locate the position and then mark and drill the hole and thus the machine tool now known as a jig borer was born. This is the second significant contribution of horology to precision engineering (the first being the Swiss sliding head automatic lathe) for the tiny watch pointing machine has been developed for precision work in larger sizes.

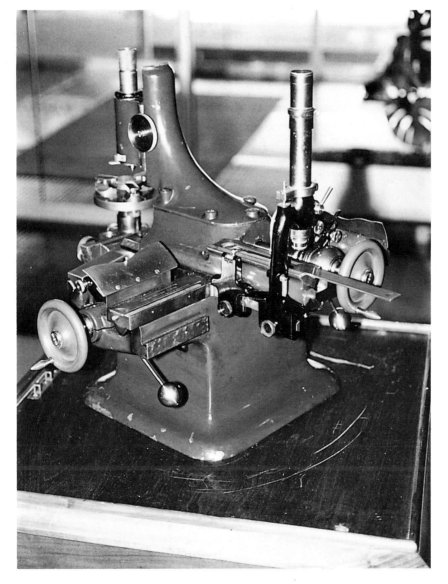

Plate 148 The original Dixi pointing machine made in 1912 in order to precisely locate position by rectangular coordinates. The two wheels to move the pointer (top left of the picture) may be seen at the bottom left and middle right. The object to be marked is held on the platform below the 'pointer'

With the introduction of the pointing machine the watchmaker could determine position with the necessary accuracy. Initially used for drilling holes in master plates and for die manufacture it has enabled machine watchmaking techniques to change so that the methods of 1920 will appear different to those of 1950 in the later discussion. Since it is not possible to describe all the special machines produced between 1850 and 1980 it can only be suggested that patents[13] and contemporary literature are examined.[1,2,3,6,14]

It would be fortunate if there were 'textbooks' specifically devoted to factory watchmaking methods. There appear to be no American books for the pioneering period but there is publicity material which contains simple descriptions of processes at Elgin[6] and Waltham.[15] There is also information in Marsh[3] and Moore.[16] For the small British industry there are the factory visits referenced in Chapter 7, in particular, The Lancashire Watch Company (reference 47) has some contemporary detail reprinted from *The American Jeweller* of 1893. For the revival period in the 1950s there are two engineering papers which give considerable detail of the processes and machines used.[14,17] None of these are complete books but there are two which describe watchmaking in detail at different periods of time. The earlier is a Swiss series of books entitled 'Bibliothèque Horlogère' of which three volumes are of particular interest describing the situation in about 1920.[2] The later work is Russian, written specifically as a textbook for technical colleges in 1956. The Swiss books are in French but the Russian book has been translated into English.[1] These books make the change in watchmaking technology between 1920 and 1950 clear, the Swiss book describing watchmaking with engineering assistance and the Russian book describing production engineering applied to watch manufacture. There is no way of detailing the information in these volumes (which total some 800 pages) in this chapter but an outline should suffice to explain the change in technology.

It was clear that traditional watchmaking was finished by the time that the Swiss books were written between 1900 and 1925 by W. Favre-Bulle. Three volumes are relevant. The first volume entitled *Le Calibre de Montre, Création Théorique et Graphique* is concerned with the design specification of a 23.6mm calibre, lever escapement watch movement. It deals with calculation of size, then decides the layout, centre distances, gear train, etc and determines the dimensions of all the parts. The second volume (sometimes called the third part since production was affected by World War I) is concerned with the planning of manufacture and takes the design described above and draws up a list of parts with dimensions followed by a plan of the operations needed to make each part (46 for a plate, 34 for a barrel bridge, 13 for a barrel, 8 for a barrel cover, 8 for a barrel arbor, etc). An experienced planner would realise that many of these operations would need to be broken down into separate processes so that the figures could be misleading. As a short example the eight barrel-cover operations are

1 Laiton en bandes, largeur (size of brass strip)
2 Un découpage (pressing)
3 Franchir le côté plat (flatten)
4 Tournage sur goutte (turn the boss)
5 Tournage en épaisseur (turn the thickness)
6 Tournage en diamètre (turn the diameter)
7 Rectifier le trou (correct the hole)
8 Tournage inclinaison du pourtour (bevel the circumference)

After the operations to make each of the watch frame parts are listed, fifty completion items are described. The remaining parts of a watch (wheels, pinions, etc) are known as 'fournitures' and similar manufacturing operations are described. For example, for a centre wheel pinion: turn, cut the teeth, wash, polish the teeth, fit the wheel, turn the pivots and polish, burnish in a lantern chuck, cut to length. Some 'fournitures' were normally bought out and their manufacture is not described (case, dial, hands, mainspring, balance and balance spring). It is however stated that there are other specialist texts for these items. This volume concludes by listing general assembly operations followed by some simple costing calculations.

The third volume is entitled *Fabrication Mécanique de la Montre, Tome III, L'ébauche* and commences with an interesting section of machine toolmakers' advertisements. The text is divided into three sections, the first dealing with measuring devices, including several pointing machines. The second section concerns itself with machines to make tools such as cutters and dies for watchmaking. The third and most interesting section describes how to follow up the information in the first two volumes systematically describing the machines to perform the operations listed in the second volume. A large number of machines are illustrated and the book is a valuable reference to those available at the time. It also enables the successful machine makers to be identified since some survive today and have been used as sources of information. The series of books is clearly still a watchmaking product rather than an engineering text and there is little about assembly so it is likely that there is another volume to cover this aspect as well as those for 'fournitures' mentioned above.

The Russian book *Technology of Watch Production* is a production engineering textbook. It does not discuss the design of the calibre but does include considerable assembly and testing information. It also includes case, dial, hand and balance spring manufacture and because the book has been translated it is possible for the interested reader to obtain a copy. The ten chapter headings give an idea of the information available;

1 Fundamentals of technology
2 Metals used in watch production
3 Stamping processes

4 Automatic turning
5 Milling the teeth of gear wheels, pinions and clutches
6 Basic machining operations for plates, bridges and cocks
7 Machining the escapement parts
8 The manufacture of cases, dials and hands
9 Finishing operations
10 Assembly and adjustment of watches

If Chapter 6 is examined as an example of the detail available we find 60 operations are used to make a plate of which 21 were presswork described in an earlier chapter and the remaining 39 are described under the general headings:

Plate 149 A watch factory photograph taken in about 1920. This clearly shows the large number of windows to allow good lighting. It has three floors, the heavy machinery would be located on ground level with lighter work on the upper floors

Turning and shaping of face planes and boring of recesses
Milling of recesses and projections
The machining of holes
Marking and decorative texturing

The chapter includes detailed instructions for setting up the machines which are to be used together with illustrations of the machines. It enables

cams to be designed, cutter paths to be planned, production rates to be calculated, etc. Indeed it gives the impression that if the machines and tools were provided we could make a watch with this manual!

Having seen how the parts are made in different eras, assembly and testing techniques complementing manufacture are vital. The Swiss book[2] says little beyond a short list of six actions and a short list to see if the watch functions. Probably at this time it was felt that irrespective of how the parts were made, the assembly techniques were still traditional and learned during apprenticeship. This would be in keeping with the feeling of watchmaking rather than engineering so that the postulated assembly book may not exist. Guidance on these techniques might be found in traditional books.[18] The Russian book[1] does describe what was happening in 1950 under the following headings:

Dimensional chains (principles of tolerances)
Sub-assemblies (sleeves, pins and jewels in bridges and cocks; wheel-pinion; barrel; pallet-lever; balance; hairspring and collet; balance and hairspring)
Watch assembly
Watch adjustment
Watch timing
Watch inspection

The assembly using the described sub-assemblies took place in eleven stages (train assembly; setting up the barrel; fitting the lever; trial mounting the balance; checking the escapement clearances; lubrication; final balance mounting; starting the movement; fitting motion work and dial; setting the hands in place; putting the movement in the case). The watch is then adjusted for timekeeping, run in six positions over several days, inspected and packed for despatch. If the testing is regarded as a self-running operation and disregarded it is clear that assembly occupies considerable time and labour and is an important contributor to the cost of a watch. It was therefore natural that with increasing competition manufacturers started to examine this facet of their business.

The efficiency of assembly was based from the early 1960s on assembly chains,[19]

Each working operation is subjected to scientific analysis and is decomposed into the primary movements of the right hand and left hand by mechanising the longest working times. The motions are then regrouped into operations of equal length.

This obscure statement means that if you make the time taken for each section of assembly the same then you can do it more efficiently with no holdups on a belt conveyor system (rather like car assembly techniques).

Plate 150 The interior of part of the Longines watch factory at St Imier photographed in about 1900 showing the work benches arranged for good lighting near windows although artificial lighting can be seen to be available. A series of machines, each of which is designed to perform a specific task, can be seen together with the operators and the foreman in charge. The machines are driven from overhead shafting which would be driven by a steam, gas or diesel engine

By this method you can reduce both the numbers and the skill level of the workforce. 'Time and motion' studies are a feature of production planning. Later (c1970) *automation* was introduced to watch assembly. To clarify this term, mechanisation might mean a plate is positioned and screws provided but a worker fits the screws whereas automation goes a stage further and the screws are fitted by machine or robot.[20] Feed of the parts to the transfer machine for automatic assembly may be by hand but this is not required in a computer-operated manufacturing system. These methods are valid in high labour cost situations for large-scale production but with the trend for watch manufacture to take place in Far Eastern countries with low labour costs it seems unlikely that full automation will be universal. In Japan the story may be different and computer driven systems may well be used for electronic products which need this technique for some of the work associated with handling integrated circuits. The traditional, hand-assembly techniques will survive in the high-quality, high price, low volume Swiss watches for it is this traditional hand-crafted image which sells these watches.

One aspect of the changing techniques of manufacture would be reorganisation of factory layout to deal with increasing output. When production is small the efficient flow of materials and parts is less crucial than in mass-production situations when the transfer of part-finished components to new locations is uneconomic of time and labour. It is also essential to balance the numbers of machines so that there is not excess capacity for making one part and to balance the skills of the workers so that all are always fully occupied. Information about layout is sparse and about the balance of machines and workers negligible. It is clear from early illustrations that factories had several floors and often had several wings.[21,22] This ensured that there was plenty of wall space for windows in an age when artificial lighting was poor. This policy was continued as can be seen in illustrations almost 100 years later.[23] Drawings showing the layout of the 1874 Elgin factory[24] illustrate a two-storey T-shaped building. The ground floor has a machine shop to make tools, an engine room, etc, which are not watchmaking departments together with a press room, a plate-finishing room and a train room. All these spaces use heavy machinery and involve most of the heavy raw materials. The upper floor is concerned with flat steel work, screws, escapements, balances, jewelling, assembly and finishing. These are lighter pieces and the work requires good illumination and clean conditions. This layout sets the fashion and is logical from a gravitational viewpoint (Plates 149 and 150).

At Waltham, Dennison's original ideas were interesting but in one case too dated in that he used small spaces for individual workmen and in another case too advanced in that he considered, but did not use, moving-belt production. By 1904 Waltham had a five-storey factory with a long frontage and several wings. There were twenty departments: punching, plate finishing, train making, flat steel, pinion polishing, escapement, balance, hairspring, jewelling, jewel making, gilding and nickel finishing, two dial departments, mainspring, finishing, adjusting, machine shop, engineering, carpentry and packing, the last four not being concerned directly with making watches.[25] Detailed illustrations of the layout in 1913 are given in Moore.[16] These show punching on the ground floor (first floor), plate work on the second, train work on the third, jewelling, escapement and assembly on the fourth and finishing on the fifth. Again heavy work was at ground level and light work at the top. However organised this sounds the text suggests that in practice there was some chaos with little integration. Progressive reorganisation from 1923 is shown in a 1938 layout but the text still suggests some 'flow problems'. The new arrangement kept heavy work on the ground (first) floor but the light work was arranged for 'gravity flow' from the fifth floor with finishing on the third, packing on the second and despatch on the ground floors. Clearly the efficient organisation of production is very important to avoid costly delays due to badly planned routes. It is also obvious that it is not easy to make a dramatic reorganisation without a closed period and workforce co-operation. One modern answer to these problems is the

transfer machine discussed earlier in which a series of operations can be performed sequentially in one machine, so obviating some of the movement of part-finished components. The idea of transferring parts was used from about 1880 in both America[3] and Switzerland[4] but these were single-purpose machines lacking the flexibility of the modern design (Plate 151).

The manufacture of quartz movements can be divided into two sections. Analogue movements will still need a plate and motion work to convert the stepper motor (Chapter 12) drive into rotation of the hands. Thus for these designs there is some conventional manufacture. Obviously the manufacture of dials, hands, and cases which has not been discussed may also follow conventional methods although there is increasing use of moulded plastic materials (Plate 152). Thus turning, presswork, milling and gear cutting will still be apparent in a factory. For the electronic parts of analogue quartz movements and for complete digital quartz movements the methods of manufacture are beyond the scope of this chapter and information should be sought in specialist literature.[26] The equipment needed is completely dedicated to the product and for this reason most makers buy the components or complete movements from specialist suppliers.

It has been demonstrated in this chapter that production engineering has developed as an important feature of watch manufacture. It is also apparent with the increasing dominance of the electronic watch that the role of the watch designer has assumed a styling aspect in a rapidly changing market place. Failure to offer the right style could result in business failure. This is the outcome of just over a century of change from the long established traditional methods of mechanical watchmaking. Some comfort for those who regret the change is the probable continued production of traditional, mechanical watches by small firms for customers who can afford the price of individualism, and for those who do not consider this real tradition there is still an adequate supply of good Victorian watches which are not expensive and which can be restored to good working order.

Plate 151 These two rows show a sequence of operations on components. The *upper* component is a bridge (i) blanked (ii) drilled (iii) recessed (iv) drilled again and locating pins fitted; the *lower* component is a cock which is part finished on the far left and then successively brought closer to completion

Plate 152 An assembly sequence of a Swatch quartz watch. This is designed so that the case forms an integral part of the watch movement. Starting from the *top left* successive components are added automatically as the case moves along the assembly line

12 Electrical and electronic watches

Since 1975 the mechanical watch has been largely replaced by the electronic watch. Tracing the development of this new timekeeper shows why it has had this effect. Since it is a radically different product the manufacturing methods have also changed.

The history of horology has been one of continuous progress towards accurate timekeeping. As machine-made watches began to dominate the market the limit of timekeeping ability for balance-controlled watches had almost been reached. Not all the available methods were incorporated in the machine-made watch for many required costly hand adjustments but the capability of good timekeeping was proven. It was not perfect and since the earliest days of electric and magnetic effects men had been hopefully experimenting with this source of battery-stored power. In the first instance clocks, rather than watches, were constructed and their development leads to the electric watch.[1,2,3]

In a conventional timepiece the power supplied by the weight or spring applies impulse to the pendulum or balance at the correct instant which also moves the hands. Power supply and impulse are the two functions that need to be achieved electrically and the first significant clock was that of Alexander Bain patented in 1845. In Bain's designs there is either a pendulum containing a coil of wire swinging along the axis of magnets or a pendulum with magnets swinging between two coils of wire. The swing of the pendulum operates switch gear to connect a battery to the coils causing a reaction with the magnetic field to produce a force to maintain the swing of the pendulum. The hands are moved using a ratchet and pawl from the pendulum. The later and more familiar Bulle clock uses the same principle but the Eureka clock uses a balance wheel which has an electromagnet across a diameter which is energised from a battery via a contact switch. When excited the balance magnet is attracted to a piece of soft iron and impulsed. This clock is the ancestor of the early electro-mechanical watches.

The fundamental problems of electric clocks are inconsistent impulse due to poor switching and batteries. Steady development overcame these difficulties and an electric clock known as the Shortt free pendulum was used as the standard observatory clock from the 1920s until the advent of quartz clocks. In quartz clocks the timekeeping is based on the vibrations of a piece of quartz. The vibrations were sustained by thermionic valve circuits which were bulky and power hungry and not suited to battery operation. Watches however needed small components. First a battery no bigger than the spring barrel was vital to any electromechanical design and, if a quartz crystal oscillator was to be used, miniature components were needed in the form of the transistor integrated circuits to replace the bulky thermionic valves. When these two objectives were achieved it was found that not only was it possible to have a watch of phenomenal accuracy but that the eventual production costs were so small that the price was less than that of the mechanical watch. Complex electric circuits enable all the complications (day, date, alarm, chronograph, etc) to be included with little extra expense. The two factors, accuracy and cost, explain the dramatic demise of the conventional watch and associated industry. Maintenance costs were also minimal. The impetus to produce small quartz timekeepers came from the space programme where navigation problems of a very demanding nature became apparent. It is convenient here to summarise the principles used in these electrical watches.

(1) Electromechanical watches (which only needed the miniature battery to be feasible) operate by energising an electromagnet with a switch. The excited magnet sustains the balance vibration which drives the watch hands. Switching can be by mechanical or electronic transistor devices.
(2) Electronic quartz watches operate by exciting a quartz crystal to vibrate and counting the vibrations with part of an integrated circuit. This count may be used to operate a motor to drive the hands or to operate electronic cells to give digital display.

Batteries became available from about 1950 but needed development to hold enough charge to avoid frequent changing. Transistor switches were devised in 1953–4 and applied to watches in 1959. Integrated circuits for quartz watches became available in 1967–8.

The timetable of events shown below has been put together by reading trade journals.[4]

Electromechanical watches with mechanical switching
1952 Announcement of intended development by Lip (France) and Elgin (USA).
1957 First battery-driven watch for sale, Hamilton 500 (USA).
1958 Lip watch on sale.
1960 Ebauches SA calibre L4750 on sale (Swiss) (Plate 153).

Plate 153 The Ebauches SA calibre L 4750 electro-mechanical watch movement with mechanical switching. The mu-metal cruciform balance can be seen with the electromagnet impulsing poles to the left and right of the balance centre. The rest of the electromagnet is circumferential at the movement perimeter. The switchgear is under the balance and cannot be seen

Electromechanical watches with transistor switching (Fig 18)

1948 Invention of transistor.

1953 Les Etablissements Léon Hatot (Paris) patent a transistor amplifier system (also British patent 746,465 of 1954) for clocks.

1959 Bulova Accutron watch (USA) announced (on sale 1960). This watch used a tuning fork oscillator, not a balance wheel.

1967 Ebauches SA calibre 9150 (Dynotron) watch with balance wheel (Plate 154).

Electronic watches with quartz oscillator and integrated circuit

1960 Integrated circuit technology.

1967 Seiko (Japan) hybrid circuit watch (sold 1969) (Plates 155 and 156).

1968 CEH (Horological Electronic Centre, Switzerland) announce prototype quartz crystal watch (Beta 21) with integrated circuit (Plate 157).

1969 Longines quartz watch *without* integrated circuit but with separate miniature components.

1969–70 Wider use of analogue display quartz crystal, integrated circuit watches.

1970 Bulova Accuquartz and Longines available.

1970 Hamilton Pulsar (USA), the first LED (light emitting diode) display watch.

1972 First LCD (liquid crystal display) systems by Société des Gardes-Temps SA (Switzerland), Longines and Seiko (Plate 158).

1973 Gray develops long-life LCD system in England.

Some watches and the vital developments are discussed below.

Plate 154 The Ebauches SA calibre 9150 electro-mechanical watch movement with transistor switching. The magnets are on the twin balance at the 10 o'clock position. The coils lie between the balance discs also at the 10 o'clock position. The electronic circuit is arranged around the left periphery. The battery power supply can be clearly seen on the right

HAMILTON 500 WATCH[5]

This watch, marketed in 1957, has a hairspring controlled balance with a coil of wire fixed to the rim. This coil is energised from the miniature battery by the closing of a mechanical switch operated by a jewelled pin on the balance roller. The balance is situated over magnets whose field interacts with the energised coil to impulse the balance in one direction only. The watch hands are moved by a train driven by a ratchet wheel moved one tooth at a time by another balance roller jewel.

LIP ELECTRIC WATCH[6]

The hairspring controlled balance has a special rim made of mu-metal. Two electromagnets are arranged adjacent to this rim and when they are energised from the battery by a mechanical switch operated by the balance roller the mu-metal rim and balance are impulsed in one direction only. The hands are moved in a similar way to those of the Hamilton 500. The layout of this watch and the Hamilton differ in the placing of the coil to be energised. In the Hamilton this is on the balance whereas in the Lip it forms part of the static electromagnet.

EBAUCHES SA L4750 MOVEMENT [7]

This movement was fitted to a number of 'makes' of watch including Avia and Mira in Britain. The design is similar to the Lip with a mu-metal cruciform balance impulsed by a static electromagnet. The switching is mechanical and is operated by the balance roller to allow impulse in both directions of swing. The hands are moved using a conventional-looking lever to increment the train. The watch was cheaper than the Hamilton or Lip, easier to maintain but of lower quality and with less good timekeeping (Plate 153).

THE TRANSISTOR AND THE HATOT AMPLIFIER

The transistor is a small piece of silicon (or other suitable material) processed to produce two forms known as p-type silicon or n-type silicon. By forming junctions between these two types particular electrical characteristics can be achieved. A transistor is formed by joining p–n–p or n–p–n in a component about 1mm square by 0.1mm thick which has to be encapsulated to make it suitable to handle. In a watch the transistor operates as a switch and amplifier. In the Hatot amplifier the transistor switches 'on' due to input induced magnetic effects as the balance swings and the amplified transistor output energises the electromagnet to impulse the balance. The transistor switches 'off' on the return swing. This small electric circuit can therefore replace the mechanical switching in an electric watch and avoid sparking and wear at the contacts.

Plates **155** and **156**. The Seiko 35SQ 'Astron' watch is shown in **Plate 155**. It was the first analogue electronic quartz watch being announced in 1967 and marketed in 1969. **Plate 156** shows the movement, which did not use a full integrated circuit

BULOVA ACCUTRON WATCH[8]

Besides using a Hatot amplifier transistor system for switching, the Accutron is notable because it uses a tuning fork as the vibrating system rather than a hairspring and balance wheel. The tuning fork has an electromagnet fitted on the free ends of the fork. The magnet is shaped as a tapered cylinder and is surrounded by a cylindrical iron cup. The space between the cup and magnet which both vibrate with the tuning fork is filled with a stationary wire coil. The wire coil is in two parts, one of which acts as a sensor to switch 'on' the Germanium transistor in the Hatot amplifier and the other which receives the amplified output to impulse the tuning fork vibrations. The watch hands are moved by a train driven by an indexing arm which vibrates with the tuning fork and rotates a tiny ratchet wheel (300 ratchet teeth on a wheel 2.4mm diameter). The vibration rate is 360Hz (Fig 18). 1Hz is one vibration per second.

EBAUCHES SA 9150 (DYNOTRON) MOVEMENT[9]

This is a conventional hairspring and balance wheel movement with electronic switching in place of mechanical switching. The balance consists of two identical discs each carrying two magnets arranged to face each other so that there are two magnetic fields in the gap. There are also two fixed

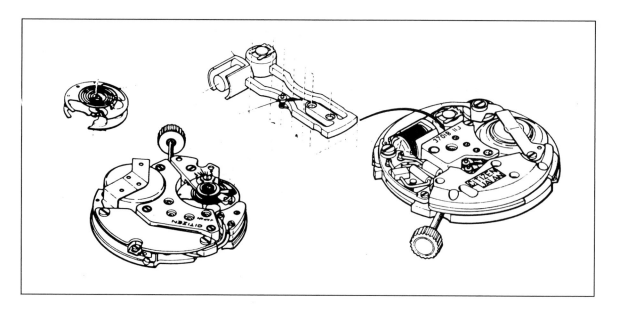

Fig 18 Two Citizen (Japan) electromechanical movements: *(left)* a balance wheel type similar to the Dynotron and *(right)* a tuning fork type similar to the Accutron but with a single cup and electromagnet

coils in the gap, one of which acts as a sensor to switch on the silicon transistor in the Hatot amplifier and the other which receives the amplified output to impulse the balance vibration in one direction only. The hands are driven using a jewelled lever to increment the train (Fig 18 and Plate 154).

THE QUARTZ CRYSTAL OSCILLATOR[10]

Any system can be made to vibrate at its natural frequency but the vibrations die away due to losses unless energy is added at the correct frequency. The losses in a quartz oscillator are ten thousand times less than those of a balance-wheel system so that it needs little power input. Because the frequency of vibration of quartz is high and the amplitude (size) of vibration is small a quartz oscillator is not suited to a mechanical system. Fortunately quartz is a piezoelectric substance which means that it physically deforms when electric charge is applied to it. Thus if an electric circuit applies charge at the correct frequency the quartz will vibrate. To sustain the vibration a transistor sensor switch and amplifier are again used. The frequency of vibration has to be interpreted by the electronic system in order to calculate the 'time'.

INTEGRATED CIRCUITS

To operate a quartz crystal watch we need a circuit to detect the vibrations and apply the sustaining electric charge. We also need a circuit to count the vibrations and to divide the frequency down to levels suitable to display the time either by analogue or digital means. This requires a large number of transistors suitably arranged to provide amplification, frequency division and display logic. Even with the transistor this would be bulky but the development of complete circuit formation (known as integrated circuits) on a single silicon chip by special manufacturing processes solved this and many other similar problems (computer chip, etc). The manufacture of integrated circuits will not be discussed but it should be emphasised that the processing of silicon is in no way similar to joining conventional electrical components and such circuits are not repairable. Complete replacement is required for malfunction. A 1973 integrated circuit in an Omega watch has 1,238 transistors in a 3.8mm square chip. Such a small device has to be encapsulated to be fit to handle. Because the circuits are mass produced they are not expensive.

OUTPUT METHODS: ANALOGUE, LIGHT EMITTING DIODE AND LIQUID CRYSTAL DISPLAY

The integrated circuit output is used to drive the method chosen to indicate the time. In the first quartz crystal watches conventional dials and hands were used. This is now known as analogue display. The early quartz analogue watches chose mechanical transducers to transmit the output from the integrated circuit (see Beta 21 and Accuquartz below). These methods soon became obsolete and the most common method used today is the stepper motor. This is an electric motor using a rotor with six peripheral, alternate North and South magnetic poles. When the motor stator, which is an electromagnet, is excited, the rotor turns through one pole, that is one sixth of a revolution. Thus, with a 10 to 1 gear ratio it can move a hand in one second steps. The integrated circuit must therefore supply pulses at one second intervals so that if, for example, the crystal vibrates at 8,192Hz this is arranged by the frequency dividing section of the circuit. The other hands, date indication, etc in analogue display are moved by further gears in the train. Other designs of electric motor are sometimes used.

Although analogue display is at present popular it will not necessarily remain so and there are other purely electrical forms of digital display. The feature of watches using this form is that there are no mechanical moving parts in the watch and they are often extremely cheap. The first electrical display used light-emitting diodes (LED). A transistor can be arranged to act as a diode. A diode conducts electricity in one direction but acts as a resistor in the other. Energy supplied to a resistor is usually emitted as heat (eg an electric fire) but in the LED it is dissipated as light. By making a 'double box' of seven LED cells and incorporating suitable logic in the integrated circuit the appropriate cells light up to display the time digitally. Unfortunately diodes consume power and a continuous display rapidly uses all the stored battery power and LED watches need to have a button pushed to make them display. This is not a convenient action as it requires a free hand.

A less power-consuming method is to use reflected light liquid crystal display (LCD). However LCD display is not visible in the dark so push-button night time illumination is required. Early LCD systems used cells filled with needle-shaped crystals whose light-transmitting properties changed when electrically excited. The same 'double box' of seven cells is used and dark non-light-transmitting cells stand out to indicate time. Unfortunately these designs had a short life and in 1973 Gray devised a polarised light system. This is best understood by taking two polarised sunglass lenses and observing that if one lens is rotated through a right angle no light passes. In the watch display system the electrically excited dark cells stand out. In both LCD systems the integrated circuit logic is used to excite the appropriate cells in the correct sequence. Polarised light systems last for several years.

EBAUCHES SA BETA 21 QUARTZ WATCH[11]

This was announced in 1968 and sold from 1970 and used an 8,192Hz crystal which was divided to 256Hz. A stepper motor was not used but a vibrating resonant reed indexed a ratchet wheel and pawl system to drive the analogue display. There are three units: the crystal, the integrated circuit and the reed motor (Plate 157).

Plate 157 The Ebauches SA Beta 21 movement which was the first quartz movement to use an integrated circuit. It was announced in 1968 and marketed in 1970

BULOVA ACCUQUARTZ WATCH[12]

This watch was also available from 1970 and did not use a stepper motor. Instead, Accutron experience was used and the divided crystal frequency was used to drive a tuning fork, ratchet wheel system.

HAMILTON PULSAR WATCH[13]

This was the first LED watch and therefore the first watch with no moving parts. The crystal frequency was 32,768Hz divided to 1Hz to drive the display. The battery was rechargeable at six-month intervals and a spare battery and charger were included with the watch. To conserve power the display lit on demand by push piece for 1¼ seconds. The initial price of this new watch was $1,500 in 1971 which should be compared fifteen years later with the price of a simple digital display LCD watch (free?).

EARLY LCD WATCHES[14]

In 1972 the first LCD watches appeared on the market. The Société de Garde-Temps SA announced one in April 1972. Longines and Seiko had

Plate 158 The Longines liquid crystal display (LCD) watch sold in 1972. This was one of the first on the market and had the co-operation of Texas Instruments in the design of the movement

similar starting dates. It is also clear that Ebauches SA had a model at this time. All these firms used technology aid from companies such as Texas Instruments, Optel Corporation, etc. At this stage the display system was the original short life design so that presumably surviving models have no display facility. However LCD watches with long-life display systems are now available for unbelievably low prices with considerable complications (Plate 158).

It should not be thought that there will be no further developments. Crystal frequency is temperature dependent and one recent improvement has been the incorporation of temperature compensation.[15] Another improvement over the years is the use of higher crystal frequencies which are obtained from shorter lengths of quartz which enable smaller calibres to be produced.

SUMMARY

In a period of sixteen to seventeen years from 1957–1973 the horological industry moved through three phases of electric watch. In doing so they have made much of their plant redundant and the process of change is still going on as more nations turn to watch 'manufacture'. This often consists of casing up movements from the available sources. It is interesting to reflect that in 1886 the problems came from America to threaten the European industry and now the threat is from the Far East and the multinational corporations producing in the cheapest situation.

In 1984 mechanical watches comprised about 30 per cent of European and Japanese outputs. However both locations have established mechanical production lines which are unlikely to be renewed when worn. Mechanical watches will soon only be available as expensive 'hand-made' products and most middle-market watches will have traditional analogue display with quartz movements. LCD watches will supply customers who require special features or a very cheap simple watch.

13 *Collecting and repair*

COLLECTING

Watch collections have traditionally been concerned with antiques. The definition of an antique seems flexible in these modern times but in the watch context it normally means those made by traditional methods rather than by machines in factories. In this discussion we will mainly consider the collecting of mechanical watches made in factories from 1850 onwards. These watches are rapidly becoming things of the past as the quartz watch now dominates the market. In the period considered the transient electromagnetic watch and the early electronic models are also considered to be collectable items.[1]

Watch collectors have not completely ignored this post-1850 period and two fields can be identified as well established. These are the high-quality watch which very often has a number of complications and the rare varieties of American watch. Both these fields require considerable investment but in the lower price ranges there are plenty of openings with collecting potential. Bearing in mind the enormous number of watches made in the period considered this is not surprising, but what is surprising is how few of these appear on the market because of the throw-away mentality that has developed in the modern consumer society.

It is important for a collector to realise that the external, visible condition of a watch is very important in determining the value and when the normally unseen movement is examined not only is the visible condition important but also the working order. A watch may not be working due to damage or missing parts, it may work in an imperfect fashion due to dirt or wear, or it may appear to work well. Most collectors like their watches to work well and indeed, in a modern collection, to be useable so that this capability must be assessed before purchase. Movements can be repaired but damaged dials or cases and missing hands in a modern watch may create greater problems than for an antique watch. These comments should be treated with caution because some watches are uncommon and the state may have to bow to the rarity. The John Bull watch shown in Plate 58 has no winding stem and button (these can be made) but since only 5,000 were reputed to have been produced it would have been unwise for the owner not to have made the purchase when the imperfect specimen became available.

What sort of watches might the collector consider in this post-1850 period? Chapter 6 gave an idea of the range of watches available. The choice made will depend on the individual taste but sooner or later by reading and by researching any watches already acquired a field of interest will probably appear. Examples might be watches from one maker or one country, watches in one style or with one type of escapement, stop watches, pocket watches, wrist watches, ladies' watches, military watches, railway watches, electromagnetic watches, LED designs, etc. Even if the collector's interest changes, provided the cost was correct for the condition, watches can be resold without too great a loss for the pleasure gained and even perhaps at a small profit. Although money is important to a collector it is the author's view that collecting should not be considered as investment and the money spent seen as that used in supporting a hobby. If it so happens that values rise, that is fine but a fall in value should not be a disaster if there was no expectation of gain.

A very important part of a modern watch collection arises from the fact that during the period under consideration watches were often sold in cases or boxes which themselves add to the collection. Similarly there have been advertisements, brochures, journal articles reporting on style and manufacture, spare parts catalogues, etc, all of which would contribute to a properly studied and indexed collection (Plate 159). There could be a vast volume of paperwork. Since such a large number of watch calibres were produced by most makers, some of which might be too expensive or very similar to others, it is also reasonable to include photographs of watches in a collection (Plate 160). Many of the photographs used in this book have been taken by the author using an inexpensive half-scale macro lens fitted in an inexpensive SLR camera body. By having a short, fixed length stick screwed into the tripod hole in the body base the camera can be held steady at an almost fixed focus for quick pictures when the opportunity occurs. Flash can be used but often gives reflections in places which spoil the picture; however some record of a watch may be preferable to no record.[2,3]

Watch collections are built up slowly from various sources including dealers, auction sales, street markets, jumble sales and other collectors' spares. In order to know what is available it is essential to look at these sources as regularly as possible and to compare items for sale with watches that can be seen in museums[4] and other collections and that are illustrated in books that can be examined in libraries[4] or purchased. Libraries should also be used to study the literature relevant to the collector's interests for though it is exciting to find out things without help none of us is blessed with infinite time to rediscover all the data that has already been collated by others. The bibliography at the end of this book may help.

Plate 159 Collections of modern watches can be enhanced by ephemera such as this 1910 advertisement for Williamson watches. This can be compared with the movements in **Plates 62** and **72**

Enough has been said to show that there is potential to build an interesting collection of modern watches and associated ephemera to suit various tastes and pockets. However carefully this is done the problem of repair will arise and it is to this aspect we now turn attention.

REPAIR

The repair of modern watches is based on the replacement of worn or damaged parts by new ones. These parts should be identical to the damaged ones and require no alterations to make them fit. Thus in order to effect a repair there are four steps:

(i) identify the faulty part (Fig 19)
(ii) identify the movement
(iii) consult the catalogue to obtain the part number
(iv) obtain the part and repair the watch.

This process requires two distinct skills, that of 'watchmaking' to find the fault and effect the repair, and that of knowing how and where to get the information and the part. There are a large number of calibres, catalogues and tables of interchangeability so that even this task is not as simple as it sounds. Some older catalogues were mentioned in Chapter 8 and this system still applies to recent calibres. It is becoming increasingly difficult for older designs which are rapidly becoming obsolete in the changed situation brought about by the electronic revolution. The number of watch repairers and spare-part sources has fallen and will continue to do so and it is likely that there will eventually only be limited supplies of the more common requirements. These would include winding buttons, winding stems, mainsprings, balance springs, standard screws, glasses, hands, jewels, bushes, etc. It is therefore obvious that many repairs will require a return to traditional skills.

For the collector who wishes to get his watches repaired this has serious consequences for it means that if replacement parts are not available they will need to be made by a skilled watchmaker or the owner will have to make them himself. This situation also arises with 'antique' watches which were not machine made and for which interchangeable spare parts were never available. Some parts are relatively easy to make and would include those that can be made in simple watchmakers' lathes such as staffs and arbors for larger calibres. Other parts such as wheels and pinions require special machines and skills. A further group of parts including flat steel springs and detents can be made with a file. All these newly made parts would require fitting by trial and error and would therefore be expensive to have done and suited only to watches of appropriate value.

Many collectors will probably be concerned with watches of such value that expensive repairs are not justified so that they must ensure that their

Fig 19 The *upper* figures provide a glossary to the parts of a modern watch. The *lower* figures are examples of illustrations in old spare parts catalogues used to identify movements. Thus the *left hand* figure shows a 13 ligne ETA movement, calibre 173/76/77. The information below gives the part number of the balance staff (Unruhwellen, U), the winding stem (Aufzugwellen, W) and the mainspring (Zugfeder, Zf). Another section of the catalogue gives the dimensions of these parts and the interchangeability with other calibres

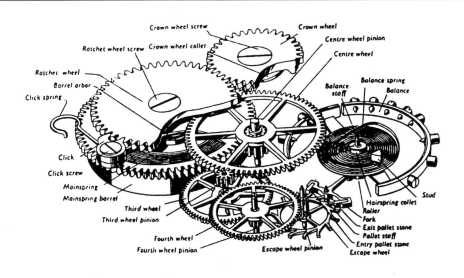

Crown wheel screw — Crown wheel
Ratchet wheel screw — Crown wheel collet — Centre wheel pinion
Ratchet wheel — Centre wheel
Barrel arbor — Balance spring
Click spring — Balance staff — Balance
Click — Stud
Click screw — Hairspring collet
Mainspring — Roller
Mainspring barrel — Fork
Third wheel — Exit pallet stone
Third wheel pinion — Pallet staff
Fourth wheel — Entry pallet stone
Fourth wheel pinion — Escape wheel pinion — Escape wheel

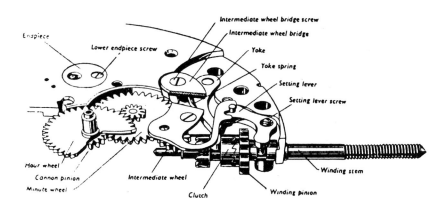

Intermediate wheel bridge screw
Endpiece — Intermediate wheel bridge
Lower endpiece screw — Yoke
Yoke spring
Setting lever
Setting lever screw
Hour wheel
Cannon pinion — Intermediate wheel — Winding stem
Minute wheel
Clutch — Winding pinion

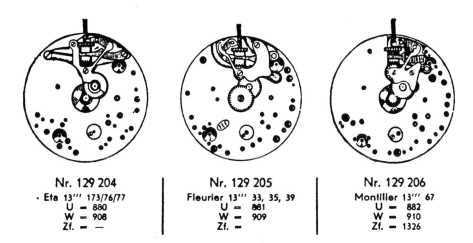

Nr. 129 204	Nr. 129 205	Nr. 129 206
· Eta 13''' 173/76/77	Fleurier 13''' 33, 35, 39	Montilier 13''' 67
U = 880	U = 881	U = 882
W = 908	W = 909	W = 910
Zf. = —	Zf. =	Zf. = 1326

purchases are in good condition or they must be prepared to undertake their own repair work. There are several courses of action available to such a person. It may be that classes in watch repair are available. Skills may be acquired by correspondence course books or by other reading[5,6,7,] backed by practical trial and error on old, valueless, broken movements until sufficient confidence is gained to tackle a watch. This learning process is slow and requires an investment in tools. The list below gives some idea of those needed.

General tools

screwdrivers	knife
tweezers	steel rule
pliers	micrometer
needle files	eyeglass
broaches	drills
small vice	hammers
stake and punches	dust covers
bench with light	calipers
centre punch	scriber
screwhead slotting file	dividers
pin vices	

Watchmakers' tools

a lathe or a set of turns	an arbor drilling tool
a staking tool	a Jacot tool
a depthing tool	spring winders
movement holders	gravers, arbors and pulleys

The use of some of the special watchmakers' tools is described below.

The simple turns operated by hand-held bow enable a variety of jobs to be tackled, such as new staffs, pivots, bushes, distorted wheels, etc. Reference should be made to texts which describe in detail how to make particular parts.[5,6] The staking tool consists of a rotating platform with a range of different-sized holes and a set of punches. The tool has a vertical guide for the punch which holds the punch with its centre exactly in line with the selected hole in the stake. Thus there is no fear of breakage or problem of lining up the work. The staking tool is used for riveting, punching, staff removal, bush insertion, etc. A depthing tool enables wheels and pinions to be tested out of the movement so saving much assembly and dismantling between adjustments. The arbor drilling tool is used to drill out a hole in an arbor which has a broken pivot. A new pivot can then be inserted. One centre in the drilling tool has a hollow end allowing the drill to be pushed through it to perform the delicate drilling operation. A Jacot tool is a special form of turns provided with supports for small diameter parts. The tool is used for burnishing pivots to improve

the surface finish and reduce friction. Spring winders coil up mainsprings so that they can be inserted into the barrel without distortion which may occur when put in by hand.

Many different faults appear in watches, the most common ones are listed below.

Plate 160 This picture shows watches in the 'lantern workshop' of Longines in about 1900. There is a regulator clock at the top centre which suggests that the watches hanging up are undergoing timekeeping trials. The boxes in which the watches are kept were the usual way of assembly and handling in this period. Period photographs like this can form part of a collection

Worn parts	*Bent parts*	*Broken parts*	*Missing parts*
pivot holes	pivots	pinions	motion work
jewels	wheels	pivots	pins, screws
pivots	arbors	wheels	wheels
		springs	jewels
		detents, ratchets	cocks, bridges
			winding gear

Other faults due to: corrosion, dirt, old oil.

Special problems due to: hands, dials, cases, glasses.

It is important to avoid causing more damage when attempting to work on a movement which, in a modern watch, is often very small. Several simple precautions are suggested.

1 Never do anything to modify undamaged parts in order to fit the new parts as better methods of repair or replacement may become available later.
2 Never dismantle a watch with the mainspring wound.
3 Always work out how the movement was assembled before dismantling. Sketches are vital and photographs may help.
4 Do not use excessive force to free an apparently jammed part. It may not be assembled in the way that has been assumed. A left-hand thread, for example, unscrews clockwise.
5 Be scrupulously clean and put away the tiny parts as they are removed.
6 When handling a rare watch, take no action until absolutely certain that no damage will result.

Modern watch movements are removed from their cases in two steps. First the winding stem is removed either by loosening a securing screw (Swiss) or by pulling the button outwards (American) which disengages the stem without removal. The two screws holding the movement to the case are then removed or slackened and the movement can then be eased through the front of the case (dial side). There are slots in some watch cases which allow the movement to be removed complete with the winding button and stem. In order to locate a fault (this is a glib statement for many malfunctions are very elusive[6]) it will probably be necessary to dismantle the movement. The first step in this process is to let down the mainspring usually by holding back the spring-loaded click so that the winding button can run backwards until the spring is unwound. To do this tension the mainspring with the winding button to push out the click, hold it out and allow the button to slip slowly through the winding finger and thumb. Once the mainspring is unwound the movement can be dismantled. Not all movements are identical but the most fragile parts are the hands and dial which should be carefully removed as identical replacements are virtually unobtainable.[6] Then the most fragile working part, the balance, should be removed and stored. The remainder of the movement is relatively robust and can be carefully dismantled. At this stage any damaged parts should be recognised and, assuming no spare parts are available, there are three courses of action.

1 It is theoretically possible that an identical movement can be found which has the vital part undamaged or which could be completely substituted.
2 The part can be repaired.
3 A new part can be made.

Only repair will be briefly considered as making a new part requires special skills and finding an identical part requires special good fortune. Some actions which may help in repair are:[5,6,7]

If no apparent damage was discovered
1 Clean the parts.
2 Check that the mainspring is not broken.
3 Reassemble the train and test for free running.
4 Add the lever and test the action.
5 Lubricate the pivots then fit the balance.
6 Make sure the balance is correctly placed so that the tick is even. (If the watch still does not work a closer examination is required.)
7 Is the balance spring free of interference?
8 Are any pivots bent?
9 Are any jewels damaged?
10 Are any pivots, jewels or holes so worn that rubbing occurs (Fig 20a).

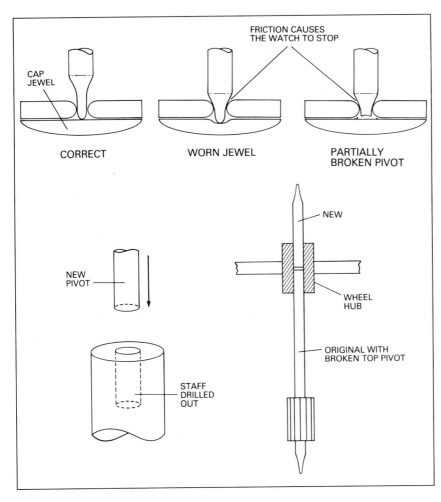

Fig 20 (a) Damage to a balance pivot or a worn cap jewel can cause a watch to stop; (b) the correct method of replacing a pivot if a new staff is not available; (c) an alternative method which may be used if a suitable 'graft' is found but which will need care in adjusting the end shake

If damage is discovered[5,6,7]

1 Repair pivots using the drilling tool and inserting a new pivot (Fig 20b).
2 Make new staffs.
3 Bush pivot holes.
4 Replace jewels.
5 Straighten bent pivots with care.
6 For broken wheel teeth, solder a new piece into the wheel and file teeth.
7 Can a file help with any other damage?

Irreparable damage requiring new parts

1 A part is missing.
2 Broken pinion teeth.
3 Broken balance spring.
4 Broken winding stem.

This list is by no means complete and again the special watch repair manuals should be studied. An interesting article of 1897 describes in some detail a fault-finding technique applied to an American machine-made watch.[8] It makes quite terrifying reading but an encouraging thought is that in the days of traditional 'hand' manufacture all the parts of a mechanical watch were made so it is possible for any mechanical watch to be repaired. This is not true for electromechanical watches or electronic watches for in the former the magnetic coils and some switches are irreparable, and in the latter so are coils and integrated circuits, although advice may help.[9,10,11] Thus spare parts are needed and these may only be available for a short period of time in the cheaper models. To detect electric faults, meters and an oscilloscope will be required together with a manual listing the test points and voltages, currents or signals which indicate malfunction in a particular model.[12,13,14] This would suggest that future collections of quartz watches may include some examples which will never be made to function except perhaps by building an external circuit which would simulate the action of the defunct internal circuit to drive the display. LCD units which have a finite life may also need external simulation in an otherwise functional watch. These actions may be feasible for an electronic expert but may not be of interest to the collector.

Appendix

WATCH SIZES

Two systems are used in this book based on the dimensions of the dial plate.

For English and American circular watch movements:
Size 0 is $1^{5}/_{30}$in diameter
Size 1 is $1^{5}/_{30} + 1/_{30}$in diameter
Size 2 is $1^{5}/_{30} + 2/_{30}$in diameter, etc

For continental circular watch movements sizes are quoted in lignes where 1 ligne is 2·255mm (about 0·088in).

Thus a 16 size watch movement is 1.7in in diameter and the comparable Swiss 19 ligne watch movement is 1.686in in diameter. Most wrist watch sizes are quoted in lignes, two dimensions being required for non-circular calibres.

Bibliography

Some readers may not wish to study the detailed chapter references and may prefer to read the more general books listed below.

Early watchmaking
Weiss, L. *Watchmaking in England, 1760–1820*, Hale, 1982.
General history
Cutmore, M. *The Pocket Watch Handbook*, David & Charles, 1985.
Landes, D. S. *Revolution in Time*, Belknap Press, 1983.
Swiss history
Jaquet, E. and Chapuis, A. *Technique and History of the Swiss Watch*, Hamlyn, 1970.
American history
Harrold, M. C. *American Watchmaking*, National Association of Watch and Clock Collectors Inc., USA, 1984.
English history
The Lancashire Watch Company, 1889–1910, Ken Roberts, USA, 1973.
Horological Theory
Rawlings, A. L. *The Science of Clocks and Watches*, Pitman, 1948.
Complicated watches
Lecoultre, F. *A Guide to the Complicated Watch,* Switzerland, 1985.
Modern manufacture
Marsh, E. A. *Watches by Automatic Machinery at Waltham,* Adams Brown, USA, 1968 (facsimile).
Tarasov, S. V. *Technology of Watch Production,* Jerusalem, 1964.
Repairs
De Carle, D. *Practical Watch Repairing*, NAG, 1947.
Pocket watch pictures
Meis, R. *Les montres de poche*, Paris, 1980.
Wrist watch pictures
Kahlert, H., Muhe, R. and Brunner, G. L. *Wristwatches*, Munich, 1987.
Negretti, G. and Neneini, F. *Ore D'Oro*, Milan, 1984.
Electric watches
Weaver, J. D. *Electrical and Electronic Clocks and Watches,* Newnes, 1982.
Dictionary
Britten's Watch & Clock Maker's Handbook, Dictionary and Guide, Methuen, 1982.

References

In this list AH denotes *Antiquarian Horology* and HJ denotes *Horological Journal*

CHAPTER 1

1 HJ, 89, August 1947, 398.
2 'The Worshipful Company of Clockmakers', AH, 13, December 1981, 140-3.
3 Gould, R. T. *The Marine Chronometer*, Holland Press, 1960.
4 Chamberlain, P. M. *It's about Time*, Holland Press, 1964.
5 Cutmore, M. *The Pocket Watch Handbook*, David & Charles, 1985.
6 Kemp, R. 'Watch movement making in Prescot', AH, 13, September 1981, 77-83.
7 Kemp, R. 'The Coventry Watch Trade', HJ, 126, March 1984, 17-20.
8 Hoult, J. 'Prescot watch-making in the XVIII century', *Trans. Historical Society of Lancashire and Cheshire*, 77, 1925, 34-53.
9 Rees, A. *Clocks, Watches and Chronometers (1819–20)*, David & Charles, 1970.
10 Nussbaum, J.-M. 'The Craft of Watchmaking', *La Suisse Horlogère et Revue Internationale de l'Horlogerie*, 80, December 1965, 3-11.
11 Jaquet, E. and Chapuis, A. *Technique and History of the Swiss Watch*, Hamlyn, 1970.
12 'Late 19th Century hand watch making', AH, 3, June 1961, 205.
13 Bickley, 'Watch Finishing', HJ, 59, 1917, 94-6 and 115-19.
14 Weiss, L. *Watchmaking in England, 1760–1820*, Hale, 1982.
15 Hatton, T. *An Introduction to the Mechanical Part of Clock and Watch work*, Turner and Devereux, 1978.
16 Britten, F. W. *Horological Hints and Helps*, Baron, 1977.
17 Saunier, C. *The Watchmaker's Handbook*, Technical Press, 1948.
18 Finch, J. 'Martin Matthews, Watch case maker', AH, 12, Winter 1980, 410-19.
19 AH, 15, December 1985, 626.
20 Parliamentary Papers, 1817 (504), 6, 71-3.
21 Wyke, J. *Catalogue of tools for watch and clock makers*, USA, 1978.

CHAPTER 2

1 Burchall, A. 'Pitt's Clock and Watch Tax: a reassessment', AH, 13, September 1982, 454-61.
2 Parliamentary Papers, 1817 (504), 6, 73-8.
3 Guye, S. 'The vital necessity and the history of mechanization in the Swiss watch industry', *La Suisse Horlogère et Revue Internationale de l'Horlogerie*, 80, December 1965, 12-18.
4 Aked, C. *Complete list of English horological patents up to 1853*, Brant Wright, 1975.
5 Alleaume, A. *Les Brevets d'Invention concernant l'Horlogerie (1792–1869)*, Paris, 1873.
6 HJ, 32, October 1889, 29-30.
7 Landes, D. S. *Revolution in Time*, Belknap Press, 1983.
8 Nussbaum, J.-M. 'The Craft of Watchmaking', *La Suisse Horlogère et Revue Internationale de l'Horlogerie*, 80, December 1965, 3-11.
9 Jaquet, E. and Chapuis, A. *Technique and History of the Swiss Watch*, Hamlyn, 1970.
10 Woodbury, R. S. 'The Legend of Eli Whitney and Interchangeable Parts', *Technology and Culture*, 1, Summer 1960, 235-53.
11 Booker, P. J. *A History of Engineering Drawing*, Northgate, 1963.

12 HJ, 37, August 1895, 165-6.
13 Carrington, R. F. and Carrington, R. W. 'Pierre Frederic Ingold and the British Watch and Clockmaking Company', AH, 10, Spring 1978, 698-714.
14 Torrens, D. S. 'Some notes on the history of machine watch-making', HJ, 89, April 1947, 177-84.
15 HJ, 32, May 1890, 144-6.
16 Waldo, L. 'The mechanical art of American watchmaking', *Jnl. Society of Arts*, 34, 1886, 740-51.
17 *American Watch Historical Information with Serial Numbers and Dates*, Minnesota Watchmakers Association, USA, c1970.
18 Harrold, M. C. *American Watchmaking*, National Association of Watch and Clock Collectors, Inc., USA, Spring 1984.
19 Wingate, R. M. 'The Pitkin Brothers revisited', *Bulletin*, National Association of Watch and Clock Collectors, Inc, USA, August 1982, 381-91.
20 Britten, F. J. *Old Clocks and Watches and their Makers*, 9th Edition, Methuen-Spon, 1982, 237.
21 Eckhardt, G. H. *United States Clock and Watch Patents, 1790–1890*, USA, 1960.

CHAPTER 3

1 Letter from A. L. Dennison, HJ, 32, June 1890, 158-9.
2 Moore, C. W. *Timing a Century*, Harvard University Press, USA, 1945.
3 Waldo, L. 'The mechanical art of American watchmaking', *Jnl. Society of Arts*, 34, 1886, 740-51.
4 Harrold, M. C. *American Watchmaking*, National Association of Watch and Clock Collectors, Inc, USA, 1984.
5 Abbott, H. G. *History of the American Waltham Watch Company*, USA, 1904.
6 'Early Vicissitudes of the American Watch Industry,' HJ, 34, July 1892, 166-8.
7 Jaquet, E. and Chapuis, A. *Technique and History of the Swiss Watch*, Hamlyn, 1970.
8 Torrens, D. S. 'Some notes on the history of machine watchmaking', HJ, 89, April 1947, 177-84.
9 'Gauges used in the watch trade', HJ, 47, December 1904, 47-51.
10 Tripplin, J. 'Recent progress in British Watch and Clockmaking', *Jnl. Society of Arts*, 38, 1890, 365-80.
11 'Review of the Mechanical Manufacture of Watches', HJ, 31, December 1888, 50-4.
12 Marsh, E. A. *Watches by Automatic Machinery at Waltham*, Adams Brown, USA, 1968 (facsimile of 1896 original).
13 Perkins, T. 'The manufacture of watches as carried on at the works of the National Watch Company, Elgin, USA', HJ, 16, January 1874, 65-75.
14 Gannay, H. 'Notes of a Horological Tour in New England', HJ, 43, August 1901, 160-2.
15 Eckhardt, G. H. *United States Clock and Watch Patents, 1790–1890*, USA, 1960.
16 Hewitt, C. J. 'Prize essay on the Horological Exhibits, British and Foreign, in the Inventions Exhibition, South Kensington', HJ, 28, 1886, 117-22 and 129-38.

17 'A master Tool Maker', HJ, 44, May 1902, 116–18.
18 Dennison, A. G. and Priestley, P. T. 'A history of the Dennison Watch Case Company', HJ, 128, March 1986, 12-16, April 1986, 8-11, May 1986, 15-17, June 1986, 10-12 and HJ, 129, July 1986, 13-16.
19 *Antique Watches*, Collector Books, Paducah, USA, 1979.
20 *American Waltham Watch Co's Materials, 1885*, Ken Roberts, Bristol, USA, 1972.
21 *Elgin Reminiscences*, Ken Roberts, Bristol, USA, 1972.
22 *American Watch Company Souvenir Catalog, 1884–85*, Ken Roberts, Bristol, USA, 1972.
23 Chamberlain, P. M. *It's about Time*, Holland Press, 1964.

CHAPTER 4

1 Centenary Number, HJ, 100, September 1958.
2 HJ, 4, 1862, 51-6, 63-6 and 77-80.
3 HJ, 9, 1867, 85-8 and 101-4.
4 HJ, 11, 1869, 89-101.
5 HJ, 16, 1874, 65-75.
6 HJ, 22, 1879-80, 43-4, 60-1 and 78.
7 HJ, 22, 1880, 57-60.
8 HJ, 22, 1880, 92-3, 125 and 140.
9 HJ, 22, 1880, 127-32 and 153-4.
10 HJ, 26, 1884, 115-20.
11 HJ, 28, 1886, 117-22, 129-38.
12 HJ, 44, 1901, 3-8.
13 HJ, 36, 1894, 116-22.
14 'Wycherley's System of Watch Movement Making', HJ, 10, October 1867, 18-21.
15 'Death of Mr John Wycherley', HJ, 34, October 1891, 17-19.

CHAPTER 5

1 Jacquet, E. and Chapuis, A. *Technique and History of the Swiss Watch*, Hamlyn, 1970.
2 Landes, D. S. *Revolution in Time*, Belknap Press, 1983.
3 Buffat, E. 'La Montre Roskopf' *Journal Suisse d'horlogerie*, 1912–14.
4 HJ, 10, 1868, 78-83, 89-92 and 97-9.
5 Bacon, D. H. 'A lathe for watchmaking', AH, 17, Summer 1988, 382-94.
6 Defossez, L. 'Some notes on the Roskopf Watch', *Swiss Watch and Jewellery Journal*, 89, 6 November 1964, 804-7.
7 'The Trip to Switzerland', HJ, 47, 1905, 171 and 178-82 and HJ, 48, 1905, 5-12.
8 HJ, 42, December 1899, 55-6 and HJ, 43, January 1901, 58-60.
9 Lecluse, J. 'Machine Watchmaking in Switzerland', HJ, 28, September 1885, 14-5.
10 Sordet, E. 'Review of the Mechanical Manufacture of Watches', HJ, 31, December 1888, 50-4.
11 HJ, 27, July 1885, 57-8.

CHAPTER 6

1 Cutmore, M. *The Pocket Watch Handbook*, David & Charles, 1985, Chapters 4, 7 and 8.
2 Chamberlain, P. M. *It's about Time*, Holland Press, 1964.
3 Grossman, M. 'Treatise on the detached lever escapement', HJ, 8, June 1866, 109-36.
4 Lossier, L. *Étude sur la théorie du reglage des montres*, Geneva, 1890. Translation by G. Walker and W. N. Barber in HJ, 36, 1893–4, 86; HJ, 37, 1894–5, 71-3, 85-8, 99-102, 113-15, 125-9, 141-5, 160-3; HJ, 38, 1895–6, 6-9, 18-22, 42-3, 45-9, 59-61, 71-3, 85-8, 99-103, 113-19, 127-31, 141-8 and HJ, 39, 1896–7, 1-6, 16-20; and Phillips, E. *Mémoire sur le spiral réglant des chronomètres et des montres*, Paris, 1861. Translation by J. D. Weaver, Monograph No 15, Antiquarian Horological Society, 1978.

5 White, T. E. 'The testing and certification of watches at the Kew Observatory and National Physical Laboratory, 1884 to 1978', HJ, 127, August 1984, 15-17.
6 Mercer, V. *The Frodshams*, Antiquarian Horological Society, 1981, 272-4.
7 Rawlings, A. L. *The Science of Clocks and Watches*, Pitman, 1948, 162-91.
8 De Carle, D. *Practical Watch Repairing*, NAG, 1946, 117-62.
9 Lecoultre, F. *A Guide to the Complicated Watch*, Switzerland, 1985.
10 Wadsworth, F. 'A History of repeating Watches', AH, 4, September 1965, 364-7; AH, 5, December 1965, 24-7, March 1966, 48-52 and June 1966, 90-2.
11 Britten, F. W. *Horological Hints and Helps*, Baron, 1977, 333-6.
12 Haswell, J. E. *Horology*, EP Publishing, 1976, 210-19.
13 Player, J. W. 'Harwood's Self-winding wrist watch', HJ, 68, September 1925, 17-19.
14 Mercer, V. 'A classification of keyless mechanisms for watches', HJ, 127, 3, September 1984; 5, November 1984; 8, February 1985; HJ, 128, 5, November 1985; 12, June 1986; HJ, 129, 7, January 1987; more parts to follow.

CHAPTER 7

1 Priestley, P. T. and Dennison, A. G. 'The History of the Dennison Watch Case Company', HJ 128, March 1986, 12-16, April 1986, 8-11, May 1986, 15-17, June 1986, 10-12 and HJ 129, July 1986, 13-16.
2 *Clocks* 2, 12, June 1980, 43-5 and *Clocks* 3, 5, November 1980, 38-40, 3, 6, December 1980, 20-3 and 3, 7, January 1981, 48-9.
3 HJ, 32, June 1890, 151.
4 HJ, 21, September 1878, 11-12.
5 Gannay, H. 'The Practical Value of Horological Schools', HJ, 22, July, 1880, 142-7.
6 Poole, J. U. 'Chronometer and Watch Manufacture', HJ, 22, April 1880, 99-104.
7 Bickley, 'The present system of English Watch Manufacture', HJ, 22, June 1880, 127-32.
8 Rigg, E. 'Watchmaking', *Jnl. Society of Arts*, 29, 1881, 663-71, 673-82, 692-8, 701-8 and 722-6.
9 Church, R. A. 'Nineteenth Century Clock Technology in Britain, US and Switzerland', *Economic History Review*, 28, 4, November 1975, 616-30.
10 *Register of Defunct and other Companies*, Thomas Skinner, 1979–80.
11 HJ, 27, August 1885, 171.
12 HJ, 28, March 1886.
13 HJ, 42, December 1899, 45.
14 HJ, 59, September 1916, 8-9.
15 William Erhhardt – obituary, HJ, 40, January 1898, 63-5.
16 Letter from City of Birmingham reference library dated 8 July, 1985.
17 HJ, 62, March 1920, 84 and HJ, 63, March 1921, 91-6.
18 HJ, 32, December 1889, 60.
19 Letter from The Assay Office, Birmingham dated 10 October, 1986.
20 HJ, 31, February 1889, 89.
21 HJ, 32, June 1890, 160-1 and 177.
22 HJ, 42, March, 1900, 96-8, HJ, 43, March 1901, 89-90 and April 1901, 102.
23 HJ, 42 January 1900, 59-60.
24 White, T. E. 'The testing and certification of watches at the Kew Observatory', HJ, 127, August 1984, 15-17.
25 Britten, F. J. *Old Clocks and Watches and their Makers*, 9th Edition, Methuen-Spon, 1982.
26 Loomes, B. *Watchmakers and Clockmakers of the World*, Vol 2, NAG Press, 1976.
27 Searby, P. 'Watchmaking in Coventry', AH, Autumn 1977, 465-8.
28 HJ, 10, October 1867, 19.
29 Tripplin, J. 'Recent progress in British Watch and Clock Making', *Jnl. Society of Arts*, 38, 1889–90, 365-80.

30 Bailey, J. R., 'The Struggle for Survival in the Coventry Ribbon and Watch Trades 1865–1914', *Midland History*, 7, 1982, 132-52.
31 HJ, 30, December 1887, 50.
32 'Machine Watchmaking as carried on by Messrs Rotherham & Sons', HJ, 30, June 1888, 145-55.
33 HJ, 32, September 1889, 15.
34 HJ, 37, 1894, 23, 95.
35 HJ, 40, 1897, 68.
36 HJ, 42, December 1899, 44-6, January 1900, 58-61, February, 1900, 77-9.
37 HJ, 36, April 1894, 123-4.
38 HJ, 43, November 1900, 39.
39 HJ, 42, April 1900, 98.
40 HJ, 45, March 1903, 85-8.
41 Tripplin, J. 'A comparison between an English and a Swiss watch factory', HJ, 52, November 1909, 49-54.
42 HJ, 66, July 1924, 208-19.
43 HJ, 68, March 1926, 140-3; HJ, 75, September 1932, 211; HJ, 76, March 1934, 459 and HJ, 79, April 1937, 16-31.
44 HJ, 29, November 1886, 45-6.
45 HJ, 37, March 1895, 96.
46 Kemp, R. 'The Coventry Watch Trade', HJ, 126, 9, September 1984, 17-20.
47 *The Lancashire Watch Company, 1889–1910*, Ken Roberts, USA, 1973.
48 HJ, 32, February 1890, 85-9.
49 HJ, 52, June 1910, 155-6.
50 HJ, 32, May 1890, 137.
51 *The Engineer*, January 13, 1893, 36-7.
52 HJ, 37, 1894, 111.
53 HJ, 40, 1897, 81.
54 HJ, 45, March 1903, 97.
55 HJ, 46, December 1903, 57-8.
56 HJ, 47, 1905, 138.
57 Hewitt, C. J. 'The manufacture of standard screws for machine made watches', HJ, 37, 1894, 29-32 and 45-7.
58 Gustave, Richard, *Traité des Machines Outils*, Paris, 1895.
59 *Coventry Times*, 10 June 1891.
60 *Coventry Herald*, 1 November 1889.
61 HJ, 32, October 1899, 23.
62 *Midland Daily Telegraph*, 4 June, 1891.
63 HJ, 42, July and August 1900, 155 and 166.
64 HJ, 42, June 1900, 135.
65 HJ, 45, July 1903, 146-7.
66 HJ, 50, July 1908, 195.
67 'Auguste Guye – obituary', HJ, 35, February 1893, 85-6.
68 HJ, 36, 1894, 157, 178-9 and 182.
69 'Machine Watchmaking – The factory of P & A Guye', HJ, 32, January 1890, 72-4.
70 Gannay, H. 'Machine Watchmaking', HJ, 26, May 1884, 115-20.
71 HJ, 22, July 1880, 154.
72 HJ, 36, September 1894, 5-6.
73 HJ, 40, 1897, 81 and 161.
74 HJ, 47, November 1904, 44.
75 HJ, 47, May 1905, 140.
76 Mercer, V. *The Frodshams*, Antiquarian Horological Society, 1981.
77 Cutmore, M. *The Pocket Watch Handbook*, David & Charles, 1985.
78 HJ, 41, July 1899, 156.
79 'Visit to Nicole, Nielson & Co's Watch Factory', HJ, 31, July 1889, 145-6.
80 Letters from Garrard & Co Ltd dated October and November 1985.
81 'High Grade Watches made in London', HJ, 77, April 1935, 254-7.
82 Benson, J. W. *Time and Time Tellers*, 1875.
83 HJ, 121, March 1974, 3-12.
84 Letters from Library and Museum Service, Wiltshire County Council, August and September 1985, and *Salisbury Journal*, 29 May 1909 and *Watch and Clockmaker*, 15 August 1930.
85 Tucker, C. 'The British Horological Industry', HJ, 90, January 1948, 22-5.

86 HJ, 52, March 1910, 98-9.
87 HJ, 40, May 1898, 120.
88 HJ, 52, July 1910, 170.
89 HJ, 42, November 1899, 37 and March 1900, 91-3.
90 Walford, H. N. 'Fifty years of Horological Manufacture,' HJ, 63, 1958, 148-50, 230-2, 299-300 and 361.
91 HJ, 42, March 1900, 98-9 and HJ, 43, November 1900, 39-40.
92 'The Trip to Switzerland', HJ, 47, 1905, 171 and 178-82 and HJ, 48, 1905, 5-12.
93 HJ, 51, December 1908, 61.
94 *The Dial*, March 1922, 36-7.
95 HJ, 46, December 1903, 58.
96 HJ, 55, November 1912, 38-42.
97 HJ, 43-69, 72 and 74, 1901-27, 1929 and 1931, various pages with Williamson AGM.
98 HJ, 63, February 1921, 81-4.
99 HJ, 100, March 1958, 170-1.
100 HJ, 67, February 1925, 94.
101 'The Story Behind Clocks, London', HJ, 91, April 1949, 214-15.
102 *Smith and Sons Ltd. Guide to the Purchase of a Watch*, Malcolm Gardner, 1978.
103 HJ, 36, September 1893, 8-9, HJ, 37, April 1895, 110 and HJ, 108, April, 1966, 14.
104 'Obituaries, Sir Allen Gordon-Smith', HJ, 93, March 1951, 170-1.
105 Buckland, H. R. 'Production of British Escapements', HJ, 80, January 1938, 8-22 and 30.
106 HJ, 89, February 1947, 78.
107 'British Wrist Watch Factory', *The Engineer*, 1 June, 1956.
108 Fell, R. A. and Indermuhle, P. 'Contemporary Methods of Watch Production', *Proc. (A) I.Mech.E.*, 1953, 167, 2, 190-208.
109 Anglo-Celtic History; HJ, 89, April 1947, 172-3; HJ, 109, November 1966, 20-4; HJ, 100, August 1958, 487-90; HJ, 125, December 1982, 24-6 and HJ, 122, April 1980, 19.
110 HJ, 92, July 1950, 441-2 and 444.
111 Robinson, T. H. 'The Smith 1215 Wristlet Movement', HJ, 94, January 1952, 25-6.
112 Pike, W. G. 'A watch that is backing Britain', HJ, 110, April 1968, 8-10.
113 Smith repair and spare parts catalogues, 1954 onwards.
114 Pike, W. G. 'A new British Watch', HJ, 100, August 1958, 487-90.
115 Pike, W. G. 'Elite by Ingersoll', HJ, 109, August 1966, 18-27.
116 HJ, 95, October 1953, 592.
117 Correspondence with Smiths Industries PLC; HJ, 116, July 1973, 12 and HJ, 124, July 1981. 29.
118 Tschudy, R. F. 'Ingersoll', *Bulletin*, National Association of Watch and Clock Collectors Inc, USA., April 1952.
119 Edwards, F. 'The Story of Ingersoll', HJ, 126, May 1983, 12-15.
120 Cryer, C. 'Louis Newmark Ltd.', HJ, 126, July 1983, 14-17.
121 Newmark Supplement, HJ, 93, April 1951 and Newmark supplement, HJ, 97, April 1957.
122 Correspondence with Newmark PLC.
123 Landes, D. S. *Revolution in Time*, Belknap Press, 1983.
124 Townsend, G. E. *The Watch that Made the Collar Famous*, USA, 1974.
125 'Britain's latest Watch factory', HJ, 101, August 1959, 492-4.
126 Shenton, R. 'The Coventry Watch Trade', *Clocks*, November 1984, 17-21.

CHAPTER 8

1 'The evolution of the methods and means of production in the watch industry', *La Suisse Horlogère et Revue Internationale de l'horlogerie*, 87, Part 1, March 1972, 37-9.
2 Defossez, L, 'Some notes on the Roskopf Watch', *Swiss Watch and Jewellery Journal*, International Edition, 89, Part 6, November 1964, 804-7.

3 'Quality testing in the manufacture of Roskopf watch ébauches', *La Suisse Horlogère et Revue Internationale de l'horlogerie*, 87, part 3, September 1972, 46-50.

4 'The Situation of the Swiss Roskopf industry', *La Suisse Horlogère et Revue Internationale de l'horlogerie*, 87, Part 1, March 1972, 53-4.

5 HJ, 125, April 1983.

6 *The Swiss Watchmaking Industry*, Economic Research Department, Union Bank of Switzerland, Zurich, 1986.

7 HJ, 43, January 1901, 58-60.

8 HJ, 66, August 1924, 239.

9 Zienau, O. 'History of the Swiss Industry', HJ, 94, February 1952, 106-7.

10 Rohn, O. 'The Swiss Horological Industry', HJ, 89, April 1947, 174-6.

11 Joly, C.-F. 'The mechanisation and automation of the methods of watch assembly', *La Suisse Horlogère et Revue Internationale de l'horlogerie*, 87, Part 3, September 1972, 34-5.

12 *Watchmaker, Jeweller and Silversmith*, May 1985, 26.

13 Good, R. 'The Basle Fair, Year of the Quartz Crystal Watch', HJ, 112, May 1970, 5-12.

14 'The mechanical watch and clock: A year on', HJ, 120, March 1978, 23-30.

15 *Switzerland in figures*, Economic Research Department, Union Bank of Switzerland, Zurich, 1985.

16 Jobin, A.-F. *La Classification horlogère*, Switzerland, 1938. Flume, R. *Der Flume Werksuchers*, Berlin, 1947. *Catalogue Officiel des pièces d'origine pour le rhabillage des montres Suisses*, Tome I et Tome II, Switzerland, 1949. *Bestfit, #III Encyclopedia of Watch Material, Part #I*, USA, 1961. *MST, Catalogue No. 5 of interchangeable and identical watch materials for various calibres*, Switzerland, 1949.

17 Pfister, F. E. 'The reign of the pocket watch and the advent of the wrist watch', *La Suisse Horlogère et Revue Internationale de l'horlogerie*, 80, December 1965, 19-22.

18 HJ, 79, April 1937, 32.

19 'The Trip to Switzerland', HJ, 47, 1905, 171 and 178-82 and HJ, 48, 1905, 5-12.

20 Tripplin, J. 'A comparison between an English and a Swiss watch factory', HJ, 52, November 1909, 49-54.

21 'Jewelling a Büren Watch', HJ, 65, February 1923, 107-8.

22 Tolke, H. E. and King, J. *I.W.C. Schaffhausen, Switzerland since 1868*, Switzerland, 1987.

23 Huber, M. and Banbury, A. *Patek Philippe, Genève*, Germany, 1982 and *Patek Philippe (Wristwatches)*, Germany, 1987.

24 Jaquet, E. and Chapuis, A. *Technique and History of the Swiss Watch*, Hamlyn, 1970.

25 'Omega past and present', Omega press release, 1985.

26 'Important events in Longines history', Longines press release, 1984 and Francillon, A. *Histoire de la fabrique des Longines*, St Imier, 1947.

27 'Revue watches for the British Market', HJ, 93, March 1951, 164-7.

28 'Important events of the Revue-Thommen factory SA', Revue-Thommen press release, 1986, catalogues and correspondence.

29 *Watchmaker, Jeweller and Silversmith*, May 1985, 20-1.

30 *Dixi, 80th anniversary brochure*, Switzerland, 1984 and correspondence.

31 I.W.C. Catalogues, 1985 and correspondence.

32 'The History of ETA', ETA, 1983 and correspondence.

33 Oris catalogues and correspondence.

CHAPTER 9

1 Harrold, M. C. *American Watchmaking*, National Association of Watch and Clock Collectors Inc, USA, Spring 1984.

2 Townsend, G. E. *Almost Everything You Wanted to Know about American Watches and Didn't Know Who to Ask*, USA 1971 and *Encyclopedia of Dollar Watches*, USA, 1974.

3 HJ, 42, February 1900, 81-2.

4 Tschudy, R. F. 'Ingersoll', *Bulletin*, National Association of Watch and Clock Collectors, Inc., USA, April 1952.

5 HJ, 64, 1922, 133 and 169.

6 Edwards, F. 'The Story of Ingersoll', HJ, 125, May 1983, 12-15.

7 Abbott, H. G. *The Watch Factories of America*, Chicago, 1888.

8 Crossman, C. S. *The Complete History of Watchmaking in America*, reprint by Adams Brown, Exeter, USA, nd.

9 Milham, W. A. *Time and Timekeepers*, Macmillan, 1923.

10 Moore, C. W. *Timing a Century*, Harvard University Press, 1945.

11 Tricano, A. 'Inside American Watch Factories', HJ, 96, May 1954, 307-8.

12 *American Watch Historical Information*, Minnesota Watchmakers Association, USA, c1970.

13 Landes, D. S. *Revolution in Time*, Belknap Press, 1983.

14 'The American Watch industry fights competition', HJ, 101, July 1959, 429-30.

15 McKinnie, M. R. 'Webb C. Ball Watches', *Bulletin*, National Association of Watch and Clock Collectors, Inc., USA, February 1970.

CHAPTER 10

1 HJ, 29, February 1887, 94-5.

2 Forster, R. 'Horology in France', HJ, 91, June 1949, 350-2.

3 'Inside the French Horological Industry', HJ, 102, May 1960, 350-2.

4 *Europa Star*, 152-4, 1985, Geneva.

5 'Watch and Clock Making in 1900', HJ, 43, January 1901, 58-60.

6 Herkner, K. *Glashütte and seine Uhren*, Düsseldorf, 1978.

7 *Uhren 1913*, Deutsches Uhrenmuseum, Furtwangen, 1980.

8 'A Watch Industry Rebuilt', HJ, 96, September 1954, 566-9.

9 'The German Watch Industry' *La Suisse Horlogère*, 93, January 1978, 64.

10 Chenekal, V. L. *Watchmakers and Clockmakers of Russia, 1400–1850*, Antiquarian Horological Society, 1976.

11 Gibbs, J. W. *The Dueber-Hampden Story*, USA, 1954, 15-19.

12 Tremayne, A. *Everybody's Watches*, NAG, c1945.

13 'Russian Horological Progress', HJ, 101, February 1959, 105.

14 Tarasor, S.V. *Technology of Watch Production*, Moscow, 1956, translation Jerusalem, 1964.

15 HJ, 98, October 1956, 618-21.

16 Bateman, M. J. 'British Horologists visit Russia', HJ, 99, April 1957, 229-31 and May 1957, 283-4.

17 Landes, D. S. *Revolution in Time*, Belknap Press, 1983.

18 'Russian Watches Arrive', HJ, 102, February 1960, 93.

19 Pike, W. G. 'The first of the Russian Imported Watches', HJ, 102, June 1960, 360-2.

20 Good, R. 'Three Russian Watches', HJ, 109, October 1966, 14-19.

21 Pike, W. G. 'The Zarja 2014', HJ, 111, September 1968, 7-9.

22 Correspondence with Sekonda, 1987.

23 Ullyett, K. *Watch Collecting*, Muller, 1970, Chapter 6.

24 HJ, 40, August 1898, 164.

25 Hoshimi Uchida, *Osaka Watch Incorporated*, Japan, 1986.

26 'The Japanese Watch Factory,' HJ, 38, October 1895, 24-6.

27 Correspondence with Hattori-Seiko, 1986-7.

28 Correspondence with Citizen, 1986-7.

29 'Inside a Japanese Watch Factory', HJ, 93, October 1951, 642-3.

30 *General Parts Catalog for Mechanical Watches*, Citizen, 1982.

31 Correspondence with Hong Kong Trade Development Council, 1987.

32 *The Swiss Watchmaking Industry*, Economic Research Department, Union Bank of Switzerland, Zurich, 1986.

33 'Plan for Europe's Watch Industries', HJ, 99, May 1957, 297.

34 'A European Horological Community?', HJ, 102, January 1960, 24-6.

35 'China's Links with Hong Kong', HJ, 124, October 1981, 29.

36 Townsend, G. E. *Encyclopedia of Dollar Watches*, USA, 1974.

37 'Britain's latest Watch Factory', HJ, 101, August 1959, 492-4.

38 HJ, 129, May 1987, 28-9.

CHAPTER 11

1 Tarasov, S. V. *Technology of Watch Production*, Jerusalem, 1964.
2 Favre-Bulle, W. *Le Calibre de Montre*, Première Partie, Bienne, 1915; Deuxieme Partie, Bienne, 1920; *Fabrication Mécanique de la Montre*, Tome III, Bienne, 1924.
3 Marsh, E. A. *Watches by Automatic Machinery at Waltham*, Chicago, 1896.
4 Bacon, D. H. 'A lathe for Watchmaking', AH, 17, 4, Summer 1988, 382-94.
5 *The Swiss Automatic*, André Bechler, Switzerland, 1957.
6 *Elgin Reminiscences*, Ken Roberts, 1972.
7 Correspondence with Mikron-Haesler SA, Switzerland.
8 *Hauser 1898–1973*, Bienne, 1973 and correspondence with Henri Hauser SA, Switzerland.
9 Correspondence with Essa Fabrique de Machines SA Switzerland.
10 *Société Genevoise d'Instruments de Physique, 1862–1962*, Geneva, 1962.
11 Correspondence with Dixi SA, Switzerland.
12 Marre, M. *Le Comparateur Dixi*, Le Locle, 1912.
13 Eckhardt, G. H. *United States Clock and Watch Patents, 1790–1890*, USA, 1960 and Swiss patent lists from 1888.
14 Fell, R. A. and Indermuhle, P. 'Contemporary methods of Watch Production', I.Mech.E., Proc(A), 167, 2. 190-228, 1953.
15 *American Watch Company, Waltham, Mass, New Orleans Exposition, 1884–5*, Ken Roberts, 1972.
16 Moore, C. W. *Timing a Century*, Harvard University Press, 1945.
17 'British Wrist Watch Factory', *The Engineer*, 1 June, 1956.
18 Saunier, C. *The Watchmaker's Handbook*, Technical Press, 1948.
19 'Assembly Chains', *La Suisse Horlogère et Revue Internationale de l'horlogerie*, 80, 4, December 1965.
20 Joly, C.-F. 'The mechanization and automatization of the methods of watch assembly', *La Suisse Horlogère et Revue Internationale de l'horlogerie*, 87, 3, September 1972.
21 Abbott, H. G. *The Watch Factories of America*, Chicago, 1880.
22 Correspondence with Omega, Longines, Oris, Switzerland.
23 'A watch industry rebuilt', HJ, 96, September 1954, 566-9.
24 Perkins, T. 'The manufacture of watches as carried on at the works of the National Watch Company, Elgin, Illinois, USA', HJ, 16, January 1874, 65-75.
25 Abbott, H. G. *The History of the American Waltham Watch Company*, Chicago, 1904.
26 *Microelectronics*, A Scientific American Book, W. H. Freeman, USA, 1977.

CHAPTER 12

1 Aked, C. K. 'Electricity, Magnetism and Clocks', AH, 7, December 1971, 398-451.
2 Hope-Jones, F. *Electrical Timekeeping*, NAG Press, 1940.

3 Weaver, J. D. *Electrical and Electronic Clocks and Watches*, Newnes, 1982.
4 HJ, 93-116, 1951–74.
5 Good, R. 'An analysis of the Electric Watch', HJ, 99, July 1957, 406-12.
6 Good, R. 'An analysis of the LIP electric watch', HJ, 102, January 1960, 18-23, 35 and February 1960, 90-3.
7 Good, R. 'An analysis of the Swiss electric watch', HJ, 102, November 1960, 696-708.
8 Good, R. 'The Accutron', HJ, 103, June 1961, 340-53.
9 Beyner, A. 'Electronic Watch with Spring Balance, Caliber ESA 9150', HJ, 110, September 1967, 10-14.
10 'Piezo Electric quartz resonators', HJ, 109, April 1967, 8-10 and May, 1967, 14-15.
11 'Quartz crystal wristwatch', HJ, 110, March 1968, 14-18.
12 Good, R. 'Year of the quartz crystal watch', HJ, 112, May 1970, 5-12.
13 'The Hamilton Pulsar', HJ, 113, July 1970, 14-15.
14 'First all electronic LCD watch', HJ, 114, April 1972, 16-18.
15 'New thermo-compensated movement', HJ, 128, April 1986, 15-16.

CHAPTER 13

1 Boullin, D. J. 'Early quartz collectables', *Clocks,* 6, 12, June 1984, 47-50.
2 Randall, A. 'The technique of photographing watches', AH, 10, Summer 1978, 835-42.
3 Walters, T. T. 'An aid to depth of field determination in Horological Photography', AH, 11, Spring 1979, 280-3.
4 Cutmore, M. *The Pocket Watch Handbook*, Chapter 12, David & Charles, 1985.
5 Britten, F. J. *Horological Hints and Helps*, Baron, 1977.
6 De Carle, D. *Practical Watch Repairing*, NAG Press, 1947 and *The Watchmaker's lathe*, Hale, 1980.
7 *Correspondence course in Technical Horology* (3 grades), British Horological Institute, 1960.
8 'Examining and repairing a worn American watch', HJ, 40, 1897, 21-4 and 29-35.
9 Freid, H. B. *The Electric Watch Repair Manual*, USA, 1972.
10 Freid, H. B. *Repairing Quartz Watches*, USA, 1983.
11 Zanoni, L. *The Digital Watch Repair Manual*, USA, 1980.
12 ESA L4750 Calibre, Service Instructions, Ebauches SA, January 1961.
13 *Repairing Quartz, LCD and Analog Watches*, Vols 1, 2, 3, etc, Switzerland, 1977 on.
14 Schmidlin, F. *Elektrische und elektronische Armbanduhren*, Lausanne, 1970.

Acknowledgements

In trying to acknowledge assistance from various sources requested over a five-year period it is very easy to forget someone. For this, I apologise. I do however acknowledge the help given by the following firms, institutions and individuals.

BRITAIN

Alfex (UK), Global Watches, Muller and Company, Louis Newmark PLC, H. Samuel, Sears PLC, SIP-DIXI (UK), Smiths Industries PLC, Tornos Bechler (UK), Assay Office (Birmingham), British Library, City of Birmingham Library, Coventry City Record Office, Guildhall Library, Hackney College, Institution of Mechanical Engineers Library, Prescot Museum, Patent Office, Plymouth Polytechnic LRC, Science Museum, Science Museum Library, Science Reference Library, Shoreditch Library, Swiss Embassy, West Yorkshire Archive Service, Wiltshire County Council.

Also, R. Burki, R. Heywood-Waddington, B. Hutchinson, K. Shanks, F. Wadsworth.

SWITZERLAND

Aubry Frères SA, Dixi SA, Essa AG, ETA (SMH), Eterna AG, Girard Perregaux SA, H. Hauser SA, International Watch Company, Longines Francillon SA, Mikron Haesler Ltd, Omega SA, Oris SA, Revue-Thommen SA (Marvin and Vulcain & Studio), Roamer SA, Rolex SA, Ronda SA, Tornos Bechler SA, Union Bank of Switzerland, Vacheron and Constantin SA, Zenith SA.

Bibliothèque Nationale Suisse, Bundesamt für geistiges Eigentum, Musée Internationale, La Chaux de Fonds, Technorama der Schweiz, Winterthur

E. Moos, R. Portmann, K. Straumann.

AMERICA

Mike Harrold.

JAPAN

Citizen Watch Company, Hattori-Seiko Company.

HONG KONG

Hong Kong Trade Development Council.

William R. Milligan took the photographs in Plates 1, 15, 16, 21, 22, 23, 25, 26, 37, 41, 44, 55, 79, 80, 83, 84, 106, 107 and 141. Mike Harrold and Roy Ehrhardt supplied Plates 5, 6, 7, 8, 9, 10, 14, 19, 20, 118, 119, 122 and 123. Longines supplied Plates 29, 87, 97, 99, 150, 158 and 160. Omega supplied Plates 30, 33, 34, 35, 36, 85, 86, 88, 90, 98, 100, 102 and the upper drawings of Fig 19.

Hattori-Seiko supplied Plates 133, 134, 135, 136, 137, 138, 155 and 156. Citizen supplied the drawings for Fig 18. ETA supplied Plates 146, 153, 154 and 157. Girard Perregaux supplied Plate 101. Revue-Thommen supplied Plate 103. Tornos Bechler supplied Plate 144. Oris supplied Plate 109. Louis Newmark supplied Plate 152. Plate 24 comes from *Kelly's Directory of the Watch, Clock and Jewellery Trades.* David Penney supplied Plate 3. Vacheron and Constantin supplied material for Plate 4. Plate 147 is reproduced by permission of the Royal Society of Arts.

The remaining plates are photographs taken by the author in various locations.

The line drawings in Figs 1, 2, 3, 4, 5, 6, 7, 8, 9, 10, 11, 12, 14, 15 and 20 are by Eadan Art. The marks in Fig 13 are from *The Trade Marks Journal*, 1876–1911. The jacket photographs were provided by International Watch Company, Schaffhausen.

Index

A

Accuquartz, 211, 217
Accutron, 168, 210, 213
Adjustments, 134, 202, 203
Advertisements, 220
Agassiz, A., 150
Alarm watch, 66, 73
American,
  Horologe Company, 27
  Waltham Watch Company, 29
  Watch Company, 29
  Watch Tool Company, 35, 90, 102
Anglo-American,
  Tool Company, 102
  Watch Company, 79
Anglo-Celtic Watch Company, 123,
  127
Audemars, L. 77
Ansonia Clock Company, 163, 165,
  177
Appleton, Tracy & Company, 29
A. S., 193
Assembly, 15, 134, 203
ASUAG, 141
Auburndale Watch Company, 160
Automatic,
  machines, 35, 37, 47, 56,
    58, 64, 93, 102, 105, 113, 115, 145,
    157, 194–204
  watch, 77, 124, 146
Automation, 204

B

Badollet, J. J. & Company, 61
Balance, 8, 10
Balance spring, 10, 51, 228
Ball standards, 169
Banking, 14
Bannatyne Watch Company, 163
Barrel, 8
Beaucourt, 16, 19
Benedict and Burnham, 160
Benson, J. W., 111
Bestfit catalog, 144, 179
Bonniksen, B., 72
Boston Watch Company, 27

Bragge, W., 79
Brandt, L., 149
Breguet, A. L. 11, 71
British,
  Horological Institute, 45, 117
  Industries Fair, 87, 93, 120, 122
  Watch & Clock Company, 21
  Watch Company, 88
Buck, D. A. A., 160
Bulova, 168, 210, 211, 213, 217
Buren Watch Company, 94, 115, 151,
  193

C

Calendar watch, 66, 74
Cartels, 139
Cases, 9, 39, 67, 80, 116
Casio, 182
Catalogs, 144
Chambre suisse d'horlogerie, 65,
  139
China, 183
Chronograph, 66, 75
Chronometer, 10, 146
Chrono-micrometer, 81
Church, D. H., 36, 166, 172
Citizen Watch Company, 182
Clockmaker's Company, 9
Cock, 8
Collections, 219–22
Columbus Watch Company, 43, 165
Compensations,
  balance, 10, 66, 70
  curb, 10
Complications, 9, 66, 73, 146
Costs, 30, 35
Coventry,
  industry, 17, 89, 95, 104, 115
  Cooperative Watchmaking Society,
    95
  Watch Movement Company, 95,
    104
Curtis, S., 27
Cyma, 151

D

Day, date, moon display, 66, 74

Dennison,
  Aaron, 22, 26, 79
  Howard & Davis, 27
Depthing tool, 224
Dixi, 154, 198
Dollar watches, 163
Draw, 14
Drawings, 20, 33, 45, 190
Dueber-Hampden Watch Company,
  177
Dumaine, F. C., 167
Durowe, 177

E

Ebauche, 19, 49
Ebauche S. A. 141, 146, 209, 210, 212,
  213, 216
Ehrhardt, W., 81, 84, 193
Electromechanical watches, 67, 146,
  173, 182, 184, 207, 209, 210, 228
Electronic watches, 67, 147, 181, 182,
  183, 184, 207, 209, 210, 228
Elgin National Watch Company, 42,
  45, 165, 168, 172
Elinvar, 70
Engineers and engineering in
  watchmaking, 33, 187, 190, 201
English,
  Clocks & Gramophones, 119
  Clock and Watch Manufacturers,
    119
  Watch Company, 79
Errington, C. H. 114
Errors in manufacture, 187–191
Escapement,
  cylinder, 11, 66, 137, 144–6
  detached, 10, 12
  duplex, 66, 69, 160
  English lever, 12, 66
  pin lever, 54, 66, 67, 163
  Swiss lever, 12, 66
  verge, 11
Escape wheel, 11, 12
ETA, 142, 157
Etablisseur, 51
Exports, 38, 51, 61, 136, 139, 163,
  173, 179, 182, 183, 185

F

Factory,
  early ideas, 18, 28, 35, 40, 205
  layout, 205
Favre-Perret, E., 51, 65
Fault-finding, 225–8
Fasoldt, C., 172
F. H., 139, 142
Finishing, 15, 16, 21–3, 203, 205
Fitch, E., 43, 166
Flume catalog, 144, 177, 178
Fontainemelon, 16, 19
Francillon, E., 150
French,
  watchmaking, 145, 173, 209, 212
  Watchmaking Company, 20
Friction, 10–12, 69
Fullplate, 14, 67
Fusee, 8, 14, 45, 46, 67

G

Gannay, H., 22, 85, 95, 162
General Time Corporation, 185
Geneva industry, 5
German watches, 127, 133, 145, 175
Goddard, L., 23
Going barrel, 14
Gooding, 90, 112
Greenwich,
  longitude, 169
  trails, 86
Grimshaw, Baxter and Elliot, 119, 120
Guilden, T., 167
Guillaume, C. E. 70, 92
Guye, P. & A., 107, 112, 113

H

Hallmark Watch Company, 168
Hamilton,
  500, 168, 209, 112
  Pulsar, 168, 211, 217
  Watch Company, 165, 172
Hampden Watch Company, 42, 165, 177
Hatot amplifier, 210, 212–14
Hattori, K., 181
Hewitt, T. P., 98
Hong Kong, 183
Hopkins, J. R., 160, 172
Howard,
  E., 27, 41
  & Davis, 27
Huguenin, G., 77

I

Illinois Watch Company, 165

Impulse, 11–14
India, 173
Ingersoll,
  U.K., 49, 122, 126, 164
  U.S.A., 56, 132, 163, 165, 184
Ingold, P. F.,
  machines, 20–2, 197
  watches, 20–2
Ingraham, E., 163, 165, 172
Integrated circuits, 209, 214
Interchangeability, 16, 20, 23–5, 27, 32, 45, 64, 85, 87, 107, 145, 187–93
International Watch Company, 142, 146, 156
Inventions Exhibition, 36, 47, 64
Isochronous, 10, 69

J

Jacob catalog, 177
Japan, 136, 139, 142, 172, 180–3, 185, 210
Japy, 19, 173, 197
Jeanneret-Gris, J-J., 19
JeanRichard, D., 51
Jewelling, 14, 39, 67, 78, 169, 170
Jig borer, 22, 155, 199
Jobin catalog, 145
Junghans, 176
Jura industry, 19, 44, 51

K

Karrusel, 66, 72, 86, 91, 121, 124, 170
Kelly Directory, 61, 79
Kew trails, 66, 73, 86, 91, 101, 107, 110, 121, 124, 146
Keyless watches, 40, 46, 76–8, 85, 91, 100, 105, 108, 112, 115, 160, 163
Kienzle, 176

L

Lancashire Watch Company, 47, 49, 97, 193
Lange and Sohne, A., 175
Lathes, 17, 19, 21, 32, 35, 58, 61, 115, 145, 194–5
LCD, 147, 182, 183, 211, 215, 217, 228
LED, 147, 182, 183, 211, 215, 217
LeCoultre, A., 23, 77
Lemkuhl, J., 184
Lepine, J–A., 15, 23
Leschot, G–A., 22, 51
Lip, 173, 209, 212
Longines, 64, 150

M

Machinery, 28, 32, 35–7, 58, 61, 85, 90, 102, 105, 108, 115, 116, 123, 145,
  160, 165, 167, 172, 194–202
Maintaining power, 10
Manufacturing techniques, 187
Marketing, 17, 38, 49, 129, 163, 172
Marsh, E. A., 37
Mass production, 20, 24, 25, 32, 187
Mauritius, 175
Measurements, 20, 33, 45, 47, 190, 198
Melrose Watch Company, 79
Merchandise Marks Act, 47, 86, 91, 98, 115, 122, 129
Metrology, 190
Middle temperature error, 70
Milling, 32, 195
Moseley, C., 35
Motion work, 8
Movement, 8
Mozart, D. J., 172
Muller-Schlenker, 176

N

Nashua Watch Company, 41
National Watch Company, 42
Newark Watch Company, 42
New England Watch Company, 162
New Haven Clock Company, 163
Newmark, Louis, 49, 122, 127
Newsome, S. T., 105
New York Standard Watch
  Company, 165
Nicole, A., 77
Nicole, Nielson & Company, 109, 112

O

Omega, 149
Oris Watch Company, 134, 157
Osaka Watch Company, 180
Otay Watch Company, 180
Outworkers, 15, 25, 51, 53, 115

P

Paper dials, 54, 133, 163
Patents, 18, 25
Philadelphia Exhibition, 36, 51
Phillipe, A., 54, 77
Phillipines, 10
Photography, 220
Pillar, 8
Pinion manufacture, 195
Pin lever watches, 49, 67, 99, 125, 127, 128, 132–7, 142, 163–4, 175–6, 178, 184, 185
Pitkin watches, 24
Plate, 8
Platform escapement, 54
Pointing machine, 22, 198
Population, 129, 132

Positional error, 10, 69, 71, 162
Potter, A. H., 172
Pratt and Whitney, 198
Prescot, 15, 49, 97
Press tools, 21, 32, 61, 197
Production figures, 17, 19, 37, 38, 43,
    44, 51, 61, 65, 129–31, 136, 139,
    151, 153, 157, 159, 163, 167, 168,
    172, 173, 175, 177, 178, 180, 181,
    182, 183, 184, 186
PUW,

Q

Quartz crystal,
    oscillator, 214
    watches, 75, 179, 207–9, 210,
    214–18

R

Railway watches, 133, 168–70
Reed, G. P., 39, 41, 172
Regulation, 10, 41, 66, 71
Repairs, 40, 45, 133, 144, 184,
    222–8
Repassage, 51, 52
Repeating, 66, 73
Retor, 32, 197
Revue-Thommen, 152
Richard and Tucker, Nunn, 120, 126
Robbins, R. E., 29, 36, 43, 166
Robots, 204
Rockford Watch Company, 43, 165
Rolex, 146
Roskopf,
    G-F., 54
    watches, 54–8, 132–7, 175
Rotary transfer machine, 197
Rotherham and Son, 35, 46, 50, 89,
    193
Roxbury, 26
Russia, 42, 142, 177, 186

S

Safety,
    pin, 14
    pinion, 39
Scarisbrick, E., 104
Schweizer, J., 56, 58, 194
Schwob Bros, 151
Scotland, 128, 185

Seiko, 181, 210, 217
Sekonda, 179
Seth Thomas Watch Company, 165
Set up, 9
SIP, 198
Size, variation in, 187–90
SMH, 142
Smith, S. & Sons, 49, 120, 121
Société d'émulation, 51
Société de Garde Temps, 211, 217
Spare parts, 30, 144, 222, 223, 228
Split plate, 6
Spring, 8
Springfield Illinois Watch Company,
    43
SSIH, 142
Stackfreed, 8
Staking tool, 224
Stauffer, Son, & Company, 61
Steam power, 18, 50, 64, 81, 85, 180
Stock Exchange Register, 98, 120, 121
Stop watch, 66, 75
Stratton, N., 27, 39, 41
Striking watch, 66, 73
Styles, modern, 146, 185, 218
Swiss production, 44, 51, 61, 136,
    139, 159
Swiss watchmakers, 61

T

Taiwan, 175, 179, 183
Talley Industries, 185
Tavannes, Watch Company, 151
Temperature compensation, 10, 66,
    70
Terminal curves, 11, 66, 69
Textbooks of machine manufacture,
    200–203
Thailand, 183
Thiel, 175
Three quarter plate, 67
Timekeeping, 66, 69
Timex, 128, 141, 164, 172, 177, 184
Tolerances, 189–90
Tools, 17, 23, 224
Tourbillon, 66, 71, 124, 162, 170
Tracy & Baker, 29
Trademarks, 83
Transistor, 209, 210, 212
Tremont Watch Company, 42, 79

Trenton Watch Company, 165
Trials, 73
Tucker, Nunn, 120
Tucker, Nunn and Williamson, 120
Tunisia, 175
Turns, 224
Types of watch, 66

U

Ulysse Nardin, 94
United Clock Company, 185
United States Watch Company, 42
U.S. Time Corporation, 164, 184

V

Vacheron and Constantin, 22
Vander Woerd, C., 36
Vickers, 122

W

Waddington, R., 105
Waltham Watch Company, 28–43,
    65, 110, 166–8, 205
Warren Manufacturing Company, 27
Waterbury Clock Company, 163, 164,
    184
Waterbury Watch Company, 56, 132,
    162, 165
Watchmaking instructions, 200–203
Watch sizes, 16, 39, 146, 229
Westclox, 128, 163, 185
Western Clock Company, 163, 185
Wheel manufacture, 195, 197
Williamson, H. Ltd., 108, 112, 113
Wilsdorf, H., 146
Winding mechanisms, 76
Workforce size, 17, 19, 37, 83, 86,
    91, 93, 99, 121, 125, 128, 139, 177,
    178, 183, 184
World production, 129, 136, 139, 186
Wrist watches, 124, 125, 127, 145,
    146, 167, 172, 178, 181, 185
Wycherley, J., 49, 89

Y

Yeomans, S., 104

Z

Zenith, 154